MW00856006

CARMINE and the 13th AVENUE BOYS

SURVIVING BROOKLYN'S COLOMBO MOB

By Craig McGuire
with Carmine Imbriale

FORWARD BY THOMAS DADES, FORMER NYPD DETECTIVE AND AUTHOR OF
FRIENDS OF THE FAMILY: THE INSIDE STORY OF THE MAFIA COPS CASE

WILD BLUE
P R E S S

WildBluePress.com

CARMINE AND THE 13th AVENUE BOYS published by:
WILDBLUE PRESS
P.O. Box 102440
Denver, Colorado 80250

WILDBLUE PRESS is registered at the U.S. Patent and Trademark Offices.

ISBN 978-1-957288-12-3 Hardcover
ISBN 978-1-957288-10-9 Trade Paperback
ISBN 978-1-957288-11-6 eBook

Cover design © 2022 WildBlue Press. All rights reserved.

Interior Formatting/Cover Design by Elijah Toten
www.totencreative.com

CARMINE and the 13th AVENUE BOYS

*I dedicate my life to you God, for forgiving me,
and for giving me a second chance,
saving my life more than once.
You truly are my savior.*

- Carmine Imbriale

*For Ma,
your sacrifices made all things possible,
believing in me when so many did not.*

- Craig McGuire

Table of Contents

Foreword

My name is Tommy Dades and I began my career in law enforcement as a police officer in South Brooklyn in 1984.

These are Carmine Imbriale's stories. Take it from me, Carmine can tell a hell of a great story. I should know, I arrested him. More than once.

I've listened to Carmine tell stories since long before I joined the force. I know Carmine from way back, when we dated sisters. He called their home when I was there. I answered the phone. Carmine started in on this hilarious story about a street fight, as if we were old friends. I liked him from that first conversation.

Carmine's known for his sense of humor, ironic considering his reputation as a tough guy and involvement with a violent Bensonhurst crew. But that's what makes this work unique. This is not your usual collection of ultra-violent organized crime accounts. Mixed in with the hits and hijackings, there's real humor here, and humanity.

This book also depicts an important time and a place in the annals of organized crime, the likes of which we'll never see again. South Brooklyn, specifically Bensonhurst's 13th Avenue in the 1980s, was like the Five Points of Lower Manhattan in the 19th century and Chicago's South Side during Prohibition. Imagine an insider's view into Murder Inc.'s Brownsville in the Depression, Hell's Kitchen with the Westies, East Harlem's Pleasant Avenue, or Knickerbocker

Village in the Two Bridges. In these ganglands, the right conditions came together to create truly brutal environments. I patrolled those streets. I worked those cases. I made those arrests. Along that long 13th Avenue strip, in those bars, in those social clubs, on those corners, at any given time, you had upwards of a hundred gangsters running scams. All Five Families of the New York Mafia operated there, though this was a Colombo stronghold. You had Carmine Sessa and Bobby Zam in one club; across the street, there was Greg Scarpa Sr., who at the time was not only a serial killer for the mob, a major narcotics trafficker, and bank robber, but an FBI informant.

Right on 13th Avenue, there was Neddy's Bar, The Wimpy Boys Club, The Flip Side—straight-up gangster hotspots. Within a mile radius, you had the Gambino's Veterans & Friends Club, Sammy the Bull's 2020, Carmine Sessa's Occasions, Christi Tick's 19th Hole, Anthony Spero's Bath Beach Social Club, Wild Bill's Friendly Bocce Club, and dozens of cafes crawling with hundreds of gangsters. More captains, consiglieres, and bosses either grew up there, or still lived there, than anywhere else in the city.

Right in the middle of all this disorganized organized crime, here comes Carmine, a young, tough neighborhood kid, looking for something to belong to, to believe in, and he became, as time went on, not the center of the action, but definitely neck deep in the action.

Carmine had a reputation as a tough guy. He was good with his hands, could take a shot and a half, and never backed down. I once watched Carmine fight a local kid, Danny, on the sidewalk out in front of Neddy's Bar. Danny was a tough kid from 79th Street. He had a brother stabbed to death over some stupid street beef, nothing to do with the rackets, and another brother who was a boxer, so I knew them from the gym.

Carmine was relentless. These two go back and forth, trading shots, beating the living shit out of each other. Bars emptied out to watch them go at it like two gladiators. In the end, they fought to a draw, and both walked away from that fight looking like they'd been through the war.

Then Carmine did two things. He shook Danny's hand after it was over. Remember, this is a street fight. You didn't see that on 13th Avenue. And that's in front of this crowd of wiseguys. Those guys loved that stuff, always looking for a tough local kid to add to their crew.

Then, the next day, Carmine went up to Danny in Neddy's Bar, told him not to get too cocky or they were fighting again. But Carmine said it in a way that Danny couldn't help but smile.

That's Carmine in a nutshell: wild, crazy, tough... but respectful, with a sense of honor, and a guy you have to try hard not to like. No wonder wiseguys in several crews heavily recruited Carmine.

No doubt about it, Carmine was a criminal from early on in life. This kid was sticking up drug dealers by the time he was 14, shaking down Coney Island pimps by 15. At 16, he was stealing cars by day and parking them at night outside one of the biggest gangster discos in Brooklyn, Pastels. By 17, he was a loan shark, an armed robber, building his own gambling book, and soon to be affiliated with the Colombos.

So sure, Carmine's a funny guy with outrageous stories, and they're true—take it from me. But he was also a solid earner in the thick of it with murderers, drug dealers, and violent hoods operating out of Neddy's Bar. You walked into Neddy's, and if you didn't have balls, you'd get crushed. Even if you did, you might still catch a beating. And forget about walking into Wimpy Boys or Flip Side if you didn't know any of those wiseguys.

When it was all said and done, nearly no one survived 13th Avenue.

But Carmine did.

Those 13th Avenue guys were crazy from the cradle. And they always had problems with Bath Avenue, who always had problems with 18th Avenue, and on and on and on. All these guys grew up together, stickball on Saturday afternoons, stabbing each other at the Saturday night feasts. Every St. Bernadette's Bazaar, every 18th Avenue Feast, at the beaches, in the bowling alleys, anywhere you put these guys within punching distance of each other, it wasn't a fight. It was an all-out war.

Guys like Carmine and the 13th Avenue Boys got into everything, not just the regular rackets like extortion, numbers running, and loansharking. When they started putting VINs on vehicles, backyard chop shops sprang up all over Bensonhurst. And no sooner did they put air bags in cars, these guys started ripping them out and re-selling them for ten cents on the dollar. These guys were the first dumpster divers, the first credit card shysters. High-end sunglasses, Sony Walkmans, designer cowboy boots, exotic fur coats, portable Kenwood car radios, Blaupunkt speakers, all of that 80s stuff... just... fell off the truck and into their trunks. They shook down businesses from Coney Island to Canarsie, buried bodies in backyards and basements.

How brazen were these guys? Every 4th of July, you couldn't drive down 13th Avenue with all the fireworks. They had garages overflowing all over the neighborhood, jammed with millions of dollars of the stuff they drove in from down south. Whatever they didn't sell, they lit off. Barrel fires burning on the corners, bonfires in the middle of the street, reloadable mortars packed with the kind of industrial pyrotechnics Macy's lit off over the East River, gunpowder smoke so thick it still hung over the neighborhood the next morning, like a warzone.

Carmine was doing what a hundred other hustlers were doing on 13th Avenue. But Carmine had a knack for endearing himself to some major organized crime figures, including infamous Colombo Consigliere Carmine Sessa, who personally recruited him as a street associate. That got Carmine swept up into the bloodiest Mafia civil war of the 20th century. And that's how Carmine became a key domino in bringing it all down.

Not long after Carmine left Brooklyn, I retired from the police department, and went to work in the Brooklyn DA's office in the rackets bureau. I initiated the Mob Cops case, and I worked other high-profile crimes as an investigator. That work took a toll. When they stopped funding the Police Athletic League, I volunteered to teach boxing for youth for a while. I went through personal issues. The wind went out of my sails. I wanted to fall off the face of the earth.

Then, I disappeared.

Over the years, people called all the time about cases I worked. Honestly, I don't talk to anybody. But I agreed to consult on this project because I believe Carmine gives an honest account of the true nature of organized crime during that era.

This book helps dispel the myths about Mafia loyalty and honor. Young men, many who dropped out of school, were perfect candidates to lure into organized crime, like Carmine, and were deceived by these lies.

Thing is, some still believe that the Mafia kept the peace in the neighborhoods where they operated. From firsthand experience in law enforcement, I can tell you that may have been the case long, long ago, to a very limited extent. But in reality, they did much more harm than good. The wiseguys extorted their own people. They hurt local businesses. They bullied honest men. They took resources away from the community. They murdered at will; civilians got caught in the crossfire. And they flooded New York with drugs that destroyed countless families.

Today, because of the hard work of law enforcement and the efforts of prosecutors and the judgments handed down, we made a difference in South Brooklyn. When you go to those locations now, all the social clubs throughout

Brooklyn, the corners where these wiseguys hung around— 13th Avenue, Bath Avenue, 11th Avenue, parts of Staten Island—for the most part, they're all gone. We put away a lot of people, crew after crew, with investigations that led to more investigations.

The taxpayers should know that those protecting them on the streets of New York—the agents of the Drug Enforcement Agency, the Federal Bureau of Investigation, the New York City Police Department—are the best of the best. Many of the officers in the NYPD and agents in the FBI and the DEA are still my friends to this day. Back then, in the thick of battle against organized crime, it was them, as well as leadership, who helped me, because we never would have done it without the help of government and some pretty amazing agents.

I know we did good work, locking up dozens of crews of hardened criminals, the worst of the worst.

There are many, many good detectives and agents out there who do what I did. You just don't hear about that part of law enforcement too often. And it was also guys like Carmine who were needed to connect the dots.

I don't make apologies for Carmine. He's an interesting character, but I don't hold him up for admiration. Carmine's story is simple and straightforward, but in many ways complex, representative of so much of that time, that place.

Carmine was an actor in a grand play, set in this wild place during a time of madness and chaos, the likes of which we will never see again.

Carmine paid his debt to society and learned the hard way that there is no honor amongst thieves.

Take it from me: bad people are bad people and God don't like ugly.

— Thomas "Tommy" Dades

Thomas "Tommy" Dades retired from being an NYPD detective in 2004 after investigating hundreds of cases, then joined the Brooklyn District Attorney's organized crime unit as an investigator. Dades also fought for the NYPD Boxing Team and volunteered his time teaching boxing to inner-city youths on Staten Island. He is co-author of the New York Times *bestseller,* Friends of the Family: The Inside Story of the Mafia Cops Case.

A Timeline of Events

1957   Carmine Imbriale is born late on a Friday night, July 12, at Bay Ridge Hospital.

1969   Halloween night, Carmine is caught vandalizing the home of Joseph Colombo, boss of the Colombo Family, who later recognizes him on 13th Avenue.

1970   Carmine steals his first car, a school bus, which is left running outside a local barber shop.

1972   Carmine's first arrest, for assault and kidnapping, and attempting to rob a pimp on Coney Island.

1973   Carmine is jumped by a rival gang, stabbed with an ice pick, and left for dead.

1973   Carmine lands a coveted job as a valet, parking cars at the famed 1970s South Brooklyn disco Pastels, a popular haunt of up-and-coming Mafioso.

1973	Carmine rides shotgun as Nicky Rizzo sticks up a card game run by future Colombo Underboss Gennaro "Jerry Lang" Langella. Future Colombo Solider Frank "Frankie Notch" Iannaci is also along for the ride.
1973	In the fall, Carmine leads an underdog team sponsored by Umberto's Clam House to the 1973 Brooklyn Concrete Tackle League Championship.
1975	Bath Avenue hoods attempting to shakedown Carmine's brother's store are scared off by Genovese Captain James Ida as a favor to Carmine.
1975	In June, James Ida hands Carmine $1,500 to buy a tailored suit. Instead, Carmine uses the funds for a Florida getaway, but has to answer to Ida on his return.
1976	Carmine, graduating from peddling football sheets to running card games and operating his own book, is still unaffiliated with an active crew.

1977	Carmine (unknowingly) picks up the girlfriend of homicidal Colombo Capo Joel "Joe Waverly" Cacace at a local 13th Avenue bar.
1977	When Carmine's niece is touched inappropriately, he beats the man severely in the street outside the Wimpy Boys Club, drawing the ire of notorious Colombo Greg Scarpa Jr.
1977	Carmine randomly saves a man from a beating; that man's appreciative father, John "Johnny" Rizzo Jr., Gambino solider and future trusted lieutenant for John Gotti, rewards Carmine with a New Utrecht Avenue nightclub to run.
1977	Convicted of grand theft auto, Carmine agrees to enter drug rehabilitation at Daytop, despite not being a junkie, to have his sentence vacated.
1978	Carmine is released from Daytop, and returns to South Brooklyn.

1978	Bonanno Capo Paul "Paulie Zac" Zaccaria intervenes when Greg Scarpa refuses to honor a $6,000 bet Carmine won. Following a sit-down, Scarpa agrees to honor the wager, but now harbors deep resentment towards Carmine.
1978	Carmine's brother-in-law Bucky robs Carmine's roommate of the $40,000 he "borrowed" from the bank where he worked to place a bet, resulting in a lengthy prison sentence for the friend.
1978	Carmine hijacks a truck on the LIE, supposed to be filled with electronics, only to find it filled with cheese, then learns it's secretly owned by Gambino Underboss Neil Dellacroce.
1979	When Carmine shakes down a bookie protected by Lucchese Solider Louis "Louie Bagels" Diadone, Jimmy Ida once again intervenes on Carmine's behalf.
1980	Carmine begins a short-lived romance with Cindy Spero, daughter of Thomas "Shorty" Spero, a future captain in the Colombo Family.

1980	Carmine brawls with the staff of Hong Pan, not knowing it's secretly owned by Christopher "Christie Tick" Furnari, a captain in the Lucchese Family.
1980	When Colombo Solider Michael Bolino is sentenced to five years for carrying out an extortion plot with Alphonse "Allie Boy" Persico, Carmine is forced to take on Bolino's disastrous loan shark book.
1981	Marked for murder by a Colombo solider, unaffiliated Carmine must accept the protection of rising Colombo Captain Carmine Sessa, and becomes an associate of the Colombo Family.
1981	Police find the decomposing body of Carmine's brother-in-law, Robert "Bucky" DiLeonardo, shot to death on Staten Island in a hit disguised to look like a drug deal gone wrong.
1982	Genovese Captain Matthew Joseph "Matty the Horse" Ianniello scolds Carmine for trying to use a stolen credit card in his Manhattan restaurant. The two will later serve time together in federal prison.

1982	Carmine begins driving for Joseph "Joe Brewster" DeDomenico, a Colombo solider and member of the Bypass Gang bank robbery ring.
1985	Carmine enters the federal prison in Danbury, Connecticut, to begin serving a sentence for credit card fraud and usury.
1985	Carmine wins the first of three high-stakes handball championships in prison, earning huge paydays for imprisoned high-ranking Mafioso.
1987	Already serving a 39-year sentence, Carmine Persico receives an additional 100-year term, yet refuses to relinquish control of the Colombo Family.
1987	At a secret March 11th ceremony, Carmine Sessa is inducted into the Colombo Family, with Dennis DeLucia and Robert "Bobby Zam" Zambardi.
1987	Carmine is released from federal prison.
1987	Joseph "Joe Brewster" DeDomenico is found shot to death, slumped in the backseat of his Buick Regal. Greg Scarpa Jr. later admits to the murder.

1988	Michael Sessa, Carmine's rival in the crew, is inducted into the Colombo Family.
1989	At the request of Carmine Sessa, Carmine starts sharing a portion of extortion payments from Hunt's Point Market with Bonanno Solider Benjamin "Lefty" Ruggiero.
1989	In May, Anthony "Bird" Coluccio, a well-liked Colombo associate and member of Carmine Sessa's crew, is murdered by Michael Sessa and Joey Ambrosino, in part because Michael feared retaliation for sleeping with Bird's wife while he was incarcerated.
1991	Michael Sessa is promoted to acting captain, standing in for imprisoned Robert Zambardi.
1991	When Carmine confronts Michael Sessa for unfairly charging him a higher interest rate than other crew members, Sessa begins plotting Carmine's murder.
1991	At the request of Carmine Sessa, Imbriale attends a critical sit-down in Floral Park with Vic Orena, in a last-ditch attempt to broker a peace, which fails.

1991	In the span of two weeks, Michael Sessa drives Joey Ambrosino to Carmine's home three times, intending to murder him. Only a recurring migraine saves Carmine from assassination.
1991	On June 20, Carmine Sessa, Robert Zambardi, John Pate, and Hank Smurra attempt to ambush Vic Orena at his Long Island home, but fail when Orena spots the hit team and flees.
1991	Carmine is arrested in a sting operation, learns of multiple conspiracies against him, and, facing racketeering charges and a potential life sentence, agrees to cooperate with the FBI.
1991	Carmine starts wearing a wire, then helps the FBI plant a bug in the car of Joseph Ambrosino, leading to Ambrosino's arrest. He also agrees to cooperate.
1991	The first shots are fired in the Third Colombo War, as Orena dispatches a hit team to murder Scarpa, ambushing the capo as he drives with his daughter and grandson. Scarpa and his family escape.

1991	Persico Soldier Hank Smurra is the first casualty of the war, shot to death in a car in front of a Dunkin' Donuts, while Carmine Sessa evades multiple assassination attempts.
1991	War escalates as bullets fly in Brooklyn. On December 3rd, Scarpa's team fails to murder Orena loyalist Joseph Tollino, instead killing Genovese soldier Thomas Amato; December 6th, the murders of Vincent Fusaro and Rosario Nastasa follow; and December 8th, Scarpa kills Nicky Grancio.
1991	In a case of mistaken identity, Colombo assassins gun down innocent 18-year-old Matteo Speranzo at a mob-controlled bagel shop in Bay Ridge, Brooklyn.
1992	Carmine is part of a failed attempt on his childhood friend, Frank "Frankie Notch" Iannaci.
1992	Carmine joins nightly missions led by Michael Sessa, who is later ridiculed by his brother and other crew members for hunting rivals when only garbage trucks are on the streets.

1992	Carmine is part of multiple failed attempts to kill Joseph "Joe Campi" Campanella.
1992	Following an earlier gun battle, Greg Scarpa shoots Joel Cacace in the stomach on Avenue U. At a diner in Staten Island, Imbriale captures Scarpa on a wire bragging about the shooting.
1992	Carmine Imbriale is taken off the streets after federal handlers learn he is the target of assassination.
1992	Vic Orena is taken into custody at his girlfriend's home in Long Island.
1992	Michael Sessa is convicted in a racketeering trial and sentenced to life in prison, while his brother, Carmine Sessa, remains a fugitive.
1992	Orena is convicted of racketeering, murder, and additional crimes, and sentenced to three life sentences plus 85 years in prison.
1993	In federal custody, Imbriale begins providing evidence and information helping convict upwards of 40 gangsters, including testifying in half a dozen cases.

1993	On April 8, 1993, Carmine Sessa and other Colombo mobsters are arrested at St. Patrick's Cathedral in Manhattan.
1993	Orena Captain Joseph Scopo is murdered, the last body to fall in the Third Colombo War.
1993	Scarpa Sr. is sentenced to ten years in prison after pleading guilty to two counts of murder. He dies in prison from AIDS-related complications in June 1994.
1994	Carmine Imbriale is convicted on multiple counts, receives a 10-year sentence, which is suspended due to his cooperation with the federal government. He leaves the New York tristate area to begin life in the witness protection program.
1998	Carmine and his family exit the federal witness protection program, but remain in hiding to this day.

A Product of His Environment

These are the stories of Carmine Imbriale.

Ya know, Carmine from 13th Avenue.

Carmine went by many names. Captain Crunch. Handsome Carmine. 79th Street Carmine. Federal Inmate Register Number 67563-044. Or just, *ya know,* that *Neddy's* loan shark that used to park Caddies outside Pastels as a kid... 13th Avenue Carmine.

Carmine Imbriale was many things—a gambler, a brawler, a bookie, a bandit. For two decades, Carmine was an associate in one of the most violent crews in the Colombo Family. Carmine was an armed robber, a credit card fraudster, a shylock, a hijacker, and, in the midst of a bloody South Brooklyn gang war, a survivor. Following multiple assassination attempts, he became an informant and today is a former member of the United States Federal Witness Protection Program.

To understand Carmine Imbriale is to appreciate how he is a product of his environment, a gritty South Brooklyn that now exists only in faded police photographs, grainy wedding-day reels, and *Eyewitness News'* van's sidewalk stock footage from the latter half of the last century. Even his place of birth is gone. Bay Ridge Hospital on Ovington Avenue is now a nursing home.

Carmine came up on the downside of Brooklyn's Golden Era. But in many ways, it still was a magical time for a scrappy street kid who could blast a Spaulding three sewers. That's until they started selling dime bags from corner payphones and purple double-barrels out the back of Cropsey Park.

Families in South Brooklyn were larger in those days. The Imbriales were a sprawling Italian-Irish American clan bursting through that sheetrock-and-linoleum mid-century one-family at 1245 79th Street. At the Imbriale home, it seemed like that screen door was always slamming. And they had to keep extra folding chairs in the hall closet for all the aunts, uncles, cousins, and neighbors rotating through for dinner.

The fourth of five children born to Helen Imbriale, Carmine clocked into this world late on a Friday night, July 12, 1957, moments before his father's birthday. Named Carmine, like his father and his father's father before him, he joined two brothers and a sister, with another sister trailing behind by a few years.

This was the heart of Brooklyn's Little Italy, Dyker Heights bordering Bensonhurst, nearby Bath Beach, and Bay Ridge. These last exits to Brooklyn lie along the Belt Parkway on the outer shores of Lower Hudson Bay, running off that dark stretch of water they call the Gravesend.

For generations, grim-faced Italian legions arrived here fleeing the poverty of places like Campania, Apulia, and Palermo. They brought with them their butchers, their bakers, their *braciole di manzo* makers. They lined their streets with smoky social clubs, and slung salamis in their *salumerias*, spiking the air with traces of *stromboli*, *soffritto*, *sfogliatella*, piping hot out of pastry shops, pork stores, pizzerias, and pasta emporiums, far as the eye could see.

This is the South Brooklyn of the Sunday sauce, just don't call it gravy. They played stickball in the streets and sat on stoops until late in the evening. Stray cats shrieked in alleyways strung with laundry. Dead-eyed statues of Saint Anthony guarded concrete gardens beneath banners of the green, white, and red snapping in the wind alongside the red, white, and blue.

In the mornings, street sweepers kicked up dust as men in white delivered glass bottles down blocks hung with sneakers sagging power lines like rubber hives. High above broken asphalt chalk-scarred with skelly boards, a tar beach tapestry unfolded, of rooftops, ancient water towers, church steeples, rusted fire escapes. And always, *always*, off in the distance, the Verrazano brooded and the mighty, mighty B Train rumbled out to Coney.

This was the real Brooklyn. Young bucks in white tanks on street corners sweated it out on busted beach chairs and milk crates. Ginas and Dinas and Minas in Berta 66 cut-offs reclined on car hoods preening, braiding. Someone crooked a monkey wrench out Old Man Dinardi's shed, cracked open the johnny pump to scream out the sun... until a patrol car from the 6-8 rolled 'round to shut it down. And soon, the sun slipped and dusk tripped the street lights, reminding the mothers along 13th Avenue to put down their Pall Malls and holler their kids home for dinner.

Historians mark the year Carmine was born, 1957, as the beginning of the end of Brooklyn's "Golden Era" that started way back in 1920, when the huddled masses of the Lower East Side slums fanned out across Brooklyn's broad plains on the backs of brand-spanking-new BMT and IRT lines.

The promise of the 1950s post-war boom was already a *welch* when Carmine first picked up a stickball bat on Dyker's P.S. 201 schoolyard. By the time he roofed his last Spaulding across the street, there were even fewer opportunities for the New Utrecht high school dropouts hanging out on 13th Avenue. At least not many legitimate ones.

That year, 1957, marked the peak for the Baby Boomers, born 1946 through 1964. Today, more Boomers live in Kings County zip codes than in anywhere in America.[1]

That year, 1957, the average cost of a home was $12,220. Rent in Brooklyn on a two-bedroom ran you $90. Fill your tank for 24 cents a gallon in a car that cost you $1,500, affordable on the average annual salary of $4,550 (though the day-rate down along the South Brooklyn waterfront was lower, especially after the union kickbacks).[2]

They went to the movies to take in *The Ten Commandments*, *12 Angry Men*, and *The Bridge Over the River Kwai*, while at home, watched as *Perry Mason* and *Maverick* debuted, *American Bandstand* first aired, and *I Love Lucy* cracked her last joke. They flung their Frisbees, slunk their Slinkys, and Hula-ed their Hoops. But Carmine and the 13th Avenue Boys stuck to stickball, handball, football—really anything with a rubber ball to hit, slap, smack, or chuck.

That year, 1957, was also the year of "The Great Tragedy," when the wailing of millions went up as the dastardly Walter O'Malley made good on his threat to move the Brooklyn Dodgers unless the city built him an elaborate new stadium. The mayor balked, and O'Malley walked, hijacking the beloved "Dem Bums" from Ebbets Field for Los Angeles.[3]

Rat bastard.

That year, 1957, was the year of the infamous summit of the American Mafia at the home of Joseph "Joe the Barber" Barbara, in Apalachin, New York. Mafia chieftains and their top lieutenants from as far as Italy and Cuba invaded that sleepy hamlet to crown Vito Genovese *capo di tutti capi.*

1. "The Most Popular Zip Codes for Baby Boomers: New York Challenges Sunny Locations for the Title," RENTCafé, July 16, 2019

2. "The Year 1957," ThePeopleHistory.com

3. *Brooklyn's Dodgers: The Bums, the Borough, and the Best of Baseball, 1947-1957* by Carl E. Prince, Oxford University Press, 1997

Not so fast, said suspicious local police, spoiling the party, sending dozens of gangsters stumbling into the woods in their wingtips.[4]

That round up of 60 mobsters compelled FBI Director J. Edgar Hoover to concede that, yes, in America, organized crime does exist. But Carmine and the 13th Avenue Boys could've told you that.

You see, in the neighborhood where Carmine grew up, the Mafia was everywhere. Everyone in that era of South Brooklyn knew someone, or knew someone who knew someone, in *the Life.*

You knew "a guy" who'd give you a break on something that just *fell off a truck.* Feeling lucky? You go to that other guy to *play the numbers.* Bank turned you down and need a loan fast? You're in luck. That's the other guy, the *shy.* And if you wanted to gamble, that guy had another guy for you, the one with the *book.* And all these guys were not hard to find. They were outside the club on your corner, in your local barber shops, down by the OTB a couple blocks over, or in the smoky backroom of the *Fortunata* bakery throwing the cards around.

Some of these *guys,* the ones that did well, lived in Dyker Heights, starting a block north of the Imbriale home. Growing up at the bottom of that hill on the border of Bensonhurst, Carmine saw that tale of two neighborhoods unfold.

Bensonhurst, working class, is block after block of one- and two-family homes and random red-brick apartment buildings, sliced by commercial strips like 13th Avenue. Lower-income Italian, Irish, and Jewish immigrant families settled here a hundred years prior. Dyker Heights took a bit longer to develop, a former Native American burial ground too sloped for farming, too wooded for building.

---

4. *Mafia Summit: J. Edgar Hoover, the Kennedy Brothers, and the Meeting That Unmasked the Mob* by Gil Reavill, Thomas Dunne Books, 2013

As young Carmine crossed over 12th Avenue, he saw where the wild ones went once they were done dealing in the clubs and cafés of 13th Avenue. These homes—larger, stucco-ed—were front-yarded with towering fountains and marbled lions, privacy hedged, paved in polished stone with gurgling waterfalls, dripping dandelions.

Behind those lace curtains were two types of people: those who made it, and those who'd been *made*.

In few other places (maybe Long Island, or out in Jersey) did so many cardiologists live alongside *caporegimes*. Here, medical surgeons shared driveways with Mafia soldiers, as contractors gave gardening advice to contract killers. After all, just like doctors on call preferred to live near Victory Memorial over on 7th Avenue, the wiseguys wanted to be short drives to their sit-downs.

In those days, Halloween was a big deal for the tough Italian boys of 13th Avenue. As night came down, the old Sicilian black-shawls returning from their All Hallows Eve masses at St. Bernadette's, the trick-or-treaters retreating home to savor their sweets, Carmine and his boys set out on their missions.

Across South Brooklyn, rival factions fanned out, block after block, armed for aerial combat with eggs and modified cans of Barbasol, bent on bombing the shit out of each other... or beating the shit out of each other.

Halloween night, 1969, Carmine at 12, rambling through Dyker Heights with his boys, spotted a glowing jack-o-lantern smiling wickedly down from a second-floor balcony wrapped in wrought iron. He told his boys to hold up a sec, then shimmied up that drain pipe, not knowing, not caring whose home it was.

Moments later, mid-shimmy halfway up that pipe, Carmine froze as an older Italian-American gentleman clad in a dark silk robe stepped out onto that balcony. He lit a long cigar, snorted at Carmine like he knew he was there, amused, not alarmed. He then twisted that fat Cuban in the flame as he dead-eyed Carmine.

"We looked at each other, like, forever, and he got a real good look at me," Carmine says. "He didn't seem to give a shit this kid was climbing up his house. He's all relaxed, lighting that big, fat cigar. Then he laughs, says out the corner of his mouth, 'Okay, tough guy, let's see how fast you can get down that pipe.'"

Carmine was stuck.

"I didn't think it through and couldn't really climb down the drainpipe, especially carrying a pumpkin," Carmine remembers. "Lucky for me, he just let me out of the house and told me to never come back. But he was laughing, like making a joke out of it."

Fortunate for Carmine, that sophisticated-looking older gentleman clad in dark silk found humor in the situation. Guy like that could make a body disappear out in a hole in Staten Island, pretty easy in fact.

"I didn't think much of it at the time, but I remembered that old man, and I'd see him on 13th Avenue," Carmine recalls. "He'd see me, shake a finger at me, laugh, sort of like he had his eye on me."

A friend of Carmine's witnessed one such exchange, and paused. "How do you know *him*?" he asked. Carmine laughed as he shared the Halloween story. "You don't know who *that* is?" his friend asked. "That's Joe Colombo. You know, the boss of the Colombos."

The Colombo Family? Sure, Carmine shrugged. Who hadn't heard of the Colombos? They were all over 13th Avenue, like semolina seeds on a Sunday loaf.

At the time, Carmine could not know what that name meant for his future.

Wiseguys were always eyeing talent up on the Avenue, and there were many sizing up that kid Carmine. Youth street gangs like the 13th Avenue Boys long served as farm teams for the Five Families of the New York Mafia. A generation before Carmine was crushing Joe Colombo's pumpkins, they had more colorful nicknames, like the South Brooklyn Devils, the Degraw Street Boys, the Sackett Street Boys, the Gowanus Boys, the Kane St. Midgets, the Savages, the Senators, the Little Gents, and the Young Savages.[5]

Future Colombo Boss Carmine "The Snake" Persico started out as a leader of the Garfield Boys in Downtown Brooklyn. After he killed a rival in a gang fight in Prospect Park, then beat the charges, he came to the attention of a Profaci solider, and was a *made* member of that Family (forerunners of the Colombos) by the age of 25.[6]

The morning of October 25, 1957, on the orders of Carlo Gambino and Vito Genovese, a hit team murdered mob boss Albert Anastasia while he was getting a shave in the barber shop in the lobby of the Park Sheraton Hotel in Manhattan. Persico was one of the gunmen on the hit team led by Joseph "Crazy Joe" Gallo.[7]

Profaci, Gallo, Colombo. These were the antiheroes held up by Carmine and the 13th Avenue Boys, at a time when America's teens idolized astronauts and cowboys.

By the 1970s, they no longer greased their hair in South Brooklyn or wore jackets with colorful gang names. Yet they were just as violent. They banded together by block or by avenue. The 18th Avenue Boys. The Avenue U Boys. The Bath Avenue Boys. And, of course, the 13th Avenue Boys.

The 13th Avenue Boys were not to be fucked with, armed, dangerous, stashing weapons nearby, because you never knew who'd be driving by, or when one of your boys would come running up after being jumped.

---

5. "Where the Mob Once Found Its Members," by Ed Scarpo, CosaNostraNews.com, 2014

6. *Carmine the Snake: Carmine Persico and His Murderous Mafia Family* by Frank Dimatteo and Michael Benson, Citadel Press, 2018

7. *Five Families: The Rise, Decline, and Resurgence of America's Most Powerful Mafia Empires* by Selwyn Raab, Thomas Dunne Books, 2014

"My brother Carmine was crazy as could be, which could be frightening," Maryellen Imbriale recalls. "He never shied from a fight, and so many times he should've. He got beaten up so bad, so many times, fighting people he never should've been fighting, guys ten times his size, ten years older than him. But he never backed down."

Carmine and the 13th Avenue Boys' fiercest rivalry was with the Bath Avenue Boys. The two groups brawled at every opportunity, from church fairs and carnivals to bowling alleys and beaches. Yet nowhere was that violence more explosive than at "The Feast."

The Italians brought these ancient festivals over with them to honor the saints who watched over their villages. Back when Carmine was kicking in teeth, South Brooklyn hosted feasts all summer, like the Feast of Our Lady of Mount Carmel in Williamsburg, the Feast of Santa Rosalia on 18th Avenue, the Feast of Santa Fortunata on 17th Avenue (actually two feasts), the Feast of St. Bernadette, the Harway Avenue Feast, and many others.

"It was a territory thing," Carmine recalls. "We fought everyone. Sometimes we got together with another avenue. Sometimes, just us against whoever came down. But it was always something with someone, every night a fight. We battled 14th Avenue, 15th Avenue, 17th Avenue. Sometimes you'd get the Park Slope Boys coming in looking for trouble, and we gave it to them. But mostly, we fought Bath Avenue. We hated those assholes and they hated us. But they were some tough kids, like us. And let me tell you, there sure were a hell of a lot of them."

Carmine's sister recalls one memorable fight at St. Bernadette's Bazaar, when a gang from Red Hook crashed the scene. "I was inside, and all of my friends came running up telling me my brother was in a huge fight," Maryellen says. "So, I run outside, and there's Carmine, all bloody, but now he's getting ready to continue on to the next stage of the fight."

Maryellen attempted to intervene. "I could get him under control sometimes, but not that night," Maryellen says. "I was afraid for him and I tried. But he took off with all his friends. They went down to Red Hook to settle the score. Later that night, he was arrested in Red Hook and went to jail."

Those feasts drew thousands, funneled into narrow streets barricaded on both sides by long, white vendor trailers, as bright green, white, and red lights hung overhead. As Lucy's sausage sizzled, Italian bands blared, and bingo wheels *click-click-click*ed, rival gangs charged, egged on by big-haired bangled beauties.

"The Saint Bernadette Bazaar was like gladiator school," Carmine says. "Other gangs came in, looking for trouble, and we just beat the shit out of each other, night after night. The girls loved it. But I'd never get into a fight over a girl."

Technically, sure, Carmine *almost* never beefed over girls. But it did happen one night at the St. Bernadette Bazaar.

"This jerkoff, Larry, from the neighborhood, comes over to me, and I'm dating this girl, Linda, and Larry wants Linda, so Larry wants to fight me for Linda, and Linda wants me to fight Larry for Linda." Carmine laughs. "I ask Linda if she wants to be with me or be with Larry."

Linda didn't give Carmine the answer he wanted.

"So, I said, 'I'll knock the shit outta this asshole, but I'm not fighting over you,'" Carmine says. "So sure. Fuck Larry. Fuck Linda. But no way was I letting it look like Larry backed me down. Fuck that."

Carmine fought Larry on principle. And that night, Carmine beat Larry unconscious, in front of Linda, at the Saint Bernadette Bazaar.

Then Carmine flat left Linda.

As Carmine grew, the violence grew, and 1970s South Brooklyn grew... darker, meaner. Drug dealers commandeered corners and parks. Sex workers strutted down Surf Avenue or stalked the shadows under the Gowanus, before the Industry City renaissance, when it was more abandoned warehouses and drug spots.

Crime spiked across all major categories. Security bars appeared on the windows of homes that, not too long ago, left doors unlocked. Roll-down gates now lined commercial avenues. Everyone knew someone who'd been mugged. And the theaters replaced comedies and westerns with vigilante movies like *Death Wish* and *Taxi Driver*.

Between 1969 and 1974, the city lost a half a million manufacturing jobs, the types that keep young, restless men off street corners. Unemployment grew to 10%. Rapes and burglaries jumped threefold. Assaults and auto thefts doubled.

In the fall of 1973, this was just the type of environment where a 16-year-old boy stumbling home along 12th Avenue late at night could get stabbed.

It was after midnight that September evening. The air was cool. Brooklyn cool, you know, with that crisp, early autumn edge. Carmine was on his way home after a night drinking in the P.S. 201 schoolyard with his boys and some local girls. The only sounds were the occasional sedan whooshing by, the faint plunk of the traffic light turning on the corner up ahead.

"I didn't know what hit me, didn't see them coming," Carmine says, waylaid by two assailants springing from the shadows from behind a parked van. They came at him from behind as he passed. He felt a sharp pain exploding halfway down the left side of his back, half a second before he hit the concrete; a pain, he says, that felt like getting hit with a lead pipe.

Carmine rolled to his side, saw his attackers flee on foot. He felt the cold concrete on the side of his face. A warmness spread across his back, to his legs. He was bleeding out from a stab wound. He dragged himself upright, struggled the block and a half to his home, stirring his entire family into a panic.

"Made a big scene, but turned out not to be too bad, missed my organs; but at the time, sure felt like I was dying, and there was a ton of blood," Carmine remembers. "I actually still have the icepick. Believe that? They left it in me when they ran off."

Carmine didn't know who jumped him. He only saw their backs. But he knew it wasn't random. They didn't even rob him of the fat knot of cash he picked up shaking down a pot dealer earlier.

"Knew it was two guys 'cause I saw them running away, and I heard one of them say, 'Good, you got him,'" Carmine recalls. "Yeah, they got me... in the back."

Days before, Carmine and his friends jumped some guys from another block to settle a beef he doesn't remember. "I'd put my money on them," Carmine says. "But really, could've been half dozen other guys. We had beef with everyone. Every day, different bullshit. Couldn't keep track of all the beef we had."

Doctor told Carmine that had the stab wound been an inch to the left, they'd have been laying him out at Torregrossa's two blocks over from where he got stabbed.

Carmine was back out on 13th Avenue the next night, peeling back the bandage, showing off the nasty wound bruising up half his back, like it was fresh ink from Mikey Tattoo.

In the years ahead, this toughness served Carmine well in the South Brooklyn underworld. Drugs hit the scene in a big way. The fights became more frequent, more involved weapons. Carmine's reputation as a 13th Avenue brawler grew.

Over the years, Carmine racked up more than two dozen arrests, from petty offenses up to a RICO (Racketeer Influenced and Corrupt Organizations Act) indictment. Before he even dropped out of New Utrecht High School, one judge reviewing his rap sheet scoffed, "Nice to see you again, Carmine. I notice you've gone on to bigger and better things."

It's a career that spans mostly enterprise crimes (burglary, illegal gambling, extortion, counterfeiting, and credit card fraud) and violent transgressions (aggravated assault, armed robbery). But considering his chronic violence and explosive temper, it's remarkable he was never indicted, convicted, or even accused of murder—not even manslaughter.

His first serious scrape with the law came in the summer of 1972. That night, a 15-year-old Carmine sat cuffed in the back of an NYPD blue-and-white, notching his first collar, for assault and kidnapping.

It started out as a simple Coney Island shakedown.

That sticky summer night, Carmine and two friends jumped on the Belt Parkway, rumbling eastbound toward the cigarette butt-strewn sands of CI.

Today, Coney Island is enjoying a renaissance. Millions of investment dollars pour in, with hotels, amusements, and attractions built or envisioned. A 5,000-seat amphitheater opened in 2016; nearby, the 7,500-seat Maimonides Park (aka Keyspan Park, then MCU Park), unveiled in 2001, is home to the New York Mets farm team, the Brooklyn Cyclones. The New York Aquarium got a makeover. Real estate sales and reconstructions are booming.[8]

Coney Island was once America's premier summer playground. Yet in 1972, as Carmine and his boys cruised down Cropsey, crossing the toxic Coney Island Creek, the area's former glory was a distant memory. The racetracks had closed. Dreamland shut down. The Parachute Jump was a rusted eyesore, as a cash-strapped city refused to pay to tear it down. Public housing projects were overrun

---

8. "Coney Island, home to hot dogs and the Cyclone roller coaster, sees a budding real estate boom," Daniel Bukszpan, CNBC, December 30, 2018

with drug gangs. Homeless camped under the boardwalk. Sex workers and junkies roamed boulevards with high commercial vacancy rates. With Luna Park in bankruptcy, and America's oldest wooden roller coast, the Cyclone, slated for demolition, Coney Island was recycling an old nickname.

"Sodom by the Sea."[9]

Sure, a trickle of day trippers still sought to escape Brooklyn's soupy summer heat at the beach. But now they fended off three-card monte dealers, dope fiends, sideshow freaks, and chain snatchers.

Carmine and his boys were also drawn to Coney Island, but not for the sun, nor the sand.

"We used to hit Coney Island to mug the pimps," Carmine said. "Pimp's an easy target. They always got cash. They won't run to the cops. And they beat up women. Whatever they get, they got coming. Can't feel sorry for a piece of shit who beats on women, turns 'em out like that."

Early that evening, Carmine and his boys rolled by the seedy arcades and shooting galleries along Mermaid Avenue. They spotted a mark hanging off a corner on Surf, couple blocks shy of the massive run-down Stillwell Avenue train terminus. They kept going, turned the corner, doubled back around, jumped out of the sedan, and ran up on the pimp.

They'd done this a dozen times before, always an easy score. Stun the pimp, knock his ass around, strip him of any valuables, escape up Stillwell, bang a left on Neptune, a right on Cropsey, fly back over the creek to jump back onto the Belt for the two exits back to the neighborhood.

They didn't count on one of the pimp's drug-addled sex workers leaping into the getaway vehicle, actually launching herself through the open shotgun window. Speeding away

---

9. *Coney Island: The Decline & Death of an American Icon* by Michael Malott, November 13, 2010

from the scene with her track-marked legs wiggling up in the air out the window, Carmine pulled over a couple blocks down Surf to get her out of the car.

"She wouldn't get out, and I don't beat up women, so we were stuck." Carmine laughs. "We're yelling at her. She's yelling at us. Then this nut says she wants us to drive her home, all the way out to Canarsie."

Arguing with her, Carmine never saw the squad cars until they were surrounded. He denied her accusations. All three boys were searched and cuffed curbside. Then the bloodied pimp ran up.

The patrolmen dragged Carmine, his boys, the pimp, and the sex worker all down to the 60th Precinct nearby on West 8th Street to sort things out.

Unfortunately, the boys from 13th Avenue faced more than a disorderly charge. Technically, with the sex worker physically inside the vehicle when the patrolmen rolled up, even though she jumped in, they could be charged with kidnapping, plus the assault and robbery of the pimp.

Tough spot.

After the boys were processed, they were minors and needed an adult to sign them out. "But no way I was calling my father to get me out," Carmine says. "I called this guy, I called that guy. I called everybody and their mother, but couldn't get hold of no one to get us out. And not like we had cell phones, beepers, none of that back then. Not even answering machines. We were stuck."

When none of the other boys reached their fathers, a detective asked Carmine a second time if his father was available. "When he asked again, it was funny, 'cause all my friends, at the same time, said NO." Carmine laughs. "They knew my father, knew how he'd react. We'd all rather spend the night in a Coney Island holding cell than face him."

After a few hours, the detective came back into the holding area to unlock the cell, ready to release the boys with Desk Appearance Tickets to appear in criminal court in Downtown Brooklyn and plea, but only for the disorderly charges. "The thing that saved us is that we didn't drive too far away, so the pimp was able to run up when he did," Carmine remembers. "This jerkoff forgot he had a shitload of heroin packets stuffed in his pimp hat. Then they find the prostitute had heroin stashed in her wig. Cops booked them, and let us go with DATs on the disorderly."

Even without Carmine's cooperation, the police tracked down his father. "My father walks into the holding area in the 6-0 like he owned it, pissed," Carmine says. "He's fuming, steam coming out of his ears, standing next to this cop, just waiting for him to unlock the cell. Cop unlocks it, and he's trying to rip the cell door open, but I'm holding it closed, 'cause I know he's gonna to beat the living shit out of me, cops or no cops. Both of us are in this tug of war, holding the bar so tight our knuckles are turning white, going back and forth. It's a good thing those cops were there to calm him down."

Hustling out of the precinct, Carmine caught a half dozen slaps upside the back of his head as he jumped in his father's Dodge. He rode in the front on the passenger side. His two boys slunk down in the back.

"The ride home, I'm getting backhands, I'm getting elbows, forearms, he's knocking me around at the red lights," Carmine remembers. "We get back to my house and I run inside, but my friends don't get out, two dopes looking for a ride. My father yells at them to get a cab 'cause he's not driving no delinquents home. They knew not to ask. What a scene."

Carmine never cleared up that DAT. "Never even went to court. Forgot all about it. Still comes up on my *old* record."

No wonder Carmine never got around to addressing that disorderly, considering all the company that minor charge got on his rap sheet. You see, the South Brooklyn authorities got to know Carmine Imbriale from 79th Street quite well down at central booking.

The Brooklyn House of Detention Complex, a notorious jail once located at 275 Atlantic Avenue in Downtown Brooklyn, was not a pleasant place for a teenager. Opened in 1956 adjacent to the Kings County Criminal Court, the Brooklyn House was a grim, grey 11-story fortress, built to house up to 815 male prisoners awaiting bail hearings or trial in Kings County (Brooklyn) or Richmond County (Staten Island).

"One night, they take me in, I'm wearing my football jersey, and it said on it 'CAPTAIN CRUNCH,' my nickname in the league," Carmine says. "Next week, I'm in there again on some stupid shit, and some cop says, 'Hey, look, here comes the captain again.' A week later, desk sergeant sees me coming, tells me to stick to football 'cause he says he seen me in there four times that month, so I obviously sucked at being a crook."

By then, Carmine knew the drill, including frequent court appearances.

"I was in court so many times, because I was young and my parents had to take me with them," Maryellen Imbriale remembers.

One hearing in criminal court in particular stands out for Carmine's sister, when her brother was arrested following another gang fight. "We waited for a while, so I hadn't seen him until they brought him in," Maryellen says. "He had on one of those leather camel coats they used to wear in the 70s, only it was full of blood. He was beat up pretty bad, black eyes, dried blood all over him, but he stood tall, defiant. I couldn't take it. I was so upset by seeing him like that, I just broke down crying. I'll never forget that day, seeing my brother like that."

Carmine learned the unwritten rules of lockup.

"One time, I get arrested and I'm down in the Brooklyn House with my friend, Billy," Carmine remembers. "When they put us in the cage, I tell Billy, 'Find your spot on a bench, lay down, and shut your mouth. Anyone tells you to move, you tell them to go fuck themselves. You don't move for nobody.'"

Carmine dozed off, only to wake a bit later to see Billy holding court. "Here's this kid, Billy, a good kid, who don't know nothing from nothing on the street, and he's giving a lesson about capos and consiglieres to these three Black guys."

"This was the year *The Godfather* came out, so like everyone was fascinated with that shit," Carmine says. "And here's this dope, Billy, acting like he's a wiseguy, explaining how the mob works, and they're just all wide-eyed, eating it up."

Carmine scolded Billy in front of his audience. "I said, 'Who are you? Why you opening your mouth? You don't know nothing, so shut up.' He's laughing, but you know, he was lucky he was in there with me and not some of the other guys from the Avenue. If there was a real wiseguy in that cage, what a beating Billy woulda caught. And, there *wouldna been* a damned thing I could do to help him. You're not even supposed to talk about this with nobody.

"What?" Carmine says. "You think I'm stupid, like Billy? Even back then, when I was robbing Fort Hamilton pot dealers and Coney Island pimps, I knew the rules."

Growing Up Brooklyn

Carmine Imbriale was not a bad kid.

Just wild.

"Carmine was quiet growing up, at least at home," Frank Imbriale, Carmine's brother, recalls. "Never did we expect this quiet kid here to go and get into what he got into. I mean, he was doing the Golden Gloves, and no one even knew about that. Then my father found out from someone in the neighborhood."

"My father was the authority in my home and I respected him," Carmine says. "He didn't want me to fight in the Golden Gloves, said that it'd turn my head into a meatball, so I stopped."

Frank remembers that while Carmine was easygoing at home, he was always getting into trouble in the neighborhood. Like the day Carmine came home with his latest concussion. "But this one was pretty serious, so bad that the doctor said someone had to keep an eye on him, not let him sleep all night," Frank says. "My parents were working, so I stayed up with him."

By the time Carmine was a teenager, the Imbriale home was often empty.

"My older brother was drafted, went to Vietnam," says Frank, who is three years older than Carmine. "My sister moved out and did her thing. I started working at 11, so I'm always out of the house. My parents are both working to make ends meet. So Carmine was left alone a lot, but not like he was a little kid."

Frank remembers one episode that defines Carmine.

"I'm outside, some of the local kids are passing by and they say my brother was in a big fight on 13th Avenue. We go down there, and sure, Carmine had gotten into a fight with some guy who worked in the pizzeria. But you gotta understand, Carmine's like 14 years old. This guy's in his thirties. Carmine just beat the shit outta him. Yeah, we got a ton of stories like that about Carmine."

"Felipe, guy who worked at Dom's Pizzeria, across from Torregrossa's, had a wet rag and he slapped me with it," Carmine says. "So I went after him."

Carmine was closest in age with his younger sister, Maryellen.

"Carmine was always my parents' favorite child, and that was very noticeable throughout our childhood," Maryellen says. "We all know Carmine doesn't like to follow rules, didn't follow rules, and did whatever he wanted to do."

One afternoon, Maryellen was walking in the neighborhood with friends when she was told police from the local precinct had her brother cornered. "Carmine had broken into P.S. 201 with his friends and was running around on the scaffolding outside the school, and the cops were trying to get him down," Maryellen says. "It was absolutely nuts, big crowd, fire trucks, cops all over, you name it. They took him in and *everybody* in the neighborhood knew about it. Carmine was always into something; and the whole neighborhood would be talking about it right away."

Carmine was only three years older than Maryellen.

"Not a big age difference now, but growing up, it sure was," Maryellen says. "I was the youngest sister, and Carmine was very, *very* protective, of me. Carmine made a point of getting involved in my life, sometimes without me even knowing. But I was younger, so he kept me away from everything."

In fact, Carmine forbade Maryellen from hanging out on 13th Avenue.

"All my boyfriends, he'd check them out. He knew everything about everybody, and if he didn't, he'd go and check, ask around, and then I was no longer allowed to date them."

It wasn't only Carmine who disapproved of Maryellen's matches. "I met boys, and the parents, when they heard the name Imbriale, they'd say no, no, no, forget it, because of Carmine." Maryellen laughs. "Seriously. At least two of my boyfriend's parents didn't want their sons to see me, *after* we were already dating, once they found out who my brother was."

In many respects, Carmine was shaped by his father. Yet today's fathers are much different than yesterday's dads.

Carmine Senior didn't drop everything when he got home to race outside and toss the ball around with his son. He was never his coach, his cheerleader, his Scout leader, or his shoulder to cry on. They never flew kites, pieced puzzles together, or built model airplanes.

When Carmine scored four touchdowns in a football game, his father asked what happened to the fifth. When Carmine came home with a black eye, damn straight the other kid better have two.

Still, Carmine Senior was a good man. And again, fatherhood was much different in the 1970s.

Carmine Senior was old school, even back then. He hammered into his son the importance of hard work, honesty, integrity. He couldn't stand the 13th Avenue wiseguys. Thought the local priests were crooked shysters. And he had little patience for people who acted disrespectfully.

Like Scott Baio.

In 1976, Baio dated Maryellen. Baio was about to land the role of a lifetime as Fonzi's younger cousin, Charles "Chachi" Arcola, on *Happy Days*, the highest-rated show on television. He'd soon be competing against Shaun Cassidy and Leif Garrett for teen-magazine covers.

Apparently, Carmine Senior let his subscription to *Tiger Beat* lapse.

"Scott came to my house with his new fancy car and honked the horn for my sister to come out, like some bigshot," Carmine says. "My sister went running down, but got stopped cold by my father."

The rest of the neighborhood may have been impressed with Chachi and his Ovaltine commercials, but not Carmine's father. "He hollered out to Scott that if he wanted to see his daughter, get out of the car and knock on the door like a real man," Carmine says. "And in front of the whole block, Scott did what he was told."

Sure, Carmine's father was a hard man, but not a harsh man. But he was also honest, hard-working, loyal, and righteous—all traits he tried to instill in his children.

Some of Carmine's father's lessons took. Others, not so much. Some took a lifetime to learn.

There was always something going on in the Imbriale home. Following the death of his grandfather in the late 1950s, Carmine' father became the patriarch of the extended family, and family members, from both sides, visited regularly.

"For some reason, everyone called my father Don, and they called my mother Mary, though her name was Helen." Carmine laughs. "My father was the cook in the family. I remember him cooking all the time, with a towel around his neck. He'd send me to Mona Lisa on 13th Avenue for the bread, then yell at me when I bit the heels off on the way home. But it was worth it. That was some great bread."

From time to time, Carmine Senior complained loudly how he wanted to move to Florida, or anywhere that the fishing was better. Carmine's mother nixed any idea of abandoning Brooklyn, refusing to leave her sisters, who also lived in the area.

Carmine Senior actually got along quite well with his wife's family, who were Bay Ridge Irish, and included nine siblings. He served in the United States Army at the same time as his brother-in-law, and both were at the Invasion of Normandy during World War II. "Those two, they never, ever spoke about the war, unless they were together," Carmine recalls. "Then the war stories came out."

Times were hard in Brooklyn. The short-lived recession of 1958 produced prolonged economic malaise, and by the 1960s, the post-World War II boom was way back in Brooklyn's rearview mirror. The Brooklyn Navy Yard closed in '66, throwing 12,000 blue collars out of work. Next went the factories along the waterfront near the Manhattan Bridge, relocating to more spacious container docks opening in Jersey. Thousands of jobs fled Brooklyn.

However, the South Brooklyn communities of Bensonhurst, Bath Beach, and Dyker Heights weathered the storm somewhat better than neighboring higher-crime districts like Coney Island and Sunset Park. The rents were relatively low and a hard worker with a bit of luck could make a living and raise a family.

While Carmine admired his father, their relationship grew strained as Carmine developed a wild streak. One episode in particular drove a wedge between them.

It happened while Carmine attended New Utrecht High School in the fall of 1973.

Located on 16th Avenue and 80th Street, New Utrecht opened in 1915 to handle overcrowding in nearby Bay Ridge High School. That school became an all-girls institution, while New Utrecht only enrolled boys.

By the time Carmine enrolled, it was co-educational, and the largest school in South Brooklyn, with a student body numbering nearly 4,000 teenagers.

The school gained national fame when its exterior was used for the opening and closing credits for *Welcome Back, Kotter*, the popular 70s sitcom starring New Utrecht alumnus Gabe Kaplan and a young John Travolta. Other graduates include Art Modell, Rosanna Scotto, Buddy Hackett, Shemp Howard, David Geffen, Jerry Ferrara, and many more.

"In my junior year, I stole a stack of blank report cards," Carmine says. "I'm failing everything, so I gave myself passing grades. Even gave myself an A."

Carmine handed off the forgery to his father. Carmine Senior paid his son a rare compliment, said he did a real good job. He then invited Carmine to join him downstairs.

Carmine did not know that New Utrecht High administration had just started mailing home report cards that semester.

"I'm walking downstairs and as I turn the corner, my father hit me with such a shot, knocked me into next week," Carmine remembers. When Carmine regained consciousness, his father imparted a life lesson that he carries with him to this day. "I didn't know they mailed them home, and he was holding it. He told me he would never trust me again. He said he didn't care what grades I got, didn't care what I did. He just wanted to know that I tried, and above all else, that I never lied to him."

That encounter left its mark on him, and not just a visible bruise. For months, Carmine's father did not speak to him. "It broke my heart," Carmine says. "Every time I sat down, he would get up and leave the room. And it taught me valuable lessons on how to carry myself. I decided I'm not going to make excuses. I'm going to carry myself like a man. And I never did lie to my father again."

Carmine dropped out of New Utrecht at 17, about the time his father landed a job as head custodian to supplement his retirement income. The position was at a private school in Sunset Park, Brooklyn, down on 5th Avenue. This was the mid-70s and the city was an economic mess. Good jobs like this were near impossible to find. It was hard work, decent work, and Carmine's father enjoyed the position.

There was one problem. Carmine Senior could not stand his supervisor, a short, obnoxious superintendent who, for whatever reason, harbored an intense personal dislike of his new custodian.

"He made my father miserable, so, of course, my father came home and he made us all miserable," Carmine said. "After a month of this, I said to myself, 'Enough's enough.' We were all suffering."

One day, Carmine, nearing 18 years of age, strong, a veteran of dozens of street fights, hardened by experiences both in the gym and on the corners of Brooklyn, decided to act. Carmine recruited his brother-in-law, Bucky DiLeonardo, who was more than willing to help Carmine eliminate the source of his father-in-law's constant outbursts.

They decided to pay the superintendent a visit.

"We went on a Saturday, when school was closed and my father was off from work. The door was unlocked, so we went in and walked around a bit. We found the superintendent and we dragged him into the boiler room."

Carmine and Bucky opened up the boiler, and after smacking the superintendent around, they threatened to shove him face-first into the flames. Carmine held him by the back of the head close enough to feel the heat.

"I told him, 'I'm Carmine's son,' and he'd better stop treating my father badly. I said, 'Next time you bother my father or my father comes home even a little bit aggravated, I don't care why, I'm coming back and throwing you down the chute. And God forbid my father hears of any of this, I'll come running back here.'"

Carmine Senior came home from work the next day in a great mood, actually whistling, with a six-pack under his arm.

"Sometimes, people need reminders for how they should act," Carmine says.

Carmine's father was old school, very strict.

"He didn't take shit from anyone," Janet, Carmine's wife, recalls. "He had the biggest heart underneath it all, but a very tough exterior and that's how he raised Carmine. Taught him a man doesn't cry, he doesn't take advantage of people, and he does the right thing. In his own way, he was a very loving father to all his kids and family."

Still, Carmine strayed from the path.

"Carmine got involved with the guys in the neighborhood, kind of fell into it," his brother Frank recalls. "Everybody knew who they were. I knew them. Didn't associate with them, but knew them. I mean, Greg Scarpa used to come into my shop all the time. I was on New Utrecht Avenue when Jimmy Emma got killed. I knew Sammy the Bull, saw him all the time. But again, didn't associate with him like that. So sure, we knew all those guys. That's just how it was back in the neighborhood. You couldn't really avoid them."

Frank remembers drugs altering the tone of the neighborhood. "Drugs started coming when I was about 11 or 12, and all the craziness that comes with that, and the neighborhood really changed, got darker.

"Remember, Carmine's three years younger than me, so he grew up in the neighborhood when all of that stuff on the streets was getting worse," Frank says. "We were all tough kids, not good kids, but not bad kids, just all did our thing."

And that took its toll.

"I'll tell you, most people my age group from back there, they're dead," Frank says. "There's a few left. But really, they all went to jail, or, like I said, they're dead. I think there's only one guy from the old neighborhood that I still talk to."

The Brooklyn Tackle League

Brooklyn in the 1970s was a hard place.

How hard a place was it?

Brooklyn in the 1970s was so hard, they played tackle football... on concrete.

Not three-second hold. Not two-hand touch. Not flag.

Concrete. Tackle. Football.

The Brooklyn Tackle League ran from the 1960s through the 1970s before migrating to Staten Island. Every season fielded up to 15 teams, sponsored by local businesses. Pretty much the same rules as regular tackle, but they played eight men on a side. Also, fewer flags. And no concussion-protocol tent.

They played on Sundays in the fall on the cracked concrete playgrounds of Dyker Heights Park, P.S. 201, and other schoolyards throughout Brooklyn and Staten Island.

Twelve-year-old Carmine attended every game at nearby Dyker Park. Then he started going down to practices, inching his way closer and closer on the sidelines.

In those days, no one inspired Carmine more than the hard-hitting Carmine "Keith" Hilt, aka "The Hilt."

The Hilt stood six feet four inches tall, weighing in at roughly 240 pounds, with forearms thicker than the business end of a Louisville Slugger.

The Hilt had a driver, Johnny Thompson, though Carmine can't recall what he did for a living. "I know The Hilt ran a bunch of leagues that must've taken up much of his time. But I don't know what he did for money. He wasn't the kind of guy who shared his private life."

The Hilt should have gone on to glory on the diamond or the gridiron. He made the New York Yankees farm team. However, an injury cut short his pro career just as it was getting started.

Instead, The Hilt found local fame on the playgrounds of South Brooklyn.

"The guy whose house I hit with Spauldings across the street from P.S. 201 was nice enough to throw them back, said thank God we weren't playing with hardballs." That's when the other kids in the neighborhood started calling the younger Carmine The Hilt. "That's about the biggest compliment you could get on the schoolyard back then," Carmine recalls.

The Hilt took notice of this muscled-up kid hanging around his sidelines. At some point, Carmine started collecting equipment and became the unofficial ball boy for The Hilts.

The team racked up championship after championship. "I was part of the next generation," Carmine says. "I carried helmets and duffle bags, and The Hilt took time to teach me. Not many people in the neighborhood liked him. He was a hard guy to like. But I did. He'd walk up and down the sidelines barking like a Brooklyn Bill Belichick. He knew what it took to win. Not many people do."

The comparison to the famed New England Patriots' coach, known for discipline and organization, is appropriate. "Other teams were nowhere near as organized as Hilt. This was a bullshit weekend-league thing for them. But with The Hilt, if you were late for practice, you got hit with a fine."

While other teams straggled up to the field on game day, Hilt orchestrated a spectacle.

First, before every game, as the crowd was arriving at the field, Hilt organizers his players into three lines to perform warm-ups, executed with tight precision, starting with jumping jacks with every player in perfect sync.

Then, Hilt had the team form two lines, with each line of players facing the other. As he announced the starting positions, that player ran down the middle of the formation. "He'd announce Joe-Joe playing safety, and Joe-Joe'd run through high fives. Then, Danny Grimaldi playing running back, and he'd run through high fives, and so on and so on."

Then, Hilt announced himself.

"Hilt saved himself for last, and he'd say, 'Sincerely yours, playing Left Corner, KEEEEITH HILT'," Carmine says. "And then the players would carry Hilt off the field, onto the sidelines. He did this every game, and the crowds just loved it."

When they lost, which was rare, The Hilt let The Hilts have it, berating players. But he also trained them hard and put them in the best position to succeed.

"It was all a big show," Carmine says. "The other teams, the players, the fans, even the refs, all said The Hilt was a nut, but they couldn't get enough of it and the sidelines were always filled. Maybe they don't like him, personally, but they respected him. Because more than anything, The Hilt hated to lose, refused to lose, and rarely did lose. And not for nothing, Brooklyn don't like losers. I learned a lot from The Hilt."

Carmine studied how The Hilt carried himself, how he called his plays, how he responded to pressure, manipulated opponents, physically and psychologically. One game, The Hilts faced a team captained by a brawny Tillio, a connected 13th Avenue regular active in the rackets, who likely would have been *made* if he hadn't have died in an automobile accident.

Normally an easy-going guy, even Tillio hated The Hilt.

The Hilt played mostly defense, cornerback. During one game, Tillio and Armando, another formidable player, taunted The Hilt, asking him why he won't play offense, why he only plays defense, loud enough for both sidelines to take notice.

"Next set of downs, The Hilt taps out the quarterback, comes in on offense, and every play goes through him, and he goes right at them," Carmine remembers. "Play after play, Hilt is hitting the line of scrimmage and those two huge guys, Tillio and Armando, they're just wrecking him. These are big guys banging the hell out of Hilt, smashing him down, poking thumbs in his eyes, all that stuff. But the Hilt wanted to show he wasn't afraid of no one."

The Hilts won. Again. "But this time, it wasn't *only* about winning for The Hilt. He wanted everyone to see him respond to the challenge. You couldn't disrespect The Hilt. He'd make you look bad. But it was great to watch. And remember, they're playing on concrete. You wanna talk about the greatest show on Earth. Forget the NFL. You've never seen nothing as intense as those football games."

As the ball boy, Carmine dreamed of the day he'd make his own highlight reel.

"These were my heroes," Carmine recalls. "My uncles and older brothers played. I was always at practices, always watching them go at it. Later, when I played, they'd come down to my games. I had a great time growing up with all that. It was all I wanted to do."

Many colorful characters crossed those sidelines, including Hollywood star Daniel "Danny" Grimaldi, long before playing twins Philly and Patsy Parisi on the HBO series *The Sopranos*.

"Carmine was much younger than me, but I remember him from early on," Grimaldi says. "He was a young, bright-faced kid from a great family. Carmine, growing up, was very much into sports. We all were. Brooklyn was very competitive. Sports were so much a part of our lives. Carmine got into weight lifting and did well with that. He became this really rough kid, physically strong and tough."

"My older brother and his friends used to have to watch me when I was little," Carmine recalls. "So Danny was over the house all the time."

Grimaldi played several years in the league. "To play in that league, you had to have no respect for your body. Because you had to really get into it and throw your body around. You can't do something like that halfway, especially on asphalt. Sure, there were a lot of injuries. Everyone got hurt, just part of the game. You knew you were coming home with something, shredded knees, elbows and hands ripped up. I remember those Sunday games, getting absolutely wrecked. Then us boys going to school the next day all cut up. I played until about 21 or 22. Couldn't play forever. They eventually moved it out of Brooklyn, played it on grass in Staten Island. Wasn't the same, like playing on asphalt. There was nothing like those games."

Carmine recalls a darker episode, involving Dan Grimaldi's brother. "Johnny Grimaldi, youngest of the three brothers, was a street guy, but not connected. Still, Johnny was a tough guy, and a good guy. Plenty of times, Johnny had my back over the years. He was a scrappy guy. Had a lot of balls."

One Saturday evening, Johnny Grimaldi was in line waiting to get into a crowded nightclub on 77th Street when Lawrence "Larry" Persico approached with his crew. By then, Larry's father, Carmine "The Snake" Persico, was the imprisoned boss of the Colombo Family.

Larry Persico started antagonizing Johnny Grimaldi, who tried to blow it off. Larry then ripped off a car antenna, and started whipping Johnny, who again warned him to stop. After several more whip lashes from the antenna, Johnny drew a knife and plunged it into Larry's side. The wound was life threatening, and hospitalized Larry Persico for weeks.

Johnny Grimaldi, now a marked man, went into hiding.

Johnny's sister, Louise, had dated Salvatore "Sammy the Bull" Gravano for a time. The romance didn't last, but they remained friends. With Colombo hitmen now hunting her brother, Louise implored Gravano to intervene, and he agreed to try. As Johnny laid low, both Gravano and Johnny's father Louie, a longshoreman, sought a sit-down to save the younger Grimaldi's life. "Sammy tried to go to bat for him, but never got the chance, because Carmine [Persico] didn't care, didn't want no sit-down, wanted to prove a point: that no one could touch one of his kids," Carmine recalls.[10] [11]

"Four days later, they found Johnny's body, shot dead in his car. When I heard about it, I was sick over it. It was a sin. Johnny was a good guy. He was trying to get his life together, had a restaurant and little night club thing going, and he died over that stupid bullshit. That's how fast it happened.

"I never knew exactly what went down, but I did suspect it was some guys close to Johnny who set him up and it bothered me," Carmine says. "I remember, I was so mad at them, I brought it up with Joe Brewster, who wasn't involved."

Joseph "Joe Brewster" DeDomenico, was a *made* Colombo and career bank robber, murderer, and member of two major burglary crews, one run by Greg Scarpa Sr., the other by Anthony "Gaspipe" Casso.

"Joe laughed at me, said I was in the wrong business if something like that bothered me," Carmine says. "He said, 'You can't have a heart in this thing.' I'm thinking, *how the fuck do you kill a friend?* I mean, how do you live with yourself after that? How does a guy like that sleep? I knew then that's one of their rules I'd never be able to follow."

---

10. *Underboss: Sammy the Bull Gravano's Story of Life in the Mafia* by Peter Maas, HarperCollins, 1997

11. "Puparo Present: The Roaring 1970s," Gangsters Inc.

Carmine made lasting friendships with players in the Brooklyn Tackle League, like Eddie the Beak, the quarterback for The Hilts, known for his large nose and larger heart.

"Eddie the Beak executed The Hilt's offense like a well-oiled machine, and The Hilt ran his team like an army drill sergeant, disciplined, doing jumping jacks, everyone keeping the same time, precision; it was unreal. As a local kid hauling around their helmets in green duffle bags, to be part of all that, I was in awe, just unbelievable."

Carmine remembers Eddie the Beak giving him advice. "Eddie the Beak was as tough as could be. Eddie'd get hammered, but he'd get up, no matter what. This guy wouldn't quit, such a tough ball player. He loved the competition. He was a great athlete who made the plays when it counted the most."

Eddie the Beak has about 10 years on Carmine.

"I remember Carmine as a great kid, big smile, funny, part of that next generation, you know, the younger guys coming up, playing on the teams that followed us," Eddie recalls. "We all came up on 13th Avenue and there was a great sense of being together. We were always out, always together. First, we hung out in the candy store and then when we got older, it was the bar on 78th Street, spent so much time there, made so many memories.

"Carmine, when he was young, was not just good at football, but good at many sports and had real talent. He was a good kid from a good family, who just got caught up in things and took a different path."

The league grew, as more businesses sponsored teams, local favorites like Vinny Venditti's Hair Place, Pastosa Ravioli, Marino's, J&J Catering, even the dive bar Club 1717 funded a team.

With intense rivalries and plenty of trash talking, violence broke out on more than one occasion.

"The Bath Avenue Boys had a team, sponsored by a ravioli shop on 15th Avenue, and they played against the South Brooklyn Boys one Sunday," Carmine recalls. "The players on the Bath Avenue team were terrible football players, just a crazy bunch of lunatics who didn't give two shits about nothing and they didn't care for the trash talking."

Disorganized, the Bath Avenue team was overmatched, already getting blown out in the first half; half a dozen times the players had to be separated by referees. The crowd roared. Players on both sides jawed. Halftime could not come soon enough.

There were no locker rooms in the Brooklyn Tackle League, so the teams stewed as they faced each other from opposing sidelines as the crowd jeered. Tensions flared. More insults and gestures flew back and forth.

Then, as halftime ended, the South Brooklyn Boys stepped out from the sidelines. Across that cracked asphalt, the entire Bath Avenue Boys team charged, some armed with bats and pipes. They attacked anyone wearing an opposing jersey.

"It was insane, happened so fast, caught everyone off guard," Carmine remembers. "Everyone was in a panic, running around trying to get out of the way, get away, as these nuts started batting these kids out. One guy got stabbed, another guy got his ear ripped off. Good thing they were padded up and had helmets, but even then, they needed a couple of ambulances to cart all these guys off. They suspended the Bath Avenue team for the season, but they didn't give a shit. They were terrible anyway."

Occasional violence aside, the games were very competitive. "Make no mistake, there was a lot of talent in that league," Grimaldi recalls. "In fact, many of the guys went on to athletic success and some became All American players at the college level."

This included players like Carmine Colasanto. "He was fast as lightning, just a hard-nosed football player and a great neighborhood guy," Carmine says of Colasanto.

After Colasanto retired from the league, he later left Brooklyn for the Bronx. Colasanto spent more than three decades as the celebrated head coach for Lehman High School's varsity football team, racking up more than 200 victories and earning numerous coach of the year awards. Several of Colasanto's players went on to play professionally, including Doug Marrone (head coach at Syracuse University) and Charles Puleri.

Carmine eventually got his opportunity, but not with The Hilts. At only 16, in an adult league, Carmine started at running back on a rival team sponsored by Umberto's Clam House, the Little Italy restaurant, site of the 1972 rub-out of Colombo gangster Crazy Joe Gallo.

After only a few games, a teammate hung a nickname on Carmine: Captain Crunch. Carmine asked his mother to stitch the moniker, not on the back of his jersey, but on the front, to be visible to opponents when they lined up. For his number, Carmine chose 51, emulating Dick Butkus, dreaded linebacker enforcer for the NFL's Chicago Bears.

Younger than everyone in the league, Carmine took his licks. "One game, I got nailed by Tillio on a slant over the middle," Carmine says. "Running into that guy was like hitting a brick wall." Dazed from the hit, Carmine stumbled to the wrong huddle. With the crowd roaring in laughter, Tillio guided Carmine back to his own sideline, telling Carmine's coach, "He's out. He's in no shape to go back in there."

Carmine shouted back at Tillio, "I'm out? No. You're out."

Sunday games were big events for the Imbriale family, with Carmine's father and uncles attending. One game, Carmine scored four touchdowns. "You know what my father said to me?" Carmine says. "'You let that guy hit you like that and don't do nothing back? And what about that touchdown you missed? You gotta do better.' Four touchdowns and he says I gotta do better. Just no pleasing the guy."

In typical Brooklyn fashion, Captain Crunch faced off against the likes of The Sheik, Pac Man, Crazy Eyes, and Joey Toothpick. Even the ref had a nickname: Vinny Cigars. "And Vinny Cigars was a gambler," Carmine says. "So if he made a bad call, we'd get on him, ask him who he bet with, and warned him that after the game, we were gonna check with his bookmaker."

Not surprising, many interesting characters rotated through the ranks of the league.

"I remember Pete Levantino, a young guy I met while working in Hunts Point," Carmine says. In 1977, Joe Levantino, Peter's father, co-founded the highly successful A&J Produce, by acquiring three units on Row A in the Hunts Point Terminal Market. Peter later made his own mark founding the Giunta's Meat Farms supermarket chain on Long Island.

"Pete's family had so much money, he sponsored his own team and was the quarterback," Carmine says. "He was a good QB, but where Pete really shined was trash talking. He talked shit to everyone, even the refs. With Pete, it was always *your mother this*, *your sister that*, just asking for it, all game long, even when they were chasing him. That league was an adventure every weekend, so many characters, so much drama, but so much fun."

Before long, Carmine made a name for himself in the league. So when the former protégé stopped carrying the ballbag and started racking up yards for the upstart Umberto's team, The Hilt took it personally.

Inevitably, Carmine faced down his football mentor in an epic showdown, pitting Umberto's squad against The Hilts. At stake? The 1973 Brooklyn Tackle League championship.

"Boy, was The Hilt mad at me." Carmine laughs. "He said he practically raised me, made me the player I was, and he was angry, like I betrayed him. I'm sure, deep down, he respected me. I was one of the top players in the league, on both sides of the ball. But The Hilts were at the top of the mountain and we were coming to knock them off."

The two teams were evenly matched, trading the lead back and forth for the entire game. The sidelines were stacked, the crowd screaming with every play as the clock wound down, the referees getting abused.

In a critical series late in the game, with Carmine's team trailing by less than a touchdown, he spotted an opportunity to turn The Hilt's fury against him.

"In the previous series, my QB threw two out passes that I caught, and Hilt just slapped me to the ground," Carmine remembers. "Soon as I stepped across the sideline, his eyes were on me. He was looking for any opening to hammer me. The game is running down, and it's close. I'm lining up in the slot, and I tell my QB I'm running the same route, a five-step-and-out, twice in a row. But then, on the third play, I'm gonna instead fake the out and do a fly, so pump fake, then hit me on the run. I knew The Hilt would bite if I played him just right."

The Hilt seethed as he strode back and forth between plays, slapping his players, barking orders, adjusting formations—and always, eyeing Carmine.

Sure enough, on first down, after Carmine made the reception, Hilt nailed him with a bone-crushing sideline shot that sent him flying into the Dyker Park bike racks as fans scrambled. The Hilt paused over Carmine long enough to make eye contact.

"On second down, Hilt got even nastier, cracking me so hard, you heard the crowd react, like one loud *OOOOOOOOOHHHHH*," Carmine laughs. "They had to think I wasn't getting up after that one. But I got up. Then, the crowd is really going crazy, and The Hilt is shaking, he's so angry."

On that key third down, time running out, championship on the line, Carmine nodded to his QB. The center snapped the ball. Carmine faked the same out-route, but then stopped on a dime, flew up the slot, snagging the ball zipped just ahead of him. The Hilt, overconfident, overcommitted, ready to unleash another forearm hammer on his wayward pupil, got caught by surprise, tried to recover and... slipped.

Carmine ran untouched into the end zone to a roar from the sidelines, capping off the wild come-from-behind win.

The Hilt knew Carmine manipulated him into taking the bait and he was furious he'd bit, costing his team the championship game. Afterwards, you'd expect the young protégé to get a begrudging handshake from his mentor, or at least a nod, maybe a harsh pound on the back.

Not quite.

After all, this was 1970s South Brooklyn.

And it was The Hilt.

"Game's won, fans are walking off the field, I have my back turned when Hilt runs over, and he levels me, just nails me, he was so pissed off," Carmine says. "And, of course, I couldn't help myself, so I said, 'Sorry, Keith, there's a new champ in town,' and boy, did he walk off steaming."

It took weeks, but The Hilt came around. "Maybe a month later, Hilt congratulated me. He still didn't sound too happy about it, but he said, 'Okay, kid, you did it.'"

The Hilt lost more than face from playing tackle football on asphalt. Following a successful tryout, he landed a spot in the New York Yankees' farm system. Unfortunately, next season, The Hilt blew out his knee playing in the Brooklyn Tackle League, violating his contract, and the Yankees dismissed him from the team.

"Hilt wasn't supposed to be playing concrete football while on the farm team," Carmine remembers. "Richie Collier did the same thing, blew out his knee playing football in Dyker Park, and because of that, he was dismissed from the Detroit Tigers. That was another guy that had forearms bigger than baseball bats."

Carmine won another championship with Umberto's team before a knee injury forced him to retire. Though he didn't suffer the injury on the concrete gridiron.

"I thought my friend had given me a couple Dianabols," Carmine recalls. Dianabol was one of the first widely used anabolic steroids used for physique- and performance-enhancing purposes. Dianabol is now a banned substance, but back in 1960s and 1970s, especially in football, it was widely used.[12]

"So here I am thinking I'm taking Dianabols, but he'd given me a bunch of Quaaludes, on purpose," Carmine says. "Thought it was real funny, laughing at how messed up I was. I couldn't walk. And I tripped, shattering my knee falling on the corner off the curb. Ruined my knee. Never been the same."

Carmine's knee was not the only thing being ruined.

"Like I said, Carmine was much younger, and the Brooklyn he grew up in was darker than our Brooklyn," Dan Grimaldi remembers. "Our Brooklyn was more of a golden era. But as time went on, it became a much rougher neighborhood, especially once drugs were introduced, very quickly, and in a big way. The drugs changed everything; not just the addictions, but the crime and the ruined families."

"When we were kids, teenagers, there wasn't much drugs at all," Eddie the Beak remembers. "When the drugs started, I was like ten years older, so the younger guys, like Carmine, they had to deal with some things we didn't when we were their age."

They don't play tackle football on the concrete playgrounds of Bensonhurst anymore, and have not done so for decades. But those battle-hardened warriors get together

12. *Anabolic Steroid Abuse* by Geraline C. Lin, Diane Publishing, 1996

every ten years or so to share war stories, though there's one player conspicuously absent.

It's been a long time since Captain Crunch sat at that table. But he remembers.

"What a life, spending all day playing stickball and football, then be out all night drinking and getting home at 4 a.m., just to wake up and do it all over again," Carmine says. "I wouldn't trade those days for nothing. I should have stuck with sports, and not taken the path I took. But it is what it is and I can't change what I can't change."

Carmine does have one more regret.

"It's a shame there's no footage of those concrete tackle games. Ask anyone who was there, and they'll tell you that you've never seen nothing like those games. Imagine if someone had a film of that league. They'd be loaded today. Just turn it over to a good producer, make millions."

Parking Cars at Pastels

Shame Carmine Imbriale never met Henry Hill. He sure shared several things in common with the infamous Lucchese Crime Family associate.

For starters, both were half Italian, half Irish.

Both struggled in school, dropping out to focus full time on lives of crime in predominantly Italian-American enclaves in Brooklyn (Carmine in 1970s Bensonhurst, Henry in 1950s Brownsville).

Both were hijackers, credit card scammers, and armed robbers. Both dove into the neighborhood rackets at young ages. And neither were *made*.

Both spent stretches in federal prisons bunking with infamous gangsters. Both were targeted for assassination by their confederates. Both faced RICO charges, forcing them to decide between death and dealing with the federal government.

Both entered the witness protection program, and both struggled to blend into the background in Small Town, USA. (Both the drama, *Goodfellas*, based on Nicholas Pileggi's book, *Wiseguy: Life in the Mafia*,[13] and the comedy, *My Blue Heaven*, with the screenplay written by Pileggi's wife, Nora Ephron, were based on Hill's life.[14])

---

13. *Wiseguy: Life in a Mafia Family* by Nicholas Pileggi, Simon & Shuster, 1985

14. *My Blue Heaven*, by Nora Ephron, directed by Herbert Ross

"You know, I never thought in a million years, someday my life'd become something like *My Blue Heaven*. But trust me, in real life, the marshals won't mambo with you."

Similarities aside, Hill and Imbriale were very different in key areas.

Carmine never killed anyone. Carmine voluntarily exited the witness protection program, leading an honest life since his arrest. And Carmine is now an active member of his Roman Catholic parish.

Hill was a murderer. In 1987, the US Marshals bounced Hill out of the witness protection program for cocaine trafficking in Seattle. Before Hill died of heart complications in 2012, he was locked up on everything from drug offenses to public intoxication. And Hill's wife divorced him.

Two men. Two similar but separate paths.

And as teenagers, the two valeted at larger-than-life gangster hotspots.

For Hill, it was parking mid-century gas guzzling tailfins at the East New York cabstand owned by Lucchese Caporegime Paul "Paulie" Vario. Carmine valeted chromed-out Caddies and Lincolns at Pastels Night Club, the legendary 1970s club in Bay Ridge, Brooklyn.

Pastels ruled South Brooklyn's nightlife during the disco era that detonated with the *Saturday Night Fever* craze, actually filmed about a mile away. The 1977 film was based on "Tribal Rites of the New Saturday Night," a 1976 *New York Magazine* article by British journalist Nik Cohn, chronicling the wild weekend Bay Ridge nightclub scene.[15] In reality, Cohn was too much of a pussy for a place like Pastels. In a 1996 interview, he admitted that while he dropped in on a Bay Ridge club, even witnessed (from

---

15. "Tribal Rites of the New Saturday Night," by Nik Cohn, *New York Magazine*, 1976

afar) a fight at the door, he fabricated most of the story, even fictionalized Tony Manero.[16]

If the disco in *Saturday Night Fever* was too intimidating for Cohn, best that he never swung by 88th Street off 4th Avenue.

Pastels was banging once the DJ dropped his first beat for Wednesday's Ladies' Night and kept on slamming through Sunday, always mobbed, always crawling with mobsters. The scene assaulted your senses as your eyes adjusted to the flashing jellies flickered by strobes. Mist gushed from smoke machines. Basslines thumped and freestyle pumped out of towering speakers.

On the glowing dancefloor, hot young ladies drenched in Chanel No. 19 shimmied by on plastic go-go boots with matching spandex stretched to the extreme. Big hair teased out, glittered breasts busting out, tan bodies popping out. In hot-hot-hot pursuit, here comes a haze of Hai Karate hairy-chested gold-roped knuckle-draggers, bell bottomed and broad collared, lust snarling their Magnum PI-ish mustachioed lips.

Fridays and Saturdays, not on The List or palming one of those little pink Pastels VIP Cards? Back of the line, snaking down 88th Street, soon to be littered by a million lipstick-lipped Marlboro Red butts.

Standing curbside on the business side of Bay Ridge's first velvet rope was a teenage Carmine Imbriale, with a big smile and broad hand outstretched, ready to catch your keys.

Ya know, that kid Carmine, from 13th Avenue.

Carmine snared that primo valet gig through his friendship with Colombo wiseguy Joe Brewster, a Pastels' regular. Pastels was secretly owned by Alphonse "Allie Shades" Malangone, a powerful mob captain who ran the Genovese Family's interest in the Fulton Fish Market.

---

16. "Disco's Saturday Night Fiction," by Nadia Khoumami, *The Guardian*, 1996

Malangone, who got his nickname for his penchant to always wear sunglasses, even indoors, conducted Family business in the club. In October 1997, Malangone was convicted for his role in the sweeping corruption of New York City's waste-hauling industry, and served 13 years in prison.[17]

Carmine worked valet at Pastels for three years at the height of the club's notoriety.

"They added extra bouncers because of all the fights," Carmine says. "It was like the St. Bernadette's Bazaars, Bath Avenue fighting 13th Avenue, 18th Avenue fighting 20th Avenue. But they didn't put up with that shit because that joint was a *frickin'* cash register."

Whenever fights broke out, they were over before they started.

"They hired goons from local gyms and they'd rip your ass outta there so fast, make your head spin. Most times, DJ didn't even stop the music. Didn't matter who was right, who was wrong. They threw out anybody who started trouble, no questions asked."

Some nights, even the talent wasn't safe.

"One Saturday night, Trammps played and at the time were a huge draw," Carmine remembers. "They're all over the radio, joint's packed, all of Brooklyn's on line outside." The Trammps charted several smash hits in the '70s, including an absolute anthem, "Disco Inferno," a number on the *Saturday Night Fever* soundtrack.

"Bands like that don't take requests. Something was said. A guy in the group's shouting back and forth with some jerkoff on the dancefloor. Before you know it, in the middle of the next song, bunch of guys rush the stage, start fighting the band. Chased them out the door. I mean, that's how it got. Crazy."

---

17. "Two Convicted as Leaders of New York Trash Cartel," by Selwyn Raab, *New York Times*, October 22, 1997

This was the pre-crack era, fueled by cocaine's popularity as a party drug, before the narcotic's true addictive nature was widely known.

"The owners didn't like the drugs in the club, but more because they weren't making money off it," Carmine says. "But you couldn't keep it out. C'mon. That was the 70s. Cocaine was everywhere. I knew better than to get involved in that shit at the club. You're taking your life in your hands. But trust me, there was a lot of drugs in Pastels, especially in the bathrooms. Bunch of times I saw guys and girls snorting coke in the bathroom, even banging in the stalls. It was wild."

Still a teen, Carmine was already a regular at Neddy's Bar, a 13th Avenue Colombo spot. But sitting on a Neddy's stool was nothing compared to standing out in front of Pastels on a Saturday night rocking that bright-red valet jacket. Almost every gangster in Brooklyn under the age of 40 passed through those ropes. "If the feds wanted to update their wiseguy photobooks, what they shoulda done was set up a surveillance van across the street from Pastels. I'm not joking. It was a parade of these guys all night, in and out."

There were the wannabees, wiseguys out to make names for themselves. Aggressive, armed, easily provoked, drunk, high, hotheads looking for hot girls on hot Saturday nights.

Then there were the young heavyweights, guys like Charlie Carneglia (assassin for John Gotti, known for torturing his victims with blowtorches[18]), Joel "Joe Waverly" Cacace Sr. (a Colombo capo who actually ordered a hit on an NYPD officer[19]), and William "Billy Fingers" Cutolo (a major labor racketeer for the Colombos who got

---

18. *Mob Killer: The Bloody Rampage of Charles Carneglia, Mafia Hit Man*, by Anthony DeStefano, Pinnacle Books, 2011

19. "Prosecutor to jurors: Mob man Joel Cacace ordered cop Ralph Dols' slay out of Envy," by John Marzulli, *New York Daily News*, November 25, 2013

his nickname for beating people to death with a baseball bat7).

"You never saw any of the old timers, like Carlo or Paul," Carmine says. "But Sammy the Bull was a regular, who was good with me; Joe Brewster, of course. Every once in a while, Chuckie Russo. Vic Amuso never came down, but Gaspipe was in there all the time; Jerry Brancato; and Georgie Goggles, who was my age, but already an associate with the Colombos, and so many others."

And they all tossed the keys to their Caddies to Carmine. *Ya know*, Carmine, from 13th Avenue.

With all these hair triggers hugging the curb, Carmine did more than park cars. Pastels was among the first, if not *the* first, Bay Ridge club with a guest list. Not on the list on Saturday night? Fuck off. Get in line or take your sorry ass down the Avenue to Hob Nails or Skinflints.

However, unlike most nightclubs, a guest list is problematic for a spot frequented by gangsters. "You had wiseguys come up, go right to the front of the line, tell the bouncer they're on the list," Carmine recalls. "But the bouncer, now, he don't know nothing from nothing. Some steroid schmuck from 3rd Avenue. So he's asking these mob guys to tell him who they are, who they're with. Under normal circumstances, those are the right questions for a bouncer to ask."

These weren't normal circumstances.

"C'mon now, you can't start naming names with these guys 'cause they can't say who they're with, unless it's to the guys they're with. On the street, you'd get in a lot of trouble for that. So right away, these guys get nasty. The bouncer, he don't know what the fuck to do. He's just a Bay Ridge Irish meathead saying, 'Just tell me who you're with.' They're like, 'Yeah, fuck you, jerkoff, I ain't telling you shit,' that quickly turns into, 'Yeah, you want to start some shit, I'll show you who the fuck I'm with,' and it just got outta hand from there."

That bouncer-bad-guy back and forth could seem like a South Brooklyn Abbott and Costello rip-off... if the consequences weren't so lethal.

"Guys with guns don't give a shit about muscles," Carmine says. "But I tell you what they did give a shit about—getting shown up by some bouncer in front of the other wiseguys. And if they were with a girl, forget about it."

Here comes Carmine from 13th Avenue to the rescue. "I knew so many of these guys, and even if I didn't know them personally, I recognized them and could put it together in my head where they're from, which was a good thing for everyone involved, especially me. Soon as I'd see it going down, I'd run up, tip the bouncer off, tell him this guy was from Bath Avenue, or this guy was from Downtown, whatever. Like magic, velvet rope flies open, bouncer apologizes. Everybody's happy, and I get the pat or the nod."

Those pats and nods had real street value. *Ya know*, that Carmine kid, from 13th Avenue. He's a good kid. Keep an eye on him.

"This place was rocking, fast work, parking cars, getting cars, hustling my ass off," Carmine remembers. "Us valet guys had these little beach chairs, but you're never sitting down. Make a hundred dollars in tips on a slow shift, easy, usually more. And this is early-70s money."

Carmine was *very* careful with the cars. "I valeted like an old widow driving to St. Bernadette's on a Sunday morning, never dinged a car, not one. But they never checked, hitting me off with tens, twenties, fifties. One night, I got a $500 tip from Charlie Carneglia from the Gambinos. Crazy money back then, like two full paychecks for my father."

Tips were great, but cash became secondary. "I fed off the recognition," Carmine says. "Everyone who was anyone was at Pastels. More wiseguys started seeing me, week in, week out. Those connections turned into some of this, some of that, you know, kinds of jobs you don't find in the back of no newspaper."

There were other benefits. "I'm out with a date, wiseguys stop at my table, say hello. The girls'd wonder how I knew these guys. Not only that, they'd buy us drinks. Few times, paid for my dinner. There was nights I didn't pull a dime out my pocket. And I'm only 16."

Pastels drew Carmine into the orbits of some powerful gangsters. "First time I ever saw Joe Waverly, he steps out the front door of Pastels like he owned the joint, beautiful girl on his arm, barks at me to get his car. Just looking at him, you'd see he's one of those guys you know not to fuck with unless you're ready to get serious."

By 1973, Joel "Joe Waverly" Cacace, 15 years older than Carmine, was on the fast track in the Colombo Family. At the outbreak of the Third Colombo War, Cacace would side with Vic Orena against the Persicos, even made a failed attempt on Greg Scarpa Sr.'s life, then was wounded in a separate gun battle with the Grim Reaper. The fact that he switched sides during the war—and was not murdered— tells you how much he was respected.

On the orders of Persico, Cacace organized a hit on a prosecutor, William Aronwald. Then Cacace's hit squad killed the wrong Aronwald, shooting to death George, the father, a judge. And Cacace even survived that disaster. Hit team members, brothers Vincent and Enrico Carini, were slain months later. Only Lucchese Associate Frank Smith survived, likely a decision Cacace regretted, as Smith later testified against him in federal court.[20]

How dangerous was Joe Waverly? One afternoon in December 1976, gunmen shot him outside the Party Room Social Club, on East 14th Street near Avenue U in Sheepshead Bay. Taking a slug to the chest, he wrestled a

20. "Mob Figure Admits Roles In Murders, Including Judge's," by William Glaberson, *New York Times,* August 14, 2004

gun from one of the robbers, shot another to death, as the rest fled the scene. He drove himself to the local precinct with the lifeless body of a would-be bandit in the backseat.[21]

"To have a guy like Joe Waverly recognize you, nod, say hello, that was a big deal for a kid like me," Carmine says. "He was a tough guy you knew right off not to cross."

Yet that's exactly what Carmine did a short while afterwards, unwittingly.

One night, Carmine stopped by a party at Sirico's on 13th Avenue to meet up with his friends when he drew the attention of a young, attractive lady. They had drinks. After a while, Carmine invited her to join him across the street, at his sister's apartment. The young lady agreed, grabbed a fur from the coat stand, and they headed out.

"So we get to my sister's and right away my brother-in-law Bucky gets this look, pulls me to the side, says I'm out of my fucking mind," Carmine says. "I'm confused, until he tells me she's Joe Waverly's girlfriend." By then, Bucky was an associate with the Colombo Family.

"Not only was this Joe's girl, but he's crazy for her. No wonder; she was gorgeous. But now I wanted no part of that. Couldn't throw her ass out of there fast enough."

Should've ended there. But nothing is ever that easy with Carmine.

Next day, Carmine gets a call from James "Little Guy" Ida. Though a captain for the Genovese, later rising to the post of consigliere[22], Ida operated for years on 13th Avenue, deep in Colombo territory, from a small shop right across the street from Sirico's.

"I get a call from Jimmy, who liked me, knew me from the Avenue, and he'd seen what happened and put it together," Carmine says. "Jimmy says to me they wanted

21. "Suspected Mob Capo, 51, Shot in Brooklyn," *New York Times*, February 27, 1992

22. "Genovese Family Counselor Is Convicted of Racketeering," by Jan Hoffman, *New York Times*, April 24, 1997

the fur coat back. Jimmy didn't know this was Joe Waverly's girlfriend, just that some girl who left with me robbed a fur coat, and it was an expensive coat. If I returned the coat, no problem. But I had no idea how to find her. So now I'm in a tough spot."

Carmine knew if he didn't cough up that coat, he'd be linked to Joe Waverly's girlfriend, leaving a club together at night. But he also didn't want to lay out thousands of dollars to replace the fur.

"I drop everything, I'm running all over Brooklyn like a lunatic, chasing leads next couple a days, and I finally, *finally* track her down."

She argued at first. "Then, I asked if she wanted to get us both whacked," Carmine says. "She just complained on and on about Joe, like he's some regular guy who won't beat us to death as we're duct taped to chairs facing each other.

"She was a whack job. But lucky for me, Joe was on a whole other level of crazy. And she's dating him, so she had to have seen it firsthand. I explain, slowly, how Joe'd take the two of us to some basement somewhere in Brooklyn and torture us. I'm not laughing now. Dead serious. She gets this look on her face, goes inside, comes back, and turns over the coat. Then, right away, I hand it off to Jimmy."

Even at that young age, Carmine knew the rules of *the Life*. And one of those rules was you don't screw around with a man's woman, especially if he's a homicidal maniac who'll be coming for you, even after you put slugs in his chest.

As for Cacace, in 1997, obsessively insecure about his ex-wife remarrying young, handsome New York Police Department Officer Ralph Dols, he ordered his underlings to murder Dols in a cowardly ambush.

Good thing Carmine tracked that coat down.

13th Avenue Hustler

Most days, Carmine Imbriale Sr. sat outside his 79th Street home like a sentinel, a wary eye out for his wayward son.

"My father sat in his tiny lawn in front of our home. He took pride in that lawn. Couldn't fit a lawn mower in there, it was so small. But he'd plant his flowers, decorate it, care for it."

One afternoon, Carmine rolled up driving a brand-new black Buick Electra. Stretching nearly sewer-to-sewer at 19 feet, it was known on the street as the 225, as in Deuce and a Quarter, for its 225-inch length. Custom leather upholstery, chromed-out grill and bumpers, velour door panels, the 225 even boasted power windows, power driver's seat, and a digital clock—rarities in the 1970s.[23]

A guy needed a well-paying job to afford a car like a 225.

"My father didn't want to know where I got the car," Carmine says, remembering his father folding up his beach chair in a huff. "When he went inside, I could hear him through the screen door tell my mom I was outside, hosing down my stolen car."

Carmine's father despised the 13th Avenue gangsters. So, out of respect, Carmine hid his illegal activities, flashy 225 aside.

---

23. The GM Collection: 1964 Buick Electra 225, The General Motors Heritage Center

"I had a record player, one of those fancy 70s stereo systems, and I cut open the back of one of the big speakers to stash my cash," Carmine says. "I think my mother knew it was there, from cleaning my room. But she'd just do the sign of the cross and move along."

The knot stashed in the speaker could be several thousand dollars. "If my father would've found it, he would've killed me. My father always said I didn't appreciate money, because he didn't see how hard I worked for it."

Carmine didn't punch a clock, but he worked hard, as a hustler, a shakedown artist, and stick-up kid.

"Every day I woke up thinking about the scams I had lined up, or had to line up, or who I was going to rob," Carmine recalls. "I'd check my dresser, see what credit cards I had to use that day. Or I'd go down to Fort Hamilton, find a drug dealer to rob. The hours weren't regular and I was into something different every day, but hustling is a job. Could finish by three in the afternoon or be chasing things down until seven. I made great money, but it was a grind."

Carmine frequented two Colombo clubhouses on 13th Avenue—the Wimpy Boys Club and Neddy's Bar. Located two blocks from each other, Wimpy Boys was run by Colombo enforcer Greg Scarpa Sr., while Neddy's was more of a local neighborhood bar. Carmine became a regular at Neddy's, though only visited Wimpy Boys for business.[24]

Neddy's Bar and Wimpy Boys were among that last generation of South Brooklyn gangster clubs, when organized crime figures still did their dirt out in the open. This was even before they started with the sidewalk strolls with hands covering their mouths to throw off the FBI lip readers.

There were a hundred spots back then, joints like Tali's Bar on 18th Avenue, Veterans & Friends on 86th Street, the

---

24. "9 New York Mafia Social Clubs: Then & Now," National. CrimeSyndicate.com

Gemini Lounge in Flatbush, the Esplanade on Bay 50th, The Wrong Number on Avenue T, The 19th Hole on 14th Avenue, and dozens of others, many without names.

A hundred years ago they would've called these spit-and-sawdust joints buckets of blood; you know, where the mop water usually turns red by the end of the night.

Carmine was partial to Neddy's, as Neddy's drew more of the younger, lower-ranking Colombos, and the associates and members of other families they did business with regularly.

From the street, Neddy's looked like any local neighborhood bar, but don't think Archie's Place or Cheers. No, this was a joint where they *better* know your name and why you came, because if they didn't, you'd get your ass handed to you.

At Neddy's, the waitress wasn't sassy, the décor wasn't classy. No ferns in brass planters, and no Trivia Nights for the trucker hats. Just a dimly lit, grimy corner gin mill. Full-length scuffed bar facing a mirror, both running the length of the room. Simple selection of draught beers, nothing imported. Bottles banging on the back bar, or sliding into the steel speed rack.

Pool table in the back good for some action, a single-serving bathroom with one of those ancient porcelain urinals extending all the way to the damp ground. A kitchen in the rear, because that used to be the law, maybe serving some light bar snacks. Jukebox that never changed, joker poker that never hit. A bowling game they bet on relentlessly, because they bet on anything and everything relentlessly. A couple of televisions always tuned into the game, with someone shouting at the screen because they're about to lose the rent betting the wrong way on their parlay.

Sure, Neddy's was infested with Colombos conspiring and conniving, but it wasn't *just* a den of thieves. This was a local where the locals ordered their usuals alongside the usual suspects, associates associated with non-associates, and everyone knew everyone since stickball on the P.S. 201 schoolyard.

Loud, rowdy, rude, drunk, high, toasting, boasting, debating, arguing, insulting, shouting, fighting... whoa, whoa, whoa, what the fuck! But also... practical jokes, memorable nights, laughter, league rivalry, comradery, and gambling on anything and its mother. But make no mistake, making a wrong move at this hole in the wall could get you a hole in your body.

Neddy's was a hard place for hard men run by a hard woman and her homely daughter. Neddy herself was an elderly, tough-as-nails South Brooklyn girl who didn't seem to need the money, or have any money, or put any money into upgrading her bar.

"Neddy was in her eighties, and she'd nod out behind the bar from time to time, leaving the cash drawer open," Carmine remembers. "My buddy used to put gum on a pool stick, fish out twenties from the register while she was snoring. If she ever woke up, she'd probably shoot him. But she never did."

That was the .22 Neddy kept handy, which everybody knew about, because in her bar, even she never knew what could happen. Yet Neddy had a soft spot for her regulars, especially Carmine and Robert. "Neddy wouldn't let strangers in, didn't like girls in the bar, and locked the door once we were bombed. She used to give me a hard time, said every time there was a problem and someone called the bar, me and Robert were the first two idiots to jump off our stools and run. She said I should let someone else do the fighting for once. She even gave us two tickets to Florida once to get outta the neighborhood for a bit."

Neddy's became sort of like a local recruiting station, but not for the US Army or NYPD.

"It was in Neddy's that I started to meet many of the local wiseguys, do favors for them," Carmine remembers. "They didn't discuss their business and you didn't ask them questions. They just told you what to do and you did it. Go here, go there, do this thing, give this to this guy, do that to that guy. And whatever they asked, you knew it was a test. There was a lot of scheming in that bar, all types of those people going in and out, that sooner or later, you're getting involved in something. You do the first thing, then it's another thing. You get in deeper and deeper, not realizing. Everything just moves so fast at that point."

With dozens of *made* members and associates floating in and out, Carmine learned who was who, who was with who, and who was with no one.

And for the trained eye, that meant opportunity.

If you operated in the South Brooklyn rackets, you had to be a member of a crew or associated with a crew to avoid being victimized. Otherwise, better cross the street when you saw Carmine from 13th Avenue coming.

Pot dealers were easy marks, easy to find. Before beepers, before delivery service, they set up on corners or under the El, sold nickels and dimes from bicycles or out the back of parks and schoolyards. Cash money.

Carmine robbed every pot dealer he could find who was not connected. Many more than once. Some just gave it up when he ran up—because not only could Carmine knock your teeth out, he was quick enough to catch your ass if you ran.

Carmine moved on from pummeling pot dealers to preying on pimps under the Gowanus in Sunset Park or out on the strip on Coney Island. Rougher trade than skinny teenage dealers, but fatter marks. A pimp on a corner always stood out, easy for Carmine to fold him up like a beach chair with a shot to the side of the head.

Soon, Carmine graduated to more flush targets. "We made a lot of money going around to the bars and clubs looking for the fugazi bookies and shylocks," Carmine says. That's *fugazi*, as in a fake-ass, phony mameluke frickin' pretenders.

Back then, the Avenue was crawling with bookmakers and loan sharks. Many paid protection. Many did not. And many said they did but lied. But no one got a free ride for long in South Brooklyn.

Spending a thousand hours pegged to a stool in Neddy's Bar, Carmine could pin out those bullshit artists. "They'd say, 'I'm with so-and-so' or 'I'm with that guy over there,' and I began to realize, most of them were full of shit," Carmine says. "That's because I knew who so-and-so was, or I knew all about that the guy over there. And I could check. These guys are connivers to start with, it's in their blood, what makes them a good book or a shy. They get greedy. And that's where I came in."

After a few robberies, Carmine adapted his play.

"You rob one of these guys once, kind of hard to rob him the second time. So instead of beating them out of their money right away, I figured I'd get more off them by playing along. If it was a shy, I'd borrow some money, pay it back. Then I'd borrow a little more money, and again, pay it back. Then I'd borrow a shit load of money, and when he came to collect, I'd rob him on top of not paying him back."

For bullshitting bookies, Carmine had a similar angle. "I'd bet small, build it up, get into the tens of thousands of dollars," Carmine says. "I win, he pays. I lose, he's beat for his money. Fuck him. And also, I rob him. Fuck's he gonna do? These guys were such assholes, running their mouths. They were everywhere. You didn't even have to look hard, because they were always the loudest guys in the bar."

Rarely did Carmine resort to extreme violence. "I could hurt people, but I never wanted to if I could avoid it. Bookies, they're not tough guys. They got loud mouths, but they're the last guys on the Avenue you'd expect to fight. Maybe have to give 'em slap or two, but usually not even that."

Not always did Carmine make the right call. Like James "Jimmy O" O'Connor, a local Irish kid Carmine played football against years earlier in the Brooklyn Tackle League. Carmine ran into Jimmy O in a Bay Ridge bar one night. Jimmy said he was a bookmaker.

"I bet with Jimmy O, ended up losing six grand with him. So I told him, you got to wait until the end of the month to get paid, even though I wasn't planning on paying him."

Jimmy O had no problem waiting. Jimmy O even told Carmine his credit was gold and Carmine could keep gambling through the end of the month. *Maybe your luck'll turn*, he encouraged Carmine.

It did. "I started winning, and ran it up to twenty-three grand, so that makes me up seventeen grand on Jimmy," Carmine recalls. "When I went to collect, Jimmy doesn't have the money, says he needs to the end of the month. Fuck that. I told him he had three days to cough up the seventeen grand."

Next day, Carmine gets a call from Mikey Bagels. "Mikey Bagels was this Genovese guy who wants to know why I'm shaking down his guy, Jimmy O. I had no idea Jimmy was working with the Genovese. Jimmy never said nothing. And I'm not with nobody at that point. But I knew people. So I get Jimmy Ida to throw a call in and straighten it out. Jimmy Ida told Mikey Bagels that O'Connor has to come up with the money, and he's Jimmy Ida, so of course, the kid comes up with the money. But I tell you, it's a good thing it went the way it did and I didn't rob this Irish kid because that would've been a big problem for me. Mikey Bagels was a *made* guy, and he'd *have* to do something to me. You can't be a *made* guy and then have someone out of nowhere smack your bookie around, and then *not* cripple that guy. It don't work like that."

Another night, Carmine was drinking in Sirico's on 13th Avenue, a popular hall with a lounge in the heart of Brooklyn Colombo territory. He overheard a conversation. "This guy's running his mouth that he's this bigtime bookmaker with the Persicos," Carmine says. "He's saying it loud, so the entire bar hears. I introduce myself, tell him I'm looking for someone to take my action. Gives me his number. Says to me no limits. I told him, 'Great, hold on, I'd be right back.' He said, 'No problem, come back whenever' I was ready."

Carmine hustled a couple blocks over to Neddy's and checked in with Michael Persico and learned this bookie had no connection with the Colombos. Incensed that this guy was using their name, the Persicos demanded Carmine drag him down the Avenue by his ankles. Carmine agreed to do so, but at a later date, after he got his hooks into him.

"I get on a winning streak with this guy, he's paying me, and then, I start losing, banging him out for a fortune. When he tries to collect, I threw him what a beating. I had to put some marks on him. It was that or drag him in to be murdered. I didn't want that. But boy, he sure was sorry he ran into me. He got what he deserved. But when you think about it, he got off lucky. The Persicos were big on making examples. You just couldn't do that on 13th Avenue and get away with it."

The problem with robbing pot dealers, pimps, and loud-mouthed bookies, though, is you run out of marks. Carmine needed a more stable source of illicit income.

So naturally, Carmine became a bookie and a shy. He had the talent. Intelligent, street savvy, a sharp memory, great with numbers. From his years competing in sports, he knew the intricacies of the games and their scoring systems. He had the people skills to attract customers, and the punishing fists to inspire them to pay. No one was getting over on Carmine easily. Yet, at the age of 16, he lacked the one thing needed most to build his "book."

Cash.

Just like on Wall Street, on 13th Avenue, money makes money. Carmine needed to put money "on the street," generating the interest to fund his operation.

Still, Carmine was reluctant to have too much money on the line with any single customer. "They're degenerates, liars, and they lose all the time, making it worse," Carmine says. "You could trust them as far as you could kick 'em. But I didn't enjoy hurting people. Trying to get a couple hundred dollars out of some jerkoff is much different when they owe you twenty grand. So with the gambling and loansharking, I capped my customers at a $500 limit. That way, I can't get hurt, they don't need to get hurt, and things don't get out of hand."

Back in those days, illegal gambling was everywhere in South Brooklyn. Many crews ran their own numbers racket, an illegal street lottery. There were money card games in the cafes and social clubs, craps games in the basements and backyards. There were smoky state-run Off-Track Betting parlors all over the city, including one right on 72nd Street and 13th Avenue. There were Joker Poker machines in the backs of candy stores from Bay Ridge out to Brighton (and they paid off, even as they were marked "For Entertainment Only"). Even the local churches sponsored casino nights.

You started gambling when you started smoking, which was before you started shaving. On the corner, you pitched coins against walls and played blackjack on car hoods. And of course, you played the football sheets.

You won't see those little green slips anymore, but back in the 1970s, football sheets were everywhere, even the playgrounds. Carmine knew his boys loved playing the sheets. You didn't need much money to play, a couple of bucks.

Basically, a football betting sheet lays out all the games for the week—college football on Saturdays and professional league play on Sundays. The games were handicapped with a "spread," or extra points assigned to the underdog to level the playing field, so to speak.

Let's say the New York Giants are playing an inferior Dallas Cowgirls team. Without a point spread, everyone bets on the Giants. So the handicapper may assign a seven-point spread. That means, before kickoff, the Cowgirls start with a seven-point lead. If you bet on the Giants, you need to win by at least eight points to collect on your bet.

The bookmaker is not performing a public service. He charges a "betting vig" (short for "vigorish"), a small fee for every wager placed, like a service charge, based on a percentage of that wager. The vig, also referred to as "the cut" or "the juice," is usually five percent of the wager.

Every Monday morning, Carmine ran down to Neddy's Bar, and Tony Palmieri, a local bookmaker, gave him a stack of those green sheets. Before Carmine dropped out of New Utrecht, really one of the only reasons he went to high school was to pass the sheets out to his regulars, collect the money—small stakes with the vig. He'd turn that over to Palmieri and, in return, receive a piece of the juice.

Football sheets were a sucker's bet, operating as a minimum-game parlay play, so you had to bet at least three games. To win, you not only need to hit on every game you select, but cover the point spread on every game, which is harder than it seems.

The more games you played, the higher the odds on the return because it's hard to cover multiple spreads. The generous payouts were published on the back of the sheet. Odds ranged from paying five dollars for every two dollars bet on a three-game pick, up to $2,000-for-$2 for picking all 15 games right, which is like hitting a royal flush in a casino—as in, that shit ain't happening unless your name's Joe Pupo.

By 16, Carmine wanted in on the real action, not just the sheets. During football season, or baseball season, a bookmaker could make hundreds, even thousands, of dollars every week.

Palmieri showed Carmine that a bookie can always make money on gambling. For one thing, if he balances his book, accepting an equal amount of bets on each side of the game, he always profits off the vig. If a larger number of bets come in on one side, he can refuse the bets, but that's bad business. Never turn away a gambler. He'll just find another book. Instead, Carmine saw how Palmieri would "lay them off," or give those bets to another book. He'd lose the vig, or a piece of the vig, but limit his risk and keep his customer.

"Rarely happens, but that's the bookmaker's dream," Carmine says. "Get 50 guys to bet the Giants, then 50 guys to go the other way on the Cowboys, and you just sit back and collect the vigs."

The book can also manipulate the line, making adjustments in his favor, as the game gets closer. Also, gamblers can become borrowers real fast. It's a grind, long hours hustling, chasing down losers. But better than ambushing pot dealers. And Carmine always got the money right, which above all else can make or break a bookie, not to mention his arms and legs.

"It's good that I started handing out football sheets for Tony Palmieri because I really didn't feel comfortable dealing directly with the wiseguys," Carmine says. "I learned fast, and I was good at it, *really* good at it. In fact, I was so good at it that before the end of that first NFL season, I had 25 customers laying bets through me. I was off and running."

As Carmine's gambling book grew, he interacted with more of the dregs of 13th Avenue.

Gambling is a sickness. Researchers at The Mayo Clinic characterize it as a disorder that "is the uncontrollable urge to keep gambling despite the toll it takes on your life. Gambling can stimulate the brain's reward system much like drugs or alcohol can, leading to addiction. If you have a problem with compulsive gambling, you may continually chase bets that lead to losses, hide your behavior, deplete savings, accumulate debt, or even resort to theft or fraud to support your addiction."[25]

Gamblers deceive—themselves, those around them, especially their bookies. For Carmine, though, violence wasn't his first option.

"When people owed me, I always offered to work out a payment plan. Sure, some would say that made me a softie, but I got results. People loved to deal with me. Some tried to take my kindness for weakness, and yes, they caught beatings. Treat me right, don't make me chase you, don't make me go to your house, don't have your wife make excuses for you, and we can work it out."

Carmine made sure he was not hard to find. "I used to hang out at a florist on 13th Avenue, and they'd come in and we'd do business. It was better than doing business in the bar. When you got your fish, you don't parade them around the other sharks."

Carmine's clientele feared him, but still tried to finagle him.

"I had one of my regulars always offering me his car to settle his debt. I hated that shit, when they offered to trade, because then I had the headache of selling their stuff. Then you gotta worry about parking all these cars. You never get what they're worth. Really, how many used cars does a guy need? I can't pay my bills with a used car. And I could steal any car I wanted."

Carmine gave his debtors *some* grace. "I told this guy, *you* sell the car, even told him where to go to sell the car, then you get me the money and we'll straighten it out," Carmine says. "So he did sell it, paid me, and we were fine. But I said, 'Don't bother me no more with this shit.' He was a nice guy, local guy, with kids, not a mob guy, used to ask me over to his barbecues. I was glad to go, and glad

---

25. "Patient Care & Health Information - Diseases & Conditions: Compulsive Gambling," The Mayo Clinic

he got out of the hole. I even passed by his wife to check in on him when I was around, and asked if he was betting or borrowing. She said no. I said, 'Okay, just let me know.'"

But not all of Carmine's customers learned their lessons.

"This other customer, on Staten Island, Peppy. Degenerate gambler, terrible gambler, bet on anything, you give him the right odds, and he never had any money," Carmine says. "He fell behind with me, big time, in the thousands, and I said, 'I'll give you some time to start making payments.' But I warned him. I better not hear he was gambling with someone else."

Sure enough, word got back to Carmine that Peppy was deep in debt to another bookie.

"I confronted him, and here's another guy who wanted to give me a car I didn't need. What's worse, it was actually his son's car, one of those old Lincolns, with the suicide doors. I said no, but gave him some time to come up with payments, which he never did. He just kept trying to give me his kid's damn Lincoln."

After a while, Peppy became harder to find.

One day, Carmine found Peppy. And Carmine took Peppy's car.

For a ride.

"Yeah, I finally ran into Peppy, I took that car, and I put him in the trunk, and I drove around all day with him banging around. And when I say drove around, I mean I'm whipping turns up and down the Avenue all afternoon."

The day after that ride, Peppy came up with the cash for Carmine.

"Sometimes, you just had to find the right motivation with these guys."

Going Away to Camp

Remember summer camp as a teen?

Sure you do. Hiking along winding trails deep into the majestic wilderness. Enjoying sun-drenched days canoeing down lazy rivers. Roasting weenies over roaring fires. Campfire singalongs with charred s'mores and chilling ghost stories.

One summer, they sent Carmine upstate to a sleepaway camp. But no lazy river rides, roasting weenies, or charred s'mores for the kid from 13th Avenue. You see, they send you to a different type of camp when you're a repeat offender teenaged car thief with a lengthy rap sheet.

Carmine stole his first vehicle at the age of 16. It started with a trip to the local barber shop.

Back in the 70s, South Brooklyn men didn't go to hair salons. They went down to the local Italian barber, but for more than a trim and a shave. They went to debate, commiserate, or get an update, because if something went down in the neighborhood, they were talking about it down at the barber shop.

Classic red, white, and blue barber's pole spinning outside. Vintage red-leather-and-chrome barber chairs facing a mirrored wall, chipped at the edges, above a ledge thick with clippers and scissors and salves and aftershaves, a jar of something menthol, a machine spitting warm shaving cream. Black-and-white checkboard floors strewn with stray hairs. Thick cloud of cigar smoke hanging from the drop ceiling. An espresso machine in the corner next to a few bottles of whiskey and Campari. A row of chairs in the back to wait. A table with crumpled racing forms, little square OTB slips, the *New York Post* and *Daily News*, dog-eared Italian magazines.

The barber was the Brooklyn Italian neighborhood's ear to the ground, ready with *the what's what*. For that end of 13th Avenue for 30 years, that man was Gus the Barber, who trimmed 10,000, including straight-razor neck shaving more than his share of colorful wiseguys.

Wedged into that small shop next door to Mike the Butcher, directly across from St. Bernadette's Church, Gus was known as much for his skill with scissors as for his smile and wit, delivered impeccably in broken English.

"Everyone in the neighborhood went to Gus the Barber, especially the wiseguys, who'd hit him off with a twenty, which was a big tip back when I was a kid," Carmine remembers. "Lay back, get a hot towel, shave, relax, he'd give you a *Playboy* magazine or the paper, maybe a cup of espresso. Gus was an artist."

What was said in Gus' barber shop stayed in Gus' barber shop, and apparently the South Brooklyn barber's code of confidentiality proved stronger than *Omertà*. Over the years, detectives took their runs at Gus. But while they got capos, consiglieres, and even a boss or three to spill the beans, they never got nothing outta Gus the Barber. "Whatta I know," Gus would croak. "I cut a da hair."

One afternoon, 16-year-old Carmine, a bit shaggy, trooped down to Gus the Barber to get a couple inches taken off the top and the back squared up.

"There's one guy ahead of me, and I sit next to him, and he goes on about how he's in a big rush, how he just left his school bus double parked, and it's running," Carmine remembers.

Gave Carmine an idea. Not a great idea. Some, like his father, would say later, a terrible idea.

"So I got up, slipped out, and took his school bus for a ride. Loaded up all the guys and rode around the neighborhood *all* afternoon. I only ditched it when we ran outta gas."

The 13th Avenue regulars shook their heads and clucked their tongues as this hollering busload of boys sped by. Carmine laughs. "Even my father saw me driving that school bus. When I got home, he gave me an earful, called me an idiot, and he was right. Who steals a school bus? Can't even bring it to the chop shop."

Not long after Carmine's wild ride, Gus the Barber gave his last shave. "When Gus passed, all the wiseguys in Brooklyn showed up, packing St. Bernadette's," Carmine remembers. "You'd think an actual wiseguy died with the crowd that turned out at Torregrossa's, and forget about all the flowers."

Within two years of that joyride, Carmine had dozens of car thefts under his seatbelt as automobile crime in New York City spiraled out of control.

From Brooklyn all the way out to the Bronx, the streets were pitted with rusted-out cars stripped bare, scarred by graffiti. In fiscal crisis, the city cancelled contracts with private salvage companies to haul those wrecks away. Thousands of abandoned cars soon lay in alleys and vacant lots. Taking the Belt Parkway from Bensonhurst out to Long Island along Gravesend Bay at low tide, you'd see a dozen sun-bleached junks anchored in the surf, iron-rusted skeletons yawning like urban fossils.

Welcome to the Golden Age of "Tag Jobs."

Starting in 1969, all passenger vehicles built in America, or manufactured overseas and imported here, were required to have a unique VIN (Vehicle Identification Number).[26]

---

26. "Vehicle Identification Numbers (VINs) and the Federal Parts-Marking Program," The National Highway Traffic Safety Administration

Almost overnight, an illegal secondary market for parts sprang up. Thieves like Carmine stole a specific make and model, then a mechanic in a so-called "chop shop" switched the VIN plates with those of an identical vehicle that had been wrecked.

These operations flooded the market with thousands of "tag job" cars, sold privately through back-page classifieds, through public auctions, or exported overseas. At one point, there were more than 1,000 chop shops set up alongside auto-body yards in commercial districts from Flatbush out to Hunts Point.[27]

Depending upon the make and the model, a vehicle swiped by Carmine, then stripped and flipped for parts, netted up to four times its original value. Carmine was part of an army of teenage car thieves in the 1970s who, on average, boosted a car in New York City every five minutes.[28]

Carmine not only stole vehicles to fill specifics orders, he used them for personal use. "This guy up the block from Neddy's Bar had this beautiful cream-colored Impala," Carmine says. "I robbed it on a Friday. But once I got inside, it was like the back of a garbage truck. I took all the crap out, cleaned it inside completely, washed it, waxed it, and drove it around for the entire weekend. Then, I put it back on Monday where I found it."

Carmine left a note warning the owner to keep his car clean or he'd steal it again. This became a running joke among the regulars at Neddy's. "Every time he drove by, my friends said, 'Here comes your guy with the dirty Impala,'" Carmine says. "And you know what? The guy never left his car on the street dirty again. And trust me, I checked."

---

27. "Car Reported Stolen Every Five Minutes on New York Streets," by Barbara Basler, *New York Times*, April 18, 1982

28. "Amateurs Fading in World of Car Theft," by M. A. Farber, *New York Times*, December 13, 1983

Stolen bus rides aside, by the 1970s, stealing cars was more about business for Carmine and the 13th Avenue Boys. According to a *New York Times* article on the auto-theft crime wave:

> Before 1970, most of the cars stolen were for "joy rides," and of the 80 percent normally recovered a relatively high percentage were in good shape. Now, however, the cars stolen in New York, most often from middle-income residential sections of Brooklyn and Queens, usually pass through several hands and wind up in parks and on piers, or in garages and repair shops, most of which are engaged in legitimate business.[28]

Nearing his 18th birthday, Carmine Imbriale was responsible for more than a hundred of those car thefts.

No wonder the Fort Hamilton pot dealers caught a breather from Carmine's beatings. Depending on the vehicle, for every car he stole, Carmine pocketed from $300 up to $500. Calculated for inflation, in today's dollars, that's $1,500 up to $2,500. Not a bad return for a Bensonhurst teenager at a time when the minimum wage at the Pantry Pride on New Utrecht Avenue was $2.10 an hour.

Cars were easier to steal back in those days. Unlike the security technology on today's vehicles, in the 1970s, you didn't have to be highly technical to steal a car.

But you did need balls.

Carmine pinned out a vehicle as he'd walk down the block, not too fast, not too slow, just right to not attract attention, usually on a secluded block with little foot traffic at a time of day less likely to have witnesses; say, late evenings or early mornings.

Carmine didn't need much time. Once he moved in, he slid a flat, thin strip of aluminum, known as a slim jim, down between the outside of the driver's side window and the door frame, jimmied it a bit, and popped the lock. Took three to five seconds, tops.

Once inside the vehicle, Carmine cranked out the ignition lock with what's called a slide hammer. This little bad boy had a thread screw that he drove into the ignition lock. Once placed, slap the hammer, ignition barrel cracks, allowing him to start the car's stripped ignition with a standard flat-head screwdriver.

Older models didn't have alarm systems, and even when those started to turn up, an experienced car thief like Carmine knew where to reach under the dash to jack a power wire and strangle the wailing screech before a handful of chirps attracted suspicion.

Any problems—a jogger popping out, someone chucking the trash, dog walkers—Carmine ran off. South Brooklyn's crowded curbs were lined with plenty of vehicles for him to boost.

Eventually, local law enforcement targeted Carmine.

"I had this tagged Park Avenue, looked brand-new, beautiful car, but I had to keep it low in the neighborhood," Carmine says. "My friend, Billy, borrowed that brand-new Park Avenue. At the time, there was a detective in the neighborhood that had a hard-on for me. I warned Billy to not drive that car around the neighborhood. Told him, 'They're looking for me and if they see that car, they'll pick you up.'"

Billy's girlfriend sure was impressed with that long Park Avenue. But Billy didn't heed Carmine's warning. He and his girlfriend were pulled over and arrested. Billy shared with Carmine the surprised looks on the faces of the arresting officers, a smug satisfaction draining into disappointment when they realized Carmine was not behind the wheel.

"The cops insisted to Billy that 'this is Carmine's car,' and Billy argued with them, said, 'No, it ain't;' said he won it at the track," Carmine remembers.

Carmine wasn't concerned with catching a collar for car theft. Everyone he heard who got pinched got off with a fine. It was a joke. Sure, car theft was exploding, but jails were overcrowded and underfunded, and non-violent criminals tended to slide. According to one account in the *New York Times*:

> Indeed, as the number of reported grand larceny motor vehicle thefts in the city alone hit a record 100,900 last year, only 19 persons in the entire state were sentenced to prison for that crime, according to figures from the State Department of Correctional Services. In 1980, the most recent year for complete city records, there were about 9,000 felony motor vehicle arrests in New York City, but the city sent only nine persons to prison for that crime, the police said.[27]

Carmine became an exception to that rule.

"I remember the day that hard-ass detective from the 6-2 pulled me over in a stolen car, took me out, handcuffed me, then stopped, like he just thought of something," Carmine remembers. "He uncuffs me, says he was giving me a chance to run, then steps back, directly behind me."

Confused, uncertain, anxious, Carmine had a decision to make. Empty street. Maybe a hundred feet of black tar before he could cut around the corner. No passing cars. No witnesses. And no way this flat foot was catching Captain Crunch.

But it wasn't the detective he'd have to outrun.

Carmine tensed, leaned in, and almost went for it.

"I felt his eyes burning into my head," Carmine recalls. "But I'm not stupid. I said, 'I'm not running.' 'Cause I knew if I ran, he'd shoot me in the back. Or shoot me in the side, then roll me over and shoot me in front, put a gun on me, put drugs on me. I slowly put my hands behind my head. And he took me in."

This officer had a history harassing criminals that came back to hurt him. Remember Jimmy the Gent, the character in *Goodfellas* based on Jimmy Burke, played by Robert De Niro? "Well, Jimmy had two sons, Frank [James Burke] and Jesse [James Burke]," Carmine says. "That's right. Named his boys after the James Gang."[29]

Carmine knew Jesse Burke from the rackets. Years later, they did time in prison together. When Burke arrived on the same tier, he came up to Carmine and said, "I got that motherfucker."

"This crazy son of a bitch ran that cop over, and not only ran him over, but backed up and ran him over again," Carmine says. "Didn't kill him, just messed him up pretty bad. I said to Jesse, 'Don't let them know you're with me.' So many cops already hated me to begin with, I didn't want to give him one more reason to pull me over. Cops back then dealt differently with the guys they didn't like. And they didn't wear no body cameras neither."

A month shy of his 18th birthday, Carmine was processed as a minor at the Brooklyn House and went before a judge. Back in 1974, the Brooklyn House also served as a remand shelter for adolescents.

"Man, it was only June, but it was hot as hell in there and crowded that weekend," Carmine remembers. "That place got really bad in the summers, just sitting in those cages waiting, sweating, stinking. I started to get a bad, bad feeling."

The Brooklyn House drew the ire of inmates' rights advocates over the years for its overcrowding, excessive violence, and poor conditions. In the summers, the incarcerated suffered through terrible heat and faulty air

---

29. Obituary: James (Jimmy the Gent) Burke, Gangster, 64, of 'Wiseguy' Fame, Reported by The Associated Press, Appeared in the *New York Times*, April 17, 1996

conditioning, then froze during winters. New York shuttered the facility in 2020 as part of a plan to overhaul the city's jail system.[30]

Carmine got called down finally to see the judge.

Not just any judge.

Just a couple weeks prior, Carmine was involved in a street fight under the El on New Utrecht Avenue, where he beat a man unconscious, injuring the man's eye. Carmine was arrested, the man taken to Maimonides Hospital. A legal aid attorney claimed Carmine acted in self-defense. There were no witnesses. The man declined to press charges or testify. Carmine's attorney pled him down to a disorderly conduct misdemeanor. The judge wasn't thrilled, slapping Carmine with a small fine, some service time— and a warning that he'd better not appear before that judge anytime soon.

Well, it was anytime soon. Again, any other defendant on an auto-theft charge most likely receives a fine. But technically, a conviction for grand theft auto could draw 54 months of incarceration.

"I already had a dozen assaults and gang fights on my record, including the one from just two weeks before, so this judge says he's not letting me off, says I needed to learn my lesson," Carmine says.

Yet as Carmine was still a minor, there was an alternative-sentencing option.

So they sent Carmine to camp.

Sort of.

"Back then, when they wanted to get you off the streets, they sent you in the service, which wasn't an option for me, or they sent you to these drug treatment places," Carmine says. "It didn't matter if you were an addict. I wasn't a junkie. But my lawyer got me into one of them programs.

30. "Brooklyn's House of Detention Closes Under De Blasio's New Jails Plan," by Sydney Pereira, *The Gothamist*, January 3, 2020

CARMINE AND THE 13TH AVENUE BOYS | 99

Right before that, my friend went to Phoenix House. They sent me to Daytop. I remember thinking it was better than prison. I didn't know how fucked up that place was."

According to his plea, if Carmine completed a court-ordered, six-month drug-rehabilitation course, his 54-month sentence would be vacated. Carmine agreed.

"My father said he told me so, that sooner or later I'd be heading to the bullpen," Carmine says. "But I *really* felt bad because my mother was ashamed. She made excuses to her church group, but word got around the neighborhood. Anyway, I was on my own."

Daytop, or Daytop Village, was founded in 1964 in Tottenville, Staten Island, as a private drug addiction treatment organization with facilities throughout New York.

> According to founder Dr. Daniel Casriel its name was originally an acronym for 'Drug Addicts Yield to Probation' as Daytop was originally a kind of "halfway house" for convicted addicts. Another account gives the name to be an acronym for "Drug Addicts Yield to Persuasion". A third account gives the name to be an acronym for "Drug Addicts Yield to Others Persuasion."[31]

Carmine was remanded to the custody of Daytop officials on a warm June morning, boarding a prison bus headed for that long ride up the New York State Thruway.

By the time Carmine entered Daytop, the organization had more than 375 full-time workers, serving some 2,000 people at 14 facilities. Carmine was shipped to one of the larger Daytop facilities in Swan Lake in New York's picturesque Catskills in Sullivan County.

The facility was housed on the site of the former Paul's Hotel, one of dozens of seasonal resorts in the Borscht

31. "A Pioneer in Residential Drug Treatment Reaches Out," by Michel Marriott, *New York Times*, November 13, 1989

Belt, that network of vacation getaways in the Catskill Mountains.[32] Remember *Dirty Dancing*? Same deal, but instead of prancing around with Patrick Swayze, you got locked in with teen drug addicts and petty criminals.

Carmine had to participate in a program based on the Therapeutic Community (TC) method, a group-based approach for treating long-term mental illness, personality disorders, and drug addictions. The approach, heavy on peer interaction, with the clients and therapists living together, includes group psychotherapy.[33] The application of the TC method on vulnerable addicts at Daytop has been both praised and criticized in the therapeutic community.[34]

This began a dark period in Carmine's young life.

"I was supposed to be out in six months, and they kept me locked up in there for 14," Carmine regrets. "I refused to cooperate with their bullshit. Fuck them. They want to break you down psychologically, destroy your self-image. Like, they'd try and make you wear a woman's dress, which I wouldn't do. Now tell me what humiliating a kid like that has anything to do with rehabilitation. I refused. I wouldn't do it."

The camp included several Italian-American boys from New York City. "Just there a couple of hours when I'm walking down a hall, and I see some kids I knew from Bath Avenue. And then they saw me."

Carmine balled his fists, squared his shoulders, ready to throw. Under normal circumstances, the Bensonhurst blood feud would have been renewed. But they gave Carmine that South Brooklyn nod, where you flick your head up slightly

32. "Catskills: New Uses For Old Hotels," by John Conway, *New York Almanac*, October 9, 2014

33. Daytop "About" Webpage, WaybackMachine.com

34. "The Daytop crisis and its impact on the global Therapeutic Community movement," by Phoebus Zafiridis, published in "Therapeutic Communities: The International Journal of Therapeutic Communities," April 29, 2020

in recognition. Carmine nodded back. They were cool; at least as long as they were in Daytop. "That made it a little better," Carmine remembers. "But I was no addict, and this program was for addicts. Many of those kids in there were really screwed up. I was just along for the ride."

Trouble found Carmine that first day. "This kid, Phil Leo, comes out of the kitchen, says to me that Eugene Polk, a Black guy locked up in there, kept testing him, and he asked me what he should do about Eugene. I walked over to this cart with silverware, picked up a fork, handed that fork to Phil Leo, and I told him to take it and go stick him right in his chest, and then he won't test you no more."

A girl seated nearby overheard the conversation and rushed over to report the boys to a director. The director called a house meeting, Carmine's first.

All the members of the dorm, a couple dozen kids, trudged into a large room, taking seats facing each other in a large circle. Phil Leo and Carmine were called to stand and questioned about the exchange, and not permitted to sit until they admitted their wrongdoing.

"I admitted it, that I told Phil to stick the kid who was bothering him," Carmine says. "So they made us shave our heads. You believe that shit? How does that rehabilitate you? They called it 'taking your poison.' And I had to take my poison three times in there, just for giving advice."

Carmine remembers Daytop as punitive, not rehabilitative, more like a criminal mental institution than a juvenile facility. "It was suffocating, just like *One Flew Over the Cuckoo's Nest* in there, and you're trapped with some pretty unstable people. When the Yankees won a game in the World Series, one guy in our group, Pat O'Connor, yelled, 'Fuck that!' They shut the TV down, just for that. So we then started yelling at the TV, pretending to be watching the game. But Pat kept it up, way after the joke was not funny no more. There was always an edge to the place. It was just not good, not healthy, not making anybody in there better."

Carmine chafed under the discipline. "If you're walking by and they tell you to pick up a piece of garbage, and you don't, they called it attitude. 'I'm not here to pick up your garbage,' I said. 'I'm only here because the court sent me.' I just wanted to do my time, and get the hell out of there."

Carmine met his fair share of shady characters in Daytop, including one roommate, Sonny from the Bronx. Boys who behaved, like Sonny, received weekend passes to go home for a brief visit.

In his time in Daytop, Carmine never qualified.

"I never got a pass because I wouldn't wear the dress. Always with that *frickin'* dress. It was all about changing your mind, brainwashing you, breaking you down psychologically. I wouldn't do it. I wanted the pass, bad— but not that bad. But what are you gonna do?"

After every weekend pass, Sonny from the Bronx returned with his duffel bag and told Carmine what an amazing weekend he had. But Sonny left out some key parts.

Then one day, during GI Day (the day assigned to clean your living space, and submit to a military-style inspection), a pair of woman's high heel shoes spilled out of Sonny's locker. He shoved them back in the locker, but not before Carmine noticed.

"I never had a problem with gay people, whatever, live and let live, not a problem for me," Carmine says. "That was his business. So I really didn't think twice about it at the time."

Two weeks later, investigators from the FBI arrived at Daytop and arrested Sonny for suspicion of committing a string of armed bank robberies, disguised in drag. "They even found a bank-money bag in his closet, along with his get-up," Carmine says. "Great scam. He had everybody in there believing he'd one day be a Daytop counselor, when really, he's playing them all along to get the weekend pass to go rob banks. Daytop was crazy like that, attracted all these nuts and junkies."

Years later, when Carmine's brother-in-law went to prison for bank robbery, Carmine received a call from none other than Sonny from the Bronx, asking Carmine to vouch for Carmine's brother-in-law, when he did his bit. Small world.

Carmine describes exhaustive truth-telling sessions, called Marathon Groups. The boys and girls were each given a bottle of water, then forced to attend these lengthy group sessions until all of them revealed some humiliating secret about themselves.

"I'm in there with Bobby from Canarsie and Patty from Sheepshead, and going around the room, and I had nothing to say, felt like I shouldn't really be there," he says. "So it goes around, hours and hours go by, and this kid Anthony blurts out he's gay and had a crush on me. I didn't even know this kid. Then another Puerto Rican kid admits he had sex with chickens until they died. Then you had girls crying about being raped by uncles. And it goes on and on. I couldn't believe some of the shit I heard in there. Real private things that should be discussed with a therapist, not admitted it in a group session with druggie kids you got to live with day in, day out. And I just had to sit there through that craziness."

To make matters worse, the (former) inmates were running the asylum. Treatment staff included addicts who'd completed the Daytop program, some not exactly well-balanced individuals.

One director took a dislike to Carmine following the initial episode with Eugene. She targeted Carmine with punishments and abuse throughout his stay. You'd think she'd have more empathy as a recovering addict who went through the Daytop program.

"About seven months after I got out of Daytop, Nicky Rizzo asked me if I wanted to work as a bouncer at this whorehouse his father ran in Manhattan, and I agreed," Carmine says. "And there she was, that director, hooked on her junk again, working on her back. I coulda made her life real miserable, for the way she treated me. But I didn't. We both knew she'd been such an asshole to me back in Daytop, and I could see it in her eyes. But I told her, I got no hard feelings. She had enough problems."

He completed the alternative sentencing rehabilitation program administered by Daytop and was released in 14 months—eight months longer than his original sentence.

The court expunged the car-theft crime on Carmine's record: a good thing, considering that pursuant to New York Penal Law section 155.30(8), it is "automatically" a felony in the state when you steal a motor vehicle, not including a motorcycle, and that vehicle is worth more than $100.[35] (In other states, the dollar-amount threshold for a felony is higher, so many automobile crimes are classified as misdemeanors.) Removed from his record, that felony would not show up on a background check performed by a potential employer or financial institution.

Now an adult, Carmine had the opportunity to go straight and not fall back into a life of crime.

He headed back to South Brooklyn.

At least for a brief time, Carmine avoided the rackets. He was released from Daytop at the same time as his friend PeeWee, another tough kid from 13th Avenue. The newly released boys rented an apartment together in Bath Beach. "PeeWee and me were tight, treated him like my younger brother."

---

35. "New York Consolidated Laws, Penal Law - PEN § 155.30 Grand Larceny in the fourth degree," FindLaw.com, Current as of January 1, 2021

Carmine can be a good friend to have in your corner, especially if you need someone to intervene on a beef with a local bookmaker reluctant to pay up on a win.

"PeeWee cleaned up on a bet he placed with a bookie named Angelo, who was a real weasel," Carmine says. "PeeWee comes back from trying to collect, and he's upset. Says Angelo told him the line was raised overnight." Basically, PeeWee placed a bet with Angelo based on a specific point spread. That should have locked in the wager. Sure, a bookie may adjust the line if, say, a star player is a scratch. But that should only affect future bets, not impact bets already placed. "I went over to Wimpy Boys and asked Angelo to step outside to discuss that bullshit."

Instead of discussing the situation calmly, Angelo told Carmine to mind his business, among other things Angelo suggested Carmine do to himself.

"So while I'm beating the shit out of Angelo, his son comes outside," Carmine says. "So I wind up beating the shit out of the son too. I even remember, Angelo's shoes fly off, so then I'm beating them both with the shoes."

Next day, Carmine gets a call for a sit-down with Kid Blast at the Wimpy Boys Social. Albert "Kid Blast" Gallo Jr. was a *made* member of the Genovese Crime Family, younger brother of notorious gangster Joseph "Crazy Joe" Gallo. Turned out, Angelo the bookie and Kid Blast were related.

"So you're the one?" Kid Blast asked Carmine as he entered Wimpy Boys. "No wonder you beat the shit outta Angelo. I'd have to hit you with a crowbar."

Once Kid Blast understood the facts, he agreed Angelo was in the wrong. You don't raise the line after the bet is placed unless you're trying to get over on someone. "He told me I could keep the money PeeWee won, about $800, as long as I didn't raise my hands to Angelo no more. 'No problem,' I says."

A few days later, though, another one of Angelo's sons took a run at Carmine. And Carmine knocked him out cold. "So I get called in for another sit-down, and now Kid Blast wanted the money back," Carmine says. "I said, 'I didn't raise my hands to Angelo.' But this time, we had to hand back the money, which me and PeeWee split."

Later, in the 1980s, Carmine took his wife and kids for a night of harness racing in Yonkers when he crossed paths with Kid Blast. "Comes in with a beautiful young girl, we shook hands like old friends. Then he pulls me to the side, says he wants to do me a favor, whispers to me to bet the four horse in the eighth race. I ask him, 'You sure?' He gives me a look. Later, I walk out of there winning about four grand. I was kicking myself for not betting heavier."

Back in 1974, Carmine was fresh out of Daytop, emerging with a positive outlook.

"So PeeWee and me get that apartment, did really well for a while, watching out for each other," Carmine recalls. "We drank a bit here and there, but we didn't go crazy and no fighting." That lasted a few weeks. "Then I started back with the gambling, then running card games. Then, before I knew it, I was back where I started, a regular at Neddy's.

"If I could go back in time and talk to that teenage version of myself, I'd tell him, 'It's not worth it for you. Go back to school, play ball, be a coach, a referee, go to one of those kind of schools. That life on 13th Avenue is just temporary, and they're not your friends. That life, in the long run, you get arrested and do life, or they take your life, so it's not gonna be worth it.'"

PeeWee didn't slide back into the 13th Avenue rackets. He landed a job at a Chase Manhattan Bank branch in Lower Manhattan and was even promoted to head teller.

Carmine and PeeWee now ran in different circles; PeeWee holding down a legitimate job at a Manhattan bank, Carmine hustling on 13th Avenue. But the South Brooklyn odd couple managed to share an apartment without driving each other crazy. Until…

"So Steve Carlton is pitching that week, and I know the Phillies never lose the first game of a series when he pitches," Carmine says. "I was joking when I said to PeeWee that he should bring some of that bank money home and bet on Carlton. It was a lock, I tell him. But I never thought PeeWee would actually do it."

The next day, PeeWee came home from work with $40,000, still wrapped in fresh bank plastic.

"He's sweating, chain smoking, and insisting I put it all on Carlton," Carmine says. "PeeWee was taking his shot."

Carmine went down to Wimpy Boys to place the bet. But that's a head-turner wager, even on 13th Avenue. His regular bookie, uncomfortable handling such a large bet, steered Carmine to Greg Scarpa.

"I put the plastic-wrapped forty thousand right on Greg's desk," Carmine says. "He took one look at it and said he wanted no part of it. Told me to get it off his desk and get the fuck out of his club."

It's harder than you'd think to place a $40,000 bet on a single baseball game, even on 13th Avenue, even for Carmine. But he made the rounds and spread it around to three separate bookies.

Sure enough, Steve Carlton pitched a gem. PeeWee won. That payday *should* have sent PeeWee sailing off into the South Brooklyn sunset. And Carmine *should* have netted a nice bonus.

That's how this story *should* have ended.

But a funny thing happened on the way to PeeWee's happily ever after.

The next day, after settling up with the bookies, Carmine ran into his brother-in-law Bucky at Neddy's Bar. Carmine casually mentioned PeeWee's windfall to Bucky. "Bucky laughed at me, told me to cut it out with the gambling,"

Carmine says. "Then he said he had a thing to take care of and left."

Carmine didn't think twice about the conversation.

No sooner had Bucky slipped out of Neddy's, then he called his brother, Michael "Mikey Scars" DiLeonardo, a Gambino soldier. The two raced across Brooklyn, ransacked the apartment Carmine shared with PeeWee, and made off with the tens of thousands of dollars in gambling winnings.

"PeeWee thought I stole it, like I set it all up," Carmine says. "I knew right away who did it, but I couldn't say nothing. I was stuck in the middle. There was not a damn thing I could do about it."

Carmine knew the 13th Avenue rackets, knew you didn't rat, especially on *made* members of crime families, even if you were roommates with the mark.

Bucky denied it. Until that day, Carmine and Bucky were close. But after the robbery, things changed between the brothers-in-law. "We still had dinner together and still saw each other all the time, but for the most part, we fell out," Carmine says. "After he did that, I didn't want to have nothing to do with him."

This was a disaster for PeeWee. It was Friday and he had until Monday morning to return the "borrowed" money at the bank.

PeeWee was dead broke.

All weekend, a desperate Pee Wee begged and borrowed some cash, but never came close to the $40,000. Monday morning, the bank discovered the theft. PeeWee was arrested. Convicted at trial, PeeWee served an 18-month prison sentence before returning to the neighborhood, broke and a convicted felon.

Afterwards, for years, Carmine and PeeWee frequented the same bar, Neddy's, even sat near each other, night after night. But nothing was ever the same between them.

"I lost a good friend," Carmine says. "PeeWee never stopped being pissed at me. Wouldn't talk to me, wouldn't sit near me, wouldn't even look at me. PeeWee and me, we went all the way back. Damn, we played stickball forever as kids, football, everything. He was a great ball player. Do you know what it was like to sit in Neddy's together, night in, night out, and not talk? It used to kill me. But what was I gonna do? I had to keep my mouth shut. You don't talk. Period."

What happened to PeeWee wasn't right. But that was life on 13th Avenue, where you can be riding high one moment, and the next, handcuffed in the back of a squad car heading down to the Brooklyn House.

Over the years, every once in a while, someone brought up Carmine's legendary stolen-bus joyride through the streets of Bensonhurst.

"Then one night, we're in some club, and Carmine Sessa pulls me to the side, says he wants me to meet a guy named Peanuts." Carmine agrees.

They walk over, Sessa makes the introductions, and with a big smile on his face, he says, "You two remember each other? Because, you should. I know it's been a while, but think back. *Way* back."

"I'm standing there, and *I know* I know this guy from somewhere, but I can't place him," Carmine says. "And by the look on his face, I know *he knows* me, but he also can't remember from where either. So we're standing there like two mopes staring real hard at each other."

Then, Sessa breaks the tension. "Carmine, you stole this guy's bus outside of Gus the Barber's shop, remember?"

And they shared the laugh.

Mr. Neil and His Cheese

Carmine's friends were baffled.

At a time like this, how could Carmine go to sleep? For crying out loud, Carmine, it's the bottom of the eighth inning. There's still a chance. Long shot. But still.

On the stolen 19-inch TV crackling in the corner of Carmine's rundown Bay 10th Street two-bedroom rental, the heavily favored Los Angeles Dodgers trailed the Philadelphia Phillies by a score of eight to one.

Carmine waved them off. He'd been down this road too many times to get his hopes up for late-inning heroics.

Carmine thought he had a lock when he wagered $6,000 on the game, based on a tip from Mike the Butcher, betting on the Dodgers to win by half a run. Earlier in the day, Mike swore up and down that the Phillies' starting pitcher would be a game-time scratch. Though it's a mystery how such sensitive MLB info made it all the way from LA to a South Brooklyn sawdust-on-the-floor-style butcher shop.

Sure enough, before that first pitch, the Dodgers' pitcher scratched.

"I don't know how he did it, but Mike the Butcher's tips were gold," Carmine says.

It wasn't just how much Carmine bet that had his friends wondering how he could turn in so early. You see, Carmine bet those six dimes with a bookmaker reporting to Greg Scarpa. More importantly, Carmine didn't have the money he bet.

"Not like I could run out on the field and pitch for the bum, though my grandmother woulda done a better job," Carmine says. "Couldn't watch no more without putting my foot through the TV. Sure, I was in trouble. But not for nothing, watching the game made it worse."

Carmine went to bed, staring at the ceiling, trying to not think about the next day. As he drifted off, a friend burst into the room shouting. "Holy shit, Carmine, you're not gonna believe it!" he hollered. "THEY ACTUALLY WON! Only you, Carmine. Could you get any luckier?" Running up nine runs in the ninth inning, the Dodgers won, 9-8. Carmine covered the bet by half a run, avoiding an uncomfortable conversation with a homicidal maniac.

Yet on 13th Avenue, sometimes when you won, you still didn't win. The next afternoon, Carmine headed down to The Wimpy Boys to collect.

Scarpa Sr. balked. "Greg said he wanted to see my money first before he'd pay," Carmine says. "That's not how this works. But he's the big shit over there and there's nothing I could do or say to change his mind."

Bookmakers generally don't want a reputation as a "welch," someone who doesn't honor his debts. But it's not like there was an official 13th Avenue Gaming Commission for Carmine to file a grievance. Scarpa didn't have to pay. And if Carmine complained too loudly? Well, they didn't call Scarpa "The Grim Reaper" for his people skills.

Bookmakers frowned on gamblers who bet beyond their means. But that's a conversation you have before you book the bet. Carmine wasn't some *chadrool* off the street. Carmine was a 13th Avenue regular, a bit player in the broader rackets, sure, but an up and comer.

But Carmine was not connected.

Scarpa was a *made* member of a crime family. He didn't hold the title of capo, but for all intents and purposes, he was the de facto leader of dozens of soldiers and associates, with his hand in multi-million-dollar rackets, from credit cards and drugs to bank robberies and securities fraud.

Carmine did plenty of dirt with 13th Avenue wiseguys. But he was on his own.

That afternoon, while dropping in at the Bath Avenue club run by Anthony Spero, Bonanno Family consigliere, Carmine hit up Paul "Paulie Zac" Zaccaria. Paulie Zac was a Brooklyn Sicilian mobster much older than Carmine, once a driver for Carlo Gambino and now a powerful Gambino captain in his own right. Paulie Zac was among the old guard who took a shine to Carmine. So when Carmine mentioned Scarpa's re-neg, Paulie Zac agreed to intervene.

The sit-down was at Wimpy Boys. Scarpa did not have to honor Carmine's bet, but he deferred to Paulie Zac and paid Carmine. And Paulie Zac did not mediate on behalf of Carmine *just* out of the kindness in his heart. "I got six grand and from that I gave Paulie twenty-five hundred," Carmine recalls.

The episode left a bad taste in Scarpa's mouth, the initiation of a mutual dislike that festered between the two for decades.

"When there's a sit-down, you may win, walk out of there high on the hog, but in the long run, you don't win shit," Carmine says. "Instead, you walk away with a new enemy."

Beforehand, Paulie Zac asked Carmine if he was *sure* he wanted to sit down with Scarpa. But Carmine was playing the short game, not realizing how that confrontation would play out.

"These guys are the cheapest bastards you ever want to meet. They don't go in their pocket for nothing. And they're all about ego bullshit. So I go in there. I know I'm in the right. Everyone at the table knows I'm in the right. What's Greg gonna say? But what I didn't realize was that whoever loses the sit-down now has hard-on for you. I got my money, sure, but I'm walking outta there getting the feeling I'd have to watch my back with Greg. That's just how this works. If you're lucky, guy like Paulie asks you twice if you really want to push *this* thing with a guy like *that*."

Hustling on 13th Avenue wasn't easy.

Carmine had thousands of dollars "out on the street" in illegal loans, at five-percent interest. That's five percent on the principle... *due every week.* Carmine also managed thousands of dollars in mostly small bets every week. That meant paying out the winners, chasing down the losers. But no matter who paid, who didn't pay, Carmine *always* had to pay up the chain. No shorts. No excuses. No joke.

Carmine was also a high-stakes sports gambler, sometimes betting money he didn't have in hand, then robbing drug dealers and unaffiliated bookies throughout South Brooklyn to cover his losses.

Between his loansharking, gambling book, and side hustles, Carmine's weekly "nut," the amount of money he coughed up, ranged anywhere from $5k to (at one point) $50k. And that's aside from a standard twenty-percent kickback he passed along from major scores.

All those 13th Avenue guys were flush one day, crying poverty the next. Sure, when Carmine was short, he'd borrow the money, like anyone else who walked into Neddy's Bar. But unaffiliated, not even an associate, Carmine didn't qualify for the *family-and-friends-of-ours* discount.

So when Jerry ambled into Neddy's one afternoon, spotted Carmine and hustled over to sit down next to him, speaking in a hushed tone about a can't-miss score, Carmine put down his beer.

It was late afternoon, Neddy's was filling up, already a dozen guys with big ears lining the bar. Carmine motioned to Jerry to quiet down. They dipped outside. Jerry, barely containing his excitement, laid out for Carmine a slam-dunk hijacking, with detailed route info on a commercial truck transporting high-end consumer electronics. He even had a guy on the inside.

Nice score. Carmine nodded. But hijacking wasn't his thing. Though a prolific armed robber, Carmine never stuck up a moving vehicle.

Hijacking wasn't as popular a racket on 13th Avenue. "Guys from the Wimpy Boys crew pulled jobs, but most of the hijacking came from the crews in Queens, Gotti's crew, Paul Vario's guys," Carmine says. "Made sense for them, since they had the airports locked up."

That was the Gambino Family crew run by John Gotti in Western Queens, and a Lucchese crew run out of a Canarsie junkyard by Lucchese capo Paul Vario.[36] Gotti's running beef with the greedy tribute Gambino boss Paul Castellano demanded from hijacking was one of the many sore points that motivated Gotti to assassinate Big Paulie.[37]

The 1970s was the high-water mark for wiseguy hijacking in the New York Tristate area. According to a 1974 *New York Times* article, "nearly 90 per cent of all the hijacks in this city can be tied to organized crime."[38]

Hijacking suits organized crime. If you're stealing a few hundred boxes of anything, especially if it's perishable, better be able to store and re-sell the goods. Say you steal a truck full of lobsters, worth tens of thousands of dollars, even with the discount. Or a shipment of fur coats, or say high-end sneakers. Where's a normal crook unloading these items? Before you peddle it door to door, someone's dropping a dime or shaking you down. And then you can't run to the cops.

That's why this tip was *so* valuable. Consumer electronics are easy to store, easy to transport, and easy to re-sell.

36. "Paul Vario, 73; Called a Leader Of Crime Group," by Mark A. Uhlig, *New York Times*, May 5, 1988

37. *Mafia Dynasty: The Rise and Fall of the Gambino Crime Family*, by John H. Davis, HarperCollins

38. "Truck Hijacking in City Is a $4.2-Million Business," *New York Times*, May 20, 1974

"It was a cheese truck, but borrowing it for this delivery, filling it with electronics," Carmine remembers. "Jerry got the tip from the regular driver. We went over the details several times, just to make sure, and he swore up and down that the information was good."

The job had one wrinkle.

"The regular driver was not scheduled to work that day," Carmine says. "But, Jerry says, that's the beauty of the thing, throws off suspicion. Some other guy was scheduled to drive, so instead of looking hard at the regular guy, they'd suspect the replacement."

Carmine wasn't concerned. This may have been his first hijacking, but not the first time he stuck a gun in someone's face on a shakedown.

Carmine recruited one of his 13th Avenue boys. He needed a driver for the truck, as he could not operate a manual transmission.

Hijacking is problematic. For starters, it's unpredictable. Timing must be right. If you get lucky, or the driver is in on the action, the truck is parked or stops for you. Otherwise, force may be required, at the point of a gun. Waving a bat at someone ain't the same.

Then there's the consequences. Committing a crime with a weapon, you may be charged with an armed robbery felony. But hijacking bumps that up to aggravated robbery, punishable by more lengthy prison sentences.

On the flip side, hijacking is lucrative. Sure, you pay for a tip, cut partners in, but there really is no overhead. The hardest part of the score is loading and unloading the stolen goods.

When things go right.

This hijacking started off well.

"So, I get the route, it's out on Long Island, and I don't know the area, but I'm able to find the truck pretty easy, and follow him along the LIE for miles," Carmine says. The LIE (Long Island Expressway), Interstate 495, spans 70 miles starting near the Queens–Midtown Tunnel, stretching east through Nassau and Suffolk Counties. This is Long Island's main artery into Manhattan, always congested. But on this clear day, good luck was with Carmine. Traffic was light.

As you head away from the city, the byways become less busy.

"I followed the truck after it left the LIE, and had to trail him for a bit," Carmine says. "I found a good spot and stopped up the road in front of him."

Carmine blocked the street. His accomplice had the hood opened, pretending to struggle. With the driver distracted, Carmine ran up, gun drawn, and barked at him to get out of the truck.

"We didn't want to hurt the guy, he's just doing his job. Lucky for me, no problems. He was surprised, didn't want no part of me, so he gave it up. The gun helped."

The driver slowly stepped down out of the cab.

"I made the driver walk a couple steps ahead of me, took him into the woods, tied him to a tree. It was a nice day out and we're in the woods, not far from the road, but far enough so he's not sticking out. I figured someone'd come along and hear him shouting."

Fighting an adrenaline high, Carmine headed back to a warehouse in Queens. When they arrived, though, he was in for a surprise.

"We get back to unload the electronics," Carmine says. "I open it up, can't believe my eyes. The truck was packed full of *frickin'* mozzarella."

Thousands of pounds of mozzarella, as well as large tins of ricotta and giant bags of pizza dough.

Carmine lost it on Jerry. "I went off on him, and he went off on the regular driver, asking him what the fuck happened. He swore he had no idea, said they tricked him too. So nobody knows who fucked up, nobody knows what to do, and I'm way out in Queens with a truck full of stolen mozzarella spoiling, and that's not electronics, but it's not nothing neither."

Carmine hit the road, to make the rounds. "We spent the day driving all over Brooklyn and Queens to I don't even know how many pizzerias, any we could find, selling the cheese at a discount they've never seen, and I tell you, I unloaded all that cheese, every box, and also all the ricotta and dough."

It wasn't the massive payday, not like a hijacked load of electronics, but for one day's work, a $17,000 profit's not bad.

Two days later, Carmine gets an ominous call.

"Joe Brewster calls me up, says I'd been *sent for* by Aniello Dellacroce," Carmine recalls. "I wracked my brain, but for the life of me, I couldn't figure out what I'd done wrong to get *sent for* by a guy like that."

Yes, *that* Aniello "Mr. Neil" Dellacroce; since 1965, Underboss of the Gambino Crime Family. Less than two years earlier, with Dellacroce imprisoned for tax evasion, on October 15, 1976, Family Boss Carlo Gambino died at home of natural causes. Before he passed, the old don appointed his cousin, Paul Castellano, to succeed him. This surprise succession infuriated many front-line Gambinos who felt Dellacroce got passed over unfairly, chief among them Captain John Gotti.[39]

Here's this Mafia lion, at the pinnacle of organized crime in America, mentor to a John Gotti on the rise, at the core of a power struggle splintering the Gambinos, the largest of New York's Five Mafia Families.

And he's looking for Carmine?

At Dellacroce's appeal hearing in 1973 for a tax-evasion conviction, Federal Judge Arnold Bauman denied bail, labeling the Gambino underboss "a top level hoodlum, a

---

39. "Reputed Organized Crime Leader Dead at 71," by Rick Hampson, The Associated Press, December 3, 1985

danger to society, a menace to the community, a parasite who lives off the life blood of honest people." 41

At another hearing, in 1979, prosecutors dubbed Dellacroce "the godfather of all crime in New York City." Dellacroce was cited by law enforcement sources for his involvement in high-profile hits, including the 1979 murder of Bonanno Boss Carmine Galante and the killing of Philadelphia Boss Angelo Bruno the following year. Dellacroce was such heavyweight, on February 25, 1985, he was indicted along with the leaders from the other New York Mafia Families as part of the epic Mafia Commission Trial. He only evaded conviction by passing away from cancer in December, later that year.[40]

"I didn't get it; what would a guy like that want with a guy like me?" Carmine remembers.

For the uninitiated, being "sent for" is a serious matter in the underworld.

"Think of the feeling you get in your gut when the IRS calls you up, out of nowhere, tells you that you're being audited and it's not looking good for you, and they want you to come down, and you're really not sure what you did, but you know they don't call you in when you did nothing," Carmine says. "It's something like that feeling, but only worse, because the IRS won't put a bullet in the back of your head or torture you in some warehouse out in Staten Island. You get sent for by someone like Mr. Neil, you come in. Or you move with your family to Nebraska."

Carmine could not think of a single reason why Dellacroce wanted to speak with him. They'd never met. He wasn't working with any Gambinos at that moment. Didn't make sense, didn't sound good. But he knew he couldn't refuse.

---

40. "Disgraced FBI agent's attorneys attack credibility of witness," by Scott Shifrel, *New York Daily News*, October 23, 2007

On his way to the meeting, Carmine sought advice from an underworld veteran he trusted.

James "Jimmy" Ida still kept tabs on Carmine. Growing up in the Little Italy neighborhood of Manhattan, Ida was inducted into the Genovese Crime Family in the late 1970s and placed in the crew of Matthew "Matty the Horse" Ianniello, serving as his captain's bodyguard and chauffeur. Ida's younger brother Joseph also served in Ianniello's crew.

Jimmy Ida operated out of storefront on 13th Avenue in Bensonhurst. Carmine would see Jimmy, often with his brother, seated outside. In the early 1970s, Carmine's brother Frank opened a Variety Hut retail shop on that same block, directly across the street, and Carmine's mother worked the counter.

"I always got along with them, especially Jimmy," Carmine says. "Jimmy was always sitting on the Avenue in his beach chair. He used to tell me to go park his car, and I'd be shitting my pants that I didn't dent it. Everyone respected Jimmy. He wasn't no guy to fool around with. And he was good to me."

One day, two thugs from Bath Avenue entered Carmine's brother's shop, demanding he cough up a street tax. "These Bath Avenue guys wanted me to be a bag man, my shop to be a drop for them," Frank says. "I turned them down, wasn't my thing."

Carmine mentioned the shakedown to Jimmy Ida.

"When they came back, Jimmy stormed into the shop right behind them, and they told Jimmy everything was okay, they were just there to talk business with my brother," Carmine recalls. "They were connected, so these guys knew who Jimmy Ida was."

"You're not talking business, because if you were talking business, you'd be talking it with me," Carmine remembers Jimmy Ida barking back at the two hoods. "This is my shop, so get the fuck outta here and go where you gotta go."

They went where they had to go, backpedaling all the way to Bath Avenue.

Jimmy turned to Carmine's mother and told her if she had any more problems with these guys, or any other guys, to just come see him across the street and he'd sort it all out for her.

"Jimmy was a street guy, tough as they come, but a gentleman, a man of his word," Carmine says. "I admired Jimmy and his brother. And Jimmy Ida was a model wiseguy, what it really meant to follow the code."

Later on, when Jimmy Ida got wind that Frank was planning to sell the shop, he approached him with a proposition. "Jimmy Ida came to my house, sat down with me and my father," Frank says. "He wanted to take over the business, wanted the location as a drop or a front. I told him I'd already sold it, and now what they do afterwards is up to the new owners, but out of my control."

One day, Carmine accepted a "gift" from Jimmy Ida.

"Jimmy calls me over and he gives me $1,500, told me he didn't like how I dressed, told me to go buy some decent dress clothes and then come meet him for dinner at Sirico's," Carmine says. He was still unaffiliated with a crew. That dinner with Jimmy Ida could have turned into something big.

Instead, Carmine jumped on a flight to South Florida and partied like a madman until the money ran out. "When I came back on the Avenue, I told Jimmy what happened, and he asked me if I was crazy. He also said I owed him the $1,500, but I never had to pay him. Jimmy liked me, and I considered him a friend."

Ida saw promise in Carmine, and attempted to recruit him to join his crew. "Looking back, I should have stuck with Jimmy. He was disappointed that I didn't go that way with him. It's one of the big regrets of my life. Jimmy did things the right way. He only went away years later. Things woulda turned out very differently had I went with Jimmy."

So Carmine stopped by 13th Avenue to ask Ida for his advice on the Dellacroce situation.

"Jimmy first asked me if I hurt anybody, and at least that week and the one before, I hadn't," Carmine recalls. "Jimmy then told me about Mr. Neil, to be prepared for a tough, no-nonsense old timer with no patience for bullshit who demanded that respect. He told me to not talk too much, follow Mr. Neil's lead, answer questions directly, and above all, be respectful and be truthful."

Then Carmine headed to Queens with Joe Brewster. When they arrived, Carmine headed in to meet with Dellacroce, while Brewster waited outside.

"As soon as I walked in, I got a bad, bad feeling," Carmine says. "That old man was about as scary as they come. No bullshit small talk, he got right to the point."

The first words out of Dellacroce's mouth froze Carmine. "You know that cheese truck was mine," Dellacroce croaked.

Carmine put it all together. "I said that of course I didn't know that that was his truck, and I apologized up and down."

Dellacroce accepted Carmine's apology, then asked what he did with all that cheese. "We're talking an entire truck of mozzarella, so he was surprised when I told him I sold it all, door to door, that day," Carmine says. "He wanted the names of all the pizzerias, insisting they had to buy from him."

Carmine didn't give up the names. "That was a tight spot, but he nodded. He was okay with me not giving up the names. I think that saved me, because I sensed he respected me, that I wouldn't give them up. But I think he was also impressed I offloaded an entire truck of cheese that fast. These guys are all about the money. Come on now. You know what that took, to sell all that in a single day, going into those shops unannounced, no appointments?"

Carmine told Dellacroce that he made $17,000. "He said, 'Okay, give me seven grand, keep the rest,'" Carmine says. "I said okay. He could've asked for it all, and got it. And he warned me not to touch his trucks again. I said no problem; I never woulda touched the truck in the first place had I known, and that's the truth. You don't rip off the underboss of the Gambinos."

It wasn't the lucrative haul of consumer electronics Carmine expected. But Carmine turned a tidy profit, and forged a new underworld connection—not to mention filing away another gangland tale he lived to tell.

"Dellacroce couldn't get over it, said I was a hell of a salesman, being able to unload a full truck of his mozzarella in under six hours." Carmine laughs. "But really, I had no choice. It would've all gone bad. You do what you gotta do."

Years later, when Carmine entered the federal witness protection program, he forgot about that hijacking, which could have had disastrous consequences. "When you enter the program, you gotta tell them all your crimes, and if you leave anything out, I mean *anything,* they got grounds to kick you out. When I remembered the hijacking, I called them back right away. For me to forget about something like that tells you what you need to know about all the shit I was into back in those days."

That wasn't the only thing that slipped Carmine's mind.

As Carmine moved to leave, Mr. Neil held up his hand. "Whoa, whoa, hold on, Carmine," Dellacroce said. "What the hell did you do with my driver?"

Carmine raced from Dellacroce's office in Queens back out to the exit off the LIE where he stashed the driver in the woods.

The poor guy was still there.

"It was two days later, but he wasn't hurt," Carmine says. "He was dehydrated and kind of a mess. I said to myself, 'Thank God the old man sent me back or this guy would've died in the woods tied to a tree.' I didn't want that.

I just figured someone would've come along sooner or later and let him go."

Lucky Like That

There's a proverb about optimism that goes *when life gives you lemons, you make lemonade.*

If there were lemonade stands on 13th Avenue back in '79, they paid protection to operate. And if anyone tried to stick a guy like Carmine with lemons, he'd punch the guy in the throat, shake him down, fence the lemons, turn a profit, kick a piece upstairs, then someone'd probably offer him a union job.

Or something like that.

How the hell did Carmine get away with so much? That question had many heads shaking on 13th Avenue over the years, especially Joe Brewster, who had a ringside seat.

For one thing, Carmine developed a knack for endearing himself to rising racketeers. "I always showed respect and carried myself the right way," Carmine says. "Besides, they'd always see me fighting, and they loved all that shit."

Sit outside Neddy's long enough, someone's coming along to wipe the curb with someone else. In the time it took smoke down a Lucky, the bar'd empty out for the matinee.

"Back in those days, we were fighting all the time. I could handle myself. I'd take on anyone, no matter how big. After it was over, I always shook hands. I think the wiseguys respected that about me. Got so I felt like I was in the draft with these guys, always being watched, evaluated, ranked."

Something to be said for being rough and ready in the wrong place, wrong time—with the right reaction.

One summer afternoon, Carmine's cruising Bensonhurst behind the wheel of his latest chromed-out Caddy tag job. He eased up, approaching a corner on New Utrecht under the elevated BMT West End Line, a Red Bird running overhead out to Coney drowning out the radio in Carmine's ride.

Stuck behind one of those long coffee-and-cake red lights, Carmine glanced left and, on the corner, spotted three goons laying into a young neighborhood guy who looked familiar. Didn't look like a jerkoff. Looked like a local kid. Didn't back down. Kept getting up, kept coming back. Kind of like Carmine.

"That's not right," Carmine says. "My father taught me a sense of fairness going back to my schoolyard days. You fight a man, settle your differences. Then afterwards, you shake hands."

Carmine palmed a short crowbar he kept handy on the floor on the shotgun side of his ride, left the car running, and leapt into the melee swinging. The three assailants wanted no part of that crowbar nor the lunatic attached to it, and fled.

Carmine helped the kid to his feet. The kid got worse than he gave, but he got his shots in, shook it off. Carmine accepted the kid's thanks, gave his name when asked for it, and they went their separate ways.

Later that afternoon, Carmine was in the P.S. 201 schoolyard, getting at-bats in on some automatics. A shiny, mile-long black Lincoln Continental four door, the one with the Rolls Royce grille, rolled to the curb. Two pairs of sunglasses, both matching the dark tint on the Lincoln, one chomping a toothpick, stepped out, started asking around for that kid Carmine.

Now there were more Carmines in that neighborhood than johnny pumps, but everyone pretty much knew who these goons were running down that day. Not the first time someone came around the schoolyard asking about Carmine Imbriale.

Carmine leaned the stickball bat against the fence, stepped forward, demanding, "Who wants to know?" Ignoring the question, the sunglasses with the toothpick turned, dipped the shades, told Carmine to get in that long Lincoln Continental.

"I'm not going with you. Kidding me?"

"Listen, Carmine, you got it all wrong" The thug softened. "This is gonna be good for you. *Trust me.*"

"Yeah, right," Carmine said, not swayed. "You must say that to everyone you take for a ride."

The goon insisted they could do this the easy way or they could do this the hard way. But either way, they were not leaving that schoolyard without Carmine in the back of that Lincoln. With a smile like a serpent, he held up an outstretched hand to beckon Carmine to come with him, again stressing that it's in his best interest to come with them.

Maybe it was the way they insisted. Maybe it was that they didn't attack him. Maybe it was the bulges from the pistols they could've pulled. Or maybe it was the half dozen witnesses on the scene.

Whatever it was, Carmine relented, with the condition that he be allowed to ride in the backseat by himself. They agreed, and for that brief ride, Carmine kept one hand on the handle, door unlocked, ready to duck and roll out into traffic.

The guys in the Lincoln drove Carmine to a well-appointed two-family in Bensonhurst, about a mile away. This was the residence of John "Johnny" Rizzo Jr., then a soldier in the Gambino Crime Family, who became one of John Gotti's trusted lieutenants. Johnny Rizzo was a well-respected, low-key career criminal who rose to captain with a crew operating throughout Brooklyn and Staten Island, including dealings in the underground New York City nightlife.

"I knew *of* Johnny Rizzo, but this was the first time I met him in person," Carmine recalls. "I remember seeing him on 13th Avenue all the time, and he'd see us play football in Torregrossa's parking lot, so he would recognize me, and nod. Right away, he reached out his hand to thank me for helping his son escape a beating earlier that day."

This surprised Carmine.

Rizzo wanted to know what compelled Carmine to help his son.

"I don't know," Carmine answered Rizzo. "I saw three guys beating up on one local guy, and it didn't seem right, so I acted without thinking it through." To this day, Carmine still has an impulse thing.

"If the guy had it coming, or it was business, then hey, that's a different story," Carmine says. "But three guys beating on a neighborhood kid, that's nowhere near right. If those guys had a real beef with the kid, they would've said something and not just ran off."

Johnny Rizzo appreciated Carmine's integrity and sense of street justice. Besides, a man who'd charge at three guys... well, a man like that could be useful, in the right capacity.

Rizzo made Carmine a proposition.

His son, Jay Rizzo, owned a gay bar on New Utrecht Avenue, a hole in the wall on a corner under the El, but it was profitable. Problem was, it drew in a rowdy crowd. Then there were unruly neighbors and local punks harassing patrons.

"Directly next door to the gay club was this smaller, after-hours joint that Johnny also owned," Carmine says. "So he offered to give me control of the after-hours spot. Had a bar, several tables, a jukebox. Could do something with that. In return, all I needed to do was provide security for the gay club. That's a pretty sweet deal."

Carmine accepted the offer.

"First, Joe Brewster comes by, and says, 'How the hell did you get Johnny Rizzo to just give you this club?'" Carmine remembers.

Johnny Rizzo also put the word out. Before long, Mafioso from all over were adding Carmine's after-hours spot to their South Brooklyn bar crawls. Even rising Gambino stars like John Gotti and Frank DeCicco were dropping by.

"On weekends, I'm pulling in thirty to forty grand a night. But I'm also making the rounds. Now, when I go to the other spots, I gotta leave a nice tip 'cause I'm expecting them to throw money around at my spot. So between the cost to run the joint, what I'm making, what I'm tipping, and what I'm giving up to Rizzo, by the end of the night, I'm coming home with ten grand. That was fine with me, but it was like a wild merry-go-round."

It was 1979. The wiseguys were everywhere in South Brooklyn. But change was in the air.

"Now I saw it on both sides of the bar," Carmine says. "The new generation coming in was very different than the old timers."

When you got down to it, there were two types of Brooklyn wiseguys. Sure, they were all pretty much violent, conniving thieves and hustlers with larcenous hearts. But those weren't mortal sins on 13th Avenue. Even murder was forgivable, as long as you got the nod from the right capo.

But there was definitely one big difference, and it ripped apart the rackets in the years ahead.

From the dons down to the dope peddlers, the hijackers, the hookers, the hustlers, and the henchmen, the crew chiefs, the captains, the car thieves, and the credit card hacks, the bank robbers, the bookies, the burglars, the leg breakers, and let's not forget the shylocks, the sneak thieves, the stick-up kids and the strong-arm union thugs...

... *all* of them.

They either followed the rules.

Or they didn't. That simple.

Not the obvious rules, like don't snitch or don't talk to the police.

Deeper.

Respect, obedience, cooperation, comradery.

Carmine followed the rules, back then. Carmine wanted to be part of something special. So sure, he may've beat the living shit outta ya. But only because you had it coming, and only because he didn't know you were connected or protected. In that case, maybe he'd still blacken both your eyes, but only after checking.

Unless you slapped him with a wet towel in front of the prettiest girl on Bath Avenue.

Fuck.

That.

We'll get to that.

You did not want to be on the business end of those knuckles. Standing a solid six feet tall and clocking in at a fighting weight of 190, Carmine was blessed with a concrete jaw and jackhammer hands.

"When I fought someone, I fought for a reason," Carmine says. "Maybe not always a great reason, but I didn't get off on hurting people. And when I fought you, I fought hard, but I'm not like these clowns out there saying they beat up every guy in the neighborhood. I beat the shit outta you or you beat the shit outta me, then I shook your hand."

Trailing behind Carmine usually was his merry band of marauders, more than happy to help bust up a Bay Ridge bar or brawl with the Bath Avenue Boys at the 18th Avenue Feast.

"We were always getting into fights inside and outside these clubs, everyone jumping in, big brawls, complete insanity. Sometimes, when I knew it was going down, I'd run to a car and rip off the antenna, and use that to whip you. Not only did that hurt you bad, it made this wicked whipping sound. You know, that's probably why they don't make cars with antennas no more. They sure made for nasty weapons and they were always around to grab."

One 1979 night stands out above the rest.

"Every time we went somewhere, we never went alone. That night, I was with Philly, Tommy, Joey, Johnny, and Louie. I remember it like yesterday. Just great guys from the old neighborhood. Been a long time. Joey and Louie joined the fire department, died on 9/11. Rest in peace. Shame. Best friends a guy could have. I was also with my girlfriend that night."

Not just any girlfriend.

Cindy Spero was the daughter of Thomas "Shorty" Spero, a future captain in the Colombo Family, and early sponsor of Salvatore "Sammy the Bull" Gravano in 1968. Following a dispute with Ralph Spero, a Colombo associate, Gravano moved over from the Colombos to the Gambinos. Ralph Spero was murdered in 1980. Several months later, Shorty Spero disappeared.[10]

Shorty Spero was murdered by Gerard "Pappa Bear" Pappa, first a Colombo associate, then a Genovese Family soldier, who took an off-the-record contract for $500,000 to whack Spero, as well as another unsanctioned hit on associate Richard Scarcella. In July 1980, Pappa had his head blown off by a Colombo hit team in the Villa Sixty-Six Restaurant on 14th Avenue and 66th Street in Bensonhurst. Years later, Pappa's son, John, a murderous drug dealer, would kill the last person in the Colombo War. He was arrested by Detective Tommy Dades on the steps of St. Ann's Church on Staten Island, participating in the wedding rehearsal of the brother of a man he murdered. John Pappa is now serving life in a federal prison.

Carmine met Cindy when she introduced herself at Hong Pan, a longtime local favorite Chinese bar-restaurant in Bensonhurst, later rebooted as Lotus Blossom. "All the girls in the neighborhood loved the drinks at Hong Pan, these coconut cocktails with the little colorful umbrellas," Carmine remembers.

Carmine sat at the end of the bar with friends, smiling as regulars pummeled Cindy with pick-up lines. She slapped away that steady stream of suitors, with a smile and a 70s-style hair flip. She was the most beautiful girl in a neighborhood known for exotic young Italian females.

Yet Carmine did not pursue Cindy. Not because he lacked the nerve. "My father always said don't chase these local girls," Carmine says. "That's not playing hard to get. That's not making a fool out of yourself. You can defend them, just don't fight over them. I took that to heart. Good advice, especially for the young guys. That night, guys were all over her, and she was a knockout."

After a couple hours, Cindy and her friends moved to leave. Walking out of the bar, she stopped, turned, sized up Carmine, and spoke to him.

"She said she saw me looking at her, and asked me why I didn't come over and talk to her," Carmine recalls. "I told her that she looked like she had enough of an audience. She laughed at that. Said she liked my confident, laidback style. Gave me her number, then left."

For a brief time in 1979, Carmine from 13th Avenue and Shorty Spero's daughter were an item.

Not long after they met, Carmine made plans with Cindy and his friends to go out, crawl a few local Bay Ridge nightclubs. First, they all met up for cocktails at Hong Pan.

Setting is important to this story. Hong Pan was on the corner of 14th Avenue and 86th Street, a busy intersection, about a half mile off the Belt Parkway. It sat amid a drab row of single-story commercial buildings, next to a gas station. There's also an American Legion Hall.

Across broad 86th Street is the Scarpaci Funeral Home, family owned and operated by five generations of Italians since 1910. More recently, Scarpaci hosted the visitation for slain Gambino boss Francesco "Franky Boy" Cali[41].

Across 14th Avenue is sprawling Dyker Beach Golf Course, with a large community park, where Carmine once played concrete tackle. The Verrazano Narrows Bridge and the Brooklyn Veterans Hospital hover off in the distance.

Next door to Hong Pan is The 19th Hole, a small bar and eatery. Its name is a riff on the golf motif, but you wouldn't find many Dyker golfers unwinding in that viper pit. That's because The 19th Hole was owned by Christopher "Christie Tick" Furnari Sr.

Tick wasn't just *any* Brooklyn gangster. Within months of that evening, Tick was promoted to consigliere in the Lucchese Crime Family. In an Italian Crime Family, a consigliere is a unique position. Unlike a captain, or even an underboss, where you may be elevated based on violence, mastery of a specific racket, or ability to generate money, a consigliere is selected for one reason.

Intelligence.

A consigliere is the don's most trusted advisor, known for his cunning and experience. The consigliere mediates disputes, weighs in on major decisions, and wields great power.

Testament to Tick's power, in 1986, though not actually a boss, he was convicted as part of the infamous Commission Trial that sent leaders of the New York Mafia Families to prison.[42] Furnari was hit with a 100-year sentence, and served 28 years before being released in 2014.[43]

---

41. "Slain mob boss Frank Cali laid to rest — as authorities look on," by Joe Marino, Kevin Sheehan, Larry Celona and Kate Sheehy, *New York Post*, March 19, 2019

42. "U.S. Jury Convicts Eight as Members of Mob Commission," by Arnold H. Lubasch, *New York Times*, November 20, 1986

43. "Christy Tick, 90, Beats the System, Departs Prison," by Ed Scarpo Saturday, Cosa Nostra News, October 4, 2014

Like a Bamboo Lounge scene with a cast out of a Scorsese walk-through, The 19th Hole bar served armed robbers, drug dealers, loan sharks, bookies, leg breakers, and other types of racketeers. Anthony Salvatore "Gaspipe" Casso, eventual underboss of the Lucchese Crime Family, and Vittorio "Little Vic" Amuso, future Lucchese boss, were regulars. Tick mentored the homicidal pair, forming the nucleus of the Bypass Gang, a wildly successful group of burglars and bank robbers.[44]

So sure, Carmine knew Christie Tick, and knew he owned The 19th Hole. Yet Carmine didn't know Tick also owned Hong Pan. That's an important wrinkle to our story.

Now a bit about Brooklyn's demographics of that era. In 1979, 11228 was still an Italian zip code, about as green, white, and red as you could find in all of America. But even then, Brooklyn's Little Italy was losing ground, transforming block by block into Brooklyn's Little Hong Kong. And like the similar Italian-Chinese rivalry raging across Manhattan's Mott Street, there was tension between the two groups in South Brooklyn.[45]

Hong Pan was staffed by hard-working Asian immigrants. But working the taps that night was a half-drunk bartender, belligerent, sloppy, cursing loudly.

Carmine makes a point of not cursing frequently, especially when he was younger and making a name for himself. Still, Carmine has no issue with profanity, as a general rule. But Carmine believes in behaving appropriately, especially in front of Shorty Spero's pride and joy.

Carmine politely (sort of) asked the bartender to cut it out.

---

44. "Most Ruthless Mafia Leader Left; Leader on the Lam Runs the Lucchese Family, Agents Say," by Selwyn Raab, *New York Times*, November 28, 1992

45. "Once Shunned, Chinese Population Booms In Bensonhurst And Dyker Heights," by Eric Jankiewicz, *The Bklyner*, January 8, 2014

The bartender brushed him off.

The bar filled up, standing room only. All tables were taken in the restaurant area. The joint was bustling with the plinks and clinks of a busy Friday night. And still, the bartender carried on with his antics.

Carmine corrected him again.

And again, the bartender blew him off.

Guess what happened next?

Go ahead. Just guess.

"The guy swung a wet towel at me and Cindy," Carmine remembers. "Can you believe it? A filthy, wet bar rag. So I reached across the bar and punched him out."

Carmine caught the bartender flush on the side of the jaw with a loud meaty *thwack* that sent him reeling into the speed rack. Cindy shouted. Bottles toppled behind the bar. Glasses crashed. Drinks spilled. The startled shouted. The surprised recoiled. The bartender stumbled into the kitchen, holding his head. Drinkers stopped drinking. Diners stopped dining. The bar crowd froze.

All eyes on Carmine.

"Then... all hell broke loose," Carmine recalls. "It was almost like these guys were waiting behind the door for this to happen, because the back emptied out so fast and it turned into this huge brawl."

The bartender charged out, trailed by angry Asian waiters and kitchen workers hollering bloody murder. Carmine put himself in front of Cindy. His friends closed ranks. Jaws tightened. Fists whitened. Patrons scrambled to get out of the way.

The fight spilled out onto busy 86th Street. Cars along the four-lane thoroughfare slowed or stopped. Passersby craned rubber necks to see the wild scene unfolding. A crowd in mourners' black outside Scarpaci across the avenue shook their heads. A group by the bus stop leaned in for better views. Even the Dyker Park pigeons paused their pecking, as Carmine and his boys put on a show.

"We beat the shit outta them," Carmine confirms. "But I have to admit, those little bastards put up a good fight. I'll give 'em that. Scrappy little fucks."

Not scrappy enough, though, as Carmine and his 13th Avenue boys held their ground, beating back their opponents, who retreated inside, locking the door behind them.

Carmine and his group dusted themselves off, then moved on to enjoy the rest of their evening.

The next day, Carmine received an urgent phone call. "Joe Brewster told me to get down to The 19th Hole. He said I needed to speak to Christie Tick. But he didn't know why." Brewster was a bank robber and member of the Bypass Gang, hence his connection with Tick, the crew's mentor.

Carmine asked Brewster to join him. "Hell no," Carmine remembers Joe Brewster saying. "Tick called you, so you go yourself."

"And," Carmine says, "before he hung up, Joe warned me that Christie Tick is not a man you make wait, so hustle up, keep my head down, and don't crack wise."

At this point, Carmine still didn't know Hong Pan was owned by Christie Tick.

Tick made Carmine nervous. Tick made everyone nervous. Tick was a tight lipped, smart, serious, and low-key gangster, terrifying in an underworld where it's the serious wiseguys you need to watch. At least with the loudmouths you know when you're in trouble.

With a man like Christie Tick, sometime you didn't see it coming.

"I go in and this big slab of muscle takes me into the back room and Christie Tick is there, and right away, he says, 'You know I own the bar where you beat the shit outta those guys last night, right?'" Carmine's blood went ice cold. "I said, 'I definitely did not know you owned it, and if I knew you owned it, I wouldn't-a had any beef there,' and

I meant it. Had to be crazy to go against Tick in his own spot."

Tick asked Carmine to apologize to three of the Asian workers mauled the night before. Carmine agreed.

"So they come in, and they all got black eyes, so there's six black eyes staring back at me. Christie, very serious, asks me, 'Okay, now, Carmine, what do you have to say?'"

Carmine was ready to apologize. "I just wanted to say what I hadda say and get the hell out of there, but these guys start jabbering away in this gibberish, all angry and all shouting at once," Carmine says. "I burst out laughing."

Tick's henchman manhandled Carmine out of the room.

"He takes me outside, tells me I can't do that, and I know that, 'cause that's Christie Tick; not a guy you screw with, at all," Carmine says. "Tick's guy tells me Tick wants an apology to these guys, so I'd better give them the apology. *Or else.* And with these guys, you know, *or else* could mean a lot of things and none of them are good for my health. So I agree. But I did tell Tick's guy, 'Come on now, tell me that's not funny.' And he did smirk for a second."

Carmine composed himself on the sidewalk outside The 19th Hole, thought hard about the severity of the situation, and re-entered.

"I go back in, I'm about to apologize, and all three of them start in with the gibberish again, and I couldn't help myself, I crack up again. I'm not lying. I tried. I really, *really* tried. But it was funny, *really* funny. And now I'm not the only one laughing. Tick's guy is trying to keep it together. Tick is pissed. His guy takes me outside again."

Carmine received an even sterner warning to cut the crap. "Same routine, deep breaths, get it together, even go in with my head down, but these guys start in with the cackling the second they see me, and I can't help myself, and this time Tick's guy has to turn around to the wall 'cause he's laughing. I swear, if Tick himself put a gun to my head, I'm still breaking up laughing."

Sure, the bodyguard liked Carmine, but he'd still put him in the Victory Memorial ICU if Tick gave the nod.

"Thank God, Tick himself breaks out laughing. And these Chinese guys are standing there confused, with their black eyes and their angry confused looks, not knowing what to do. So Tick waves them away, tells them to get back to work."

After sharing the laugh, Carmine apologized, reiterated how he meant no disrespect. Tick accepted Carmine's apology. Carmine was turning to leave, when Tick stopped him to discuss another matter.

"If you can believe it, Tick offered me a job in construction, with a union card," Carmine says. "And I tell ya, unless your uncle was a captain or something like that, those union cards were not easy to come by." And not just any union job, but a plum spot on an asbestos-removal crew, paying a handsome $28 an hour, a great rate back in 1979 (equal to approximately $120 per hour today).

Unfortunately, that gig didn't last. "That's dangerous work, removing asbestos from pipes, so they make you wear these crazy hazmat suits," Carmine says. "I'd get all suited up, and right then, I'd have to go to the bathroom. I never had a solid stomach. Can't re-use those suits. So we go through a bunch of suits and they just gave up on me. Put the call in to Tick's son and he made me a flag man, which isn't too bad neither."

When Joe Brewster heard what happened at the sit-down, he shook his head. "Are you kidding me?" Brewster asked. "You get called in to get yelled at, and come out with a union card? Only you, Carmine. Only you. You don't know how lucky you are that he didn't hurt you."

Actually, Carmine knew how lucky he was.

"But I guess I was *lucky like that* sometimes," Carmine says.

Carmine had no idea just how *lucky like that* he'd need to be.

South Brooklyn Cold Case Files – Abduction at Tommaso's

Most friendships... happen.

Two people share an interest. Or strangers meet, solve a challenge, defeat a threat.

The friendship between Carmine Imbriale and Nicky Rizzo began with a kick to the face.

Both boys were ten years old. Nicky challenged Carmine to fight after school on Bensonhurst's Public School 204 yard. Nicky was shorter than the rest of the kids, red haired, chip on his shoulder the size of a loaf of lard bread, always picking fights.

No helicopter parenting in those days. Ten-year-olds walked themselves home after school. At 3 p.m., teachers cut the kids loose, herding them through the front and side doors. A couple dozen kids slipped around to the schoolyard to form a fight circle on the cracked concrete in the shadow of that four-story orange-brick school, named for NFL Hall of Fame coach Vince Lombardi, a Sheepshead Bay native.

The scene was very *Lord of the Flies*. Kids chanting, taunting. Nicky didn't have a real reason to rumble. Carmine didn't have a real reason to refuse. Rest of the kids worked themselves up, but Nicky never needed much prodding. Carmine dropped his book bag, entered the circle. Nicky attacked.

Wasn't much of a fight. They were only ten-year-old knuckleheads. Both got shots in, but mostly wrestling, flailing, flapping, slapping, scratching, clawing—and with Carmine down on the concrete, he caught a swift kick to the face. Nicky walked off to praise. Carmine slunk away up 80th Street, alone.

Nicky's kick gave Carmine a shiner and a half. During the three blocks it took to get home, Carmine's eye swelled shut. But trudging up his stoop, Carmine knew not to cry. "My father was the kind of guy who didn't take shit from no one and expected me to not take shit from no one and told me if I ever came home crying, I'd catch a beating."

When he sat down to dinner, the swollen eye attracted attention. "My mother was upset, like any mother, when she saw the heel mark, and all my father wanted to know was, 'Did the other guy get worse?' I said he did, so my father said, 'Okay, let's eat.' Said he didn't want to know any details, we're done. So we ate. He was a strict man and respected for it in our family and in the neighborhood. My mother, she was always making the sign of the cross whenever I came home all marked up after a fight, which was pretty often."

Back at P.S. 204, Nicky wasn't done with Carmine. Couple days later, the boys exchanged hard words again. Nicky called Carmine out. Remembering the kick to his face, Carmine slipped out the side after the school bell rang.

"When I got home, my father's standing there, and I don't know why, but I told him what happened," Carmine recalls. Carmine's furious father berated his son.

"He drags me back to the schoolyard, told me to pick out Nicky. I point him out. Then my father told me to attack him. What was I gonna do? I jumped right the fuck on him. Back then, I wasn't good with my hands, didn't know how to fight. I was only ten. But we beat the living shit outta each other. I was crying. Nicky was crying. And there's my father, arms folded, watching with all these kids. Then my father separated us, made us shake hands, and we went home."

The two boys became lifelong friends. But in Bensonhurst, "lifelong" is not always a long time.

Over the years, the two got into all kinds of mischief, in the South Brooklyn sense. You know, those crazy little reindeer games the young lads play—juvenile armed robberies, grand theft auto, burglaries, ripping off drug dealers, gang assaults.

Among their exploits, Nicky and Carmine were involved in a notorious kidnapping plot that rocked 1980s Bensonhurst, sending armed gunmen into the streets to scour South Brooklyn. That cold case was never solved. The culprits were never even suspected.

Until now.

First, a bit more about the friendship between Carmine Imbriale and Nicky Rizzo.

Carmine and Nicky had plenty in common. Both had old-school, domineering fathers who were in the service. However, Nicky's *paterfamilias* had a darker streak.

See, Nicholas Rizzo Senior was a feared enforcer and hitman for the Colombo Crime Family. A World War II veteran, member of the United States Navy, and a former boxer, Nicholas Senior was that rare breed of gangster, one who enjoyed a lengthy career in the underworld with minimal incarceration. In fact, he amassed millions of dollars, legally and illegally, and didn't notch his first arrest until well into his eighties, when he was prosecuted for loan sharking in 2011.[46]

Eighty-three at the time of his arrest, Rizzo Sr. was swept up in a takedown of 127 mobsters and associates from Brooklyn down to Florida. He was sentenced to two years. His attorney sought leniency for medical conditions,

---

46. "Career NY Mobster Arrested for First Time in His 80s; Stayed Out of Limelight," by Allan Lengel, July 24, 2011

producing sworn affidavits from doctors for a litany of ailments, including prostate and bladder cancers, anxiety, depression, and others.

It worked. The judge soft-slapped the elderly Rizzo Sr. with a reduced sentence of six months in a secure medical facility, much less time than the two years in prison sought by prosecutors.

Carmine's childhood memories of his friend's father are more sinister than a gentle, aging, ailing bookmaker. "Nicky's father was every inch a stone-cold assassin, just a really frightening guy," Carmine recalls. "When we were young, you knew by looking at that maniac that Nicky's father was dangerous. I used to go over to his house and eat, and his father was just scary. Would look right through you. You know, dead-eye stare you get killing too many people. He wasn't trying to prove nothing. Not acting tough. That's how he was. I've seen eyes like that. Some guys, they see so much violence, they get numb and it shows in the eyes. Or they're just made like that. Cold, empty. Nicky's father was all of that and a half."

Nicky had two older brothers, both masons by trade, always driving around the neighborhood in a work truck. "They all came over from Italy, so the older brothers barely spoke English. They were respected and feared, but not *made* like the father. They were his little hit crew, ya know, working on construction sites during the day, going out killing people at night. That entire family was crazy dangerous."

Nicky's home life was not typical for a teenager, even by 1970s South Brooklyn standards. "Nicky'd ask me if I wanted to go downstairs, into his basement," Carmine says. "But instead of playing darts or pool like other kids, we're shooting rifles. They had it set up like a shooting gallery, with targets and all that. We weren't even in high school. Kids in other places, I don't know what they were doing. Playing ping pong maybe. We're shooting guns. I think of it now and how crazy that was. But back then, we didn't see nothing wrong with it. Boys being boys."

Other families have house pets that nip at you when you enter the home. With Nicky's pets, you prayed the gate held. But just in case, you looked for the nearest car hood to jump on. From the backyard, Carmine heard those deep barks that came from three large hunting dogs penned up in cages.

As the two boys grew, they had different interests. "Nicky wasn't a ball player, at all, and all I wanted to do was play ball, but we still got on great."

Nicky had other passions. "He just wanted to rob people," Carmine says. "I loved the kid, but he got to be too much. He wanted to rob drug dealers all the time, obsessed on it. Wanted to rob the pimps, couldn't get enough of them. And if we couldn't find any of them, he'd rob anyone, anywhere, any way he could work out an angle. Christ, like the Jews in Borough Park, snatch the fur hats off their heads and then sell them. You have any idea how expensive those hats are, even on the resale? That was a great score. He was always coming up with new schemes to rob people. He didn't care. And he was violent, would go off at any moment for the smallest things."

Nicky Rizzo was trouble. Yet Carmine was loyal to a fault. "I never questioned him, usually because I didn't want to know the answers. He'd pick me up, then Frankie, and every time, we didn't even have to ask, we knew the car was stolen." That would be Frank "Frankie Notch" Iannaci, future Colombo soldier and a gunman for the Orena faction during the Third Colombo Family War.

Back then, Carmine, Nicky, and Frankie were young hoods cruising South Brooklyn, looking for action.

One early evening, Nicky and Frankie picked up Carmine. Nicky was driving, noticed he was low on gas. They rumbled into a local station to fill up. "So, we're filling up, Nicky's running through different scores to rob people, make some money that night," Carmine says. "He pauses, looks at the dash, sees the tank is full, floors it, flies out of the parking lot like nothing, ripping out the gas pump. Sure, he had money. But Nicky wouldn't pay for nothing if he could steal it. That was Nicky."

It didn't help that Nicky was below average in height and had a crop of red hair that stood out in a neighborhood of olive skin and jet-black D.A.s.

One evening, Nicky and Carmine made the rounds at local bars, landing at an after-hours on 15th Avenue off 74th Street. After-hours bars in Brooklyn were illegal when open beyond the 4 a.m. curfew mandated by New York State's blue laws. But you didn't go to an after-hours to sip mimosas. You went there to keep the party going with other drunk, drugged-up, and dangerous people.

This charming little hole in the earth was a mess of low-level Brooklyn wiseguys and motorcycle bikers. Nicky was drunk. Nicky was loud. Nicky was asked to leave. Actually, "asked" is not the right word.

"This was a rough spot. After all the bars are closed, Tilio's there, Nicky Waves, Petey Pecs, Tommy Farace, all the local tough guys that'd stab you in a dark alley," Carmine says. "All of sudden, I don't know what happened, but they're yelling at Nicky to get out. He's yelling back. Then, they picked his ass up and threw him right through the door."

Carmine followed, trying to talk Nicky down.

"I'm getting him into Nicky's truck, which was stolen, of course, saying don't worry, forget about it, go sleep it off. And he drops me at home, says he's all good, says don't worry, he'll call me tomorrow. But see, instead, Nicky goes back home, then goes back to the bar with like a 20-foot chain attached to the truck, runs it through the front wheel of a bunch of bikes parked outside and tears off, dragging those bikes, just destroying them. Sun must've been coming up. Bar empties out and you got all these drunk, drugged-up tough guys running all over the Avenue, cursing, shouting.

Nicky drops the chain, takes off, hollering back for them to have a nice night."

Word got around the neighborhood the next day but no one knew who wrecked the bikes.

"Next day, Nicky picks me up, don't say nothing, and when it came up, first he says he wonders who did it," Carmine remembers. "But then he admitted it, couldn't hold it in. He just couldn't go home and let that lie. He knew *I knew* Tillio and Armando, all of them, all the weight-lifting guys from the Avenue, many either *made* guys or would've been *made*. Nicky didn't care. He never cared. That was his problem."

One night, Nicky rolls up in front of Tommaso's, a popular Bensonhurst restaurant frequented by Colombos and Gambinos. Carmine was shotgun that night, Frankie Notch holding down the backseat. Nicky then surprised his friends, donning a ski mask and pulling out one of his father's shotguns from the trunk. "He told me to keep the car running and ran inside. Now, there's a bunch of wiseguys in the back playing cards. But this was Jerry Lang's game."

As in, this was the personal, by-invitation-only card game run by Gennaro "Jerry Lang" Langella. With Carmine Persico imprisoned for much of the 1970s and early 1980s, Langella served as underboss and even acting boss for a time. Langella supervised labor rackets for the Family, including the Cement and Concrete Workers District Council, Local 6A, and the Colombos' stake in the infamous "Concrete Club."[7] Back then, they didn't get much bigger than Gerry Lang.

"We all knew that card game," Carmine says. "The entire neighborhood knew that card game. Of course, Nicky knew that card game. And everyone knew, you don't fuck with that card game."

Nicky Russo didn't care.

"Nicky shouted at them to put their wallets and jewelry on the table. Jerry stands up, tells Nicky he's gonna personally find out who he was and deal with him. Nicky, the crazy bastard, takes the mask off and says forget it, comes outside, and tells us what happened. Remember, all these guys know Nicky's father and know Nicky since he's a little kid. We're shitting our pants, but nothing ever came of it."

Tommaso Ristorante was an interesting spot, located on 86th Street and Bay 8th Street, right in the heart of Italian Bensonhurst. Founded in 1968, it's one of those traditional old world-style red-sauce favorites, known as much for its food as for its owner; in this case, the opera-singing Thomas "Chef Tom" Verdillo.

The Verdillo parents were Italian immigrants. Tom's older brother died at a young age of pneumonia. His mother, a former nurse at Maimonides Hospital, suffered a nervous breakdown. When she was institutionalized, young Tom was packed off to a home, along with his sister. Eventually they were reunited as a family.[47]

As Verdillo grew, the hard-working young man took ownership of Jacque Catering on 86th Street and renamed it Tommaso's Catering. When his father was killed in an automobile accident, he used the $10,000 insurance payment to expand that food-delivery business and added a restaurant. He bought the building for less than $14,000; real estate now likely valued north of a million dollars.

Tommaso's Ristorante was two blocks from Christie Tick's 19th Hole and less than a block from the Veterans & Friends Social Club, a Gambino clubhouse run by capo James "Jimmy Brown" Failla. Nearly every gangster in Brooklyn passed through there during that era. It was also where nearby Frank DeCicco was murdered by a car bomb for his role in the Castellano murder.

---

47. "Thomas Verdillo, 77, Dies; Restaurateur Went from Red Sauce to Blue Ribbon," LightlyNews.com, January 11, 2021

For years, Failla was seen on his wiseguy "walk and talks" along 86th Street. They started dropping in at nearby Tommaso's. It became a regular haunt. Later, Paul Castellano not only frequented Tommaso's with his real family, but Verdillo catered gatherings at "the White House," the nickname for the Gambino boss's Staten Island manse.[48]

On any given Saturday night, Chef Tom, in his hallmark red shirt, entertained diners, belting out arias as waiters served mouth-watering dishes like *spiedini romana alla Tommaso*, with sides of crispy *mozzarella carrozza*. With his rustic Italian comfort food a hit with the local hitmen, Chef Tom enjoyed privileged status among his notorious clientele.

One spring afternoon on the other side of the neighborhood, Carmine was home when he got an urgent call from Lukey, owner of Lukey's Candy Store. The store was on 15th Avenue and 81st Street, directly across from the same P.S. 204 where, long ago, Nicky kicked Carmine in the eye.

Carmine knew Lukey since elementary school, dropping in for cherry sodas on his way home. Lukey was a local guy. Not a wiseguy, but he knew people, people like Carmine. Lukey begged Carmine to come down to his shop, but refused to reveal what was wrong over the phone. That's a red flag.

Carmine rushed down. An agitated Lukey led him into the basement of the two-story building. There, Carmine spotted a few things out of the ordinary.

First, there was a German shepherd chained up in the corner. Carmine knew Lukey didn't have a dog. Next, Nicky Rizzo and Frankie Notch were there, and Nicky was holding large scissors.

---

48. "Chef talk: Tommaso Verdillo," by Michael Steinberger, *The Financial Times*, November 26, 2010

"You recognize this dog?" Nicky smiled to Carmine. "You should."

Again, Nicky's family had large hunting dogs Carmine remembered, but never a German shepherd. Nope. Wasn't Nicky's dog. Wasn't Lukey's dog. And it wasn't Frankie Notch's dog either. But damn it, this dog was familiar. Carmine couldn't place the dog, but he'd seen it, somewhere.

Carmine also recognized that larcenous look on Nicky's face. Something was definitely going down in Lukey's basement.

Then, it hit Carmine like a Sony Betamax falling off the back of a Crazy Eddie box truck. Of course Carmine knew that dog. He'd seen it up close, or one that looked like it, many times. And he'd seen it on lost-dog flyers posted all over the neighborhood.

He'd also heard about that dog from several people. The news was all over Bensonhurst. Everyone and their mother seemed to be looking for that dog.

"Really?" Carmine shook his head. "You stole Tommaso's dog? What were you thinking?"

"That's what I was just saying to him," Frankie Notch griped. "But you try and talk to him. He don't listen to me."

Chef Tom wasn't married, didn't have children. When his mother passed, all he had for companionship living in an apartment above his restaurant was his beloved dog, whom Rizzo was now trying to trim with those sheers.

To say that Chef Tom adored his pooch is like saying L&B Sicilians are tasty. When that dog went missing, Tom was so beside himself with grief, he shuttered his restaurant, blanketed the neighborhood with flyers, and roamed the streets, inconsolable.

Word got back to Veterans & Friends. No one was getting their *spiedini romana alla Tommaso* until Verdillo got his German shepherd back.

It didn't make sense to anyone outside Lukey's basement. Tommaso's dog never ran away, was not even the type to try to escape. And even if he slipped out somehow, all the locals knew the dog. Surely someone should have picked him up by now. This was no lap dog someone could have carried off.

Also, 86th Street is a broad, four-lane thoroughfare with cars zipping back and forth between Bay Ridge and Bensonhurst. An accident involving a dog that size stops traffic, causes a scene.

But nothing. No leads.

Of course the foul minds suspected foul play. But who would do something like that, to someone like Chef Tom?

Yep. Nicky Rizzo, that's who.

When the wiseguys learned of Tommaso's troubles, and that the restaurant was closed until further notice, they launched a massive dog-hunt.

Seriously.

So as Mafia street soldiers scoured South Brooklyn in earnest, in a basement less than a mile away, Nicky kept trying to give that damn dog a haircut. "These two nuts were trying to cut pieces of the dog's hair to include in the ransom note," Carmine remembers. "I'm not kidding. They kidnapped Tommaso's dog on purpose. I mean, not planned. They came across the dog outside the restaurant, and in the moment... Nicky dognapped him, I guess you'd call it. I couldn't believe it, even for Nicky. I know we're all supposed to be out here hustling, chasing scores, making that money, but this was embarrassing. It was stupid. I couldn't get out of that basement fast enough."

Carmine fled the canine crime scene, but not before delivering a warning.

"I'm an animal lover, so I didn't want no part of that mess, even if it wasn't Tommaso's dog. And I told them how every gangster in Brooklyn was looking for this dog, so they better get rid of it."

Nicky scoffed at Carmine's warning.

"Then I told them, do what you want, but I want no part of this. I said there's no point, you're not getting ransom money outta Tommaso. No way. Tommaso is protected. He's running right to the Gambinos. Then I look dead at Nicky, and I tell him, 'Nick, you know how this thing works. You know your father is one of the guys out there, right now, beyond pissed to be looking for a frickin' dog, swearing up and down how they're gonna kill the son of a bitch who stole him, just for all the aggravation.'"

A couple hours later, a passerby on 14th Avenue came across a wandering German shepherd, missing a couple tufts of fur.

Tommaso's Ristorante reopened for business in time for the evening rush, and the wiseguys in that small corner of South Brooklyn went back to their rackets and rigatoni.

Outside Lukey's basement, no one ever knew the truth of what really went down.

Until now.

Unfortunately, on December 27, 2021, at Lutheran Hospital, Thomas "Chef Tom" Verdillo passed on, from health complications triggered by COVID-19.[52] Rest in peace.

The statute of limitations has long since expired on the dognapping.

As for the conspirators, Frankie Iannaci went on to play a role in the Third Colombo Family War, and more recently became embroiled in another bizarre underworld dispute... over a pizza sauce recipe. Not just any recipe, mind you, but the secret sauce for those famous L&B Spumoni Gardens squares.[49]

L&B Spumoni Gardens was started on Stilwell Avenue in Gravesend in the late 1930s by Italian immigrant Ludovico Barbati as a spumoni stand. Barbati later added a

---

49. "Mob sauce summit! Colombos and Bonannos had sitdown over suspected family recipe theft from L&B Spumoni Gardens," by John Marzulli, *New York Daily News*, June 13, 2012

pizzeria and restaurant. They serve many outstanding dishes there, but are famous for the unusual way they make their Sicilian pies. Instead of the traditional style, the L&B style was to *first* put the mozzarella on the pizza dough and *then* ladle on the marinara.

Genius.

Today, an L&B square pie'll run you the best $30 you'll ever spend, if you're willing to wait in a line that sometimes stretches way out the door. There are now dozens of imitators across the Tristate area, some not too bad, some even exceptional. Many of those imposters call their take on it "Brooklyn style" or "Upside Down style." But Stillwell Avenue regulars know the real deal.

However, the style is not the only thing one guy tried to rip off from L&B Spumoni Gardens.

In 2021, Eugene Lombardo, actually an in-law of an owner of L&B, allegedly stole the secret recipe for a restaurant he opened in Staten Island on Hylan Boulevard called The Square. Iannaci was part of a Colombo crew that confronted Lombardo during a Staten Island sit-down, demanding either a piece of the business or a one-time $75,000 shakedown. Frankie Notch slapped him around during the confrontation. The dispute was settled for $4,000.

As for Nicky Rizzo, he may have balked on the dog caper, but became even more reckless.

Carmine and Nicky went to a local Bensonhurst disco one night, and this muscle guy bangs into Nicky. This steroid guy, much larger than Rizzo, goes, "Watch where the fuck you're going."

"So Nicky apologizes, and we gave Nicky a hard time for apologizing, calling him a sissy," Carmine says. "Thinking back on what happened after, we shouldn't a done that."

Later that night, Nicky introduced Carmine and some of their friends to the same muscle guy. "He says, 'This is my friend,' this muscle guy, who not even a couple hours before he had beef with, and he says he's coming with us to Bedrocks on Bath Avenue. So we're outside, kid asked Nicky to smoke a joint. They go up the block, and I remember looking down the block, and I see Nicky pull out his gun and shoot him three times. Comes back, tells us, 'What? You think I'm letting a jerkoff like that get away with it?'"

As time went by, Nicky grew more manic, more violent.

One night in '79, Carmine and Nicky in their early twenties, they're in a bar and Nicky gets into an argument. "I don't why, Nicky must've said some shit, and this girl was badmouthing him, loud, calling him carrot top, you know, because of his red hair," Carmine says. "So, Nicky, he don't skip a beat, shoves a glass right into her face, just ruins her. I didn't have no time to react, to hold him back. Now there's blood everywhere. It's a big thing. She leaves, tells her brothers, Richie and Bobby, local guys. Everybody knew everybody back then. And they knew Nicky, knew where he lived. They go and get two guys, and the four of them drive by Nicky's house, start shooting up the place."

Nicky Rizzo goes off.

"Nicky loaded up like he was going to war, he got multiple rifles lined up for battle, but all it took was one bullet. They were ready for him outside. He charged out in a rage, made himself an easy target. Shot him dead, got him with a bullet to the brain."

They were either unaware, or didn't care, that their target was the son of Colombo enforcer Nicky Rizzo Sr. Bad move. That evening, Nicky's father returned from a wedding reception to a crime scene, to find his youngest son, his namesake, murdered in front of the family home.

"Three out of the four guys, Vinny Connelly, and Bobby and Richie Utivich, disappeared off the face of the earth," Carmine says. "And believe me, Nicky's father had to have put 'em through hell. The fourth guy, Jimmy Melfie, was connected; he knew guys, like Georgie Goggles."

That didn't get Melfie a pass. This was South Brooklyn. There was only so much that could be done by George "Georgie Goggles" Conte, even if he was a rising wiseguy and future captain in the Lucchese Family.

"Georgie couldn't save him, of course not," Carmine remembers. "But because Goggles put in a word, they at least let his body be found so his mother could bury him. But all the others, they *disappeared* them, and to this day, they've never been found."

The Rizzo family suffered further tragedies over the years. Nicky's older brother, Charlie, died in an accident in '82, plunging six stories down an elevator shaft on a construction site. A third Rizzo child, a daughter, died from a drug overdose in 1990.[50]

Later, the premature deaths of the Rizzo children were taken into account when Judge Kiyo A. Matsumoto handed down a lighter sentence for the aging mobster. But soon after Rizzo's release, his parole was revoked after he was spotted in an illegal gambling den on 20th Avenue and 72nd Street run by Bonanno boss Vincent "Vinny TV" Badalamenti.[51] That set back sent him back for six months.

Rizzo may have been a successful criminal, but in the end, he's alone.

Carmine, in many respects, too is alone.

For guys who grew up on 13th Avenue like Carmine did, few childhood friendships survive.

Friendships are funny like that. They just... happen. And after all, while we can pick our friends, we don't get to decide their fates.

---

50. "Colombo mobster gets 6-month medical leave from prison," by Selim Algar, *New York Post*, September 26, 2013

51. "Mobster Nicholas Rizzo was ordered back to jail after a judge said he violated conditions of a humanitarian parole," by John Marzulli, *New York Daily News*, October 9, 2013

Always Get a Receipt

In the early 1980s, Carmine Sessa, alias Carmine Marletta, was a rising star in the Colombo Family. Ten years older than Carmine Imbriale, Sessa came up as a hitman, armed robber, and drug dealer under Greg Scarpa, and did time for bank robbery. By 1984, Sessa ran his own violent crew, featuring about a dozen hardcore crew members.

Sessa was inducted in the Colombo Family on March 11, 1987. He'd rise to captain and eventually consigliere, playing a key role throughout the Third Colombo Family War. Sessa later testified for the government about his role in 13 homicides.[52]

Carmine liked the gang boss, respected him—at least in the early days. Sessa, looking to expand his crew, took an interest in the young brawler.

"I started doing stupid shit when we were teenagers, and moved on to bigger and bigger things," Carmine says. "We started robbing the fruit store, and before you know it, we were robbing cars and pot dealers."

Sessa wasn't the only one keeping tabs on young Carmine. "I was scouted by guys from all the Five Families. They all wanted me. I was a proven earner. I had a string of robberies under my belt. I could handle myself and made money as a shylock. And most important with these guys, I followed the rules."

---

52. "Start Snitching: Inside the Witness Protection Program," by Marcus Baram, *ABC News*, October 26, 2007

Still, Carmine wasn't ready to commit to any specific crew.

"I was a good earner, involved in so many things, with so many people, but I didn't have a real plan for myself. I see now that Sessa had his own plan for me and was waiting for his opportunity to trap me. I got suckered into it, without understanding what I was getting into, because it happened so fast," Carmine says. "It started with a beef I had with a serious player."

He got into a public altercation with a *made* member from the Colombos. "This guy was a jerk, yelled at me in front of other people, so we got into it at the bar. It went from nothing to a serious thing in a second, and we had to be broken up. Then later, Carmine Sessa pulls me to the side, says I was in trouble. He says this guy now had the right to kill me because I disrespected him. And no doubt, he'd be coming after me soon to try and kill me."

Carmine Imbriale was marked for murder. Everyone was backing away. Except Carmine Sessa.

"There's no wrong or right with this. You're either part of this thing and with someone, or you're not. And if you're not, and they come for you and they want to kill you, you're nothing to no one. You're out in the cold. No one'll lift a finger to save you. In fact, they're supposed to help the other guy set you up. That's the rules."

There's no database of active wiseguys. So Carmine's rival had to make the rounds to make sure before he made his move. "He wanted to kill me, but he had to check, so he went to Carmine Sessa, who told this guy, 'Didn't you know he was with me?' The guy said no, backed off. And that was that. I was safe. But now, I was with Sessa. Either that or they'd murder me. Funny thing is, afterwards, me and this guy, we got along great. He'd always says how he felt bad that because of him, I got stuck with the Sessas." (Michael Sessa, younger brother of Carmine Sessa, was also a member of the crew and eventually rose to captain with the Colombos.)

Carmine remembers feeling overwhelmed with gratitude. "I thought Carmine was helping me, but he was using me. I was young, looking for somewhere to belong. He knew that. When I joined Carmine's crew, it felt good to be part of the Family. It felt good to know that now no one was going to mess with me or my family. I now had that title, that status, of being *with* someone, and in a place like Brooklyn, that meant everything."

Growing up on 13th Avenue, Carmine was enamored with the gangster lifestyle long before he met Carmine Sessa. "You don't realize it's a phony world with a fake code and false honor. At first, when you become part of that, it's more than just security. They pretend it's a brotherhood, to get you to do what they want you to do. That makes you feel like you're building on something, you're part of something. But in the end, it's all bullshit."

"Carmine was easily misled because he always wanted to be somebody, be something," Maryellen Imbriale notes. "I think if someone offered him a different path, he would've taken that, but he took the path that was available to him. He didn't know what else to do with his life. They got their hooks in him and he got so wrapped up in all of that, he didn't know how to get out. Thing is with Carmine, that when he started something, he didn't know how to stop until he finished."

So why did Carmine Imbriale flip later? He's transparent and doesn't recreate history. He had his reasons. Not *just* the multiple assassination attempts he survived. Not *just* the unfair vig Michael Sessa charged him, and *only* him, out of jealousy and vindictiveness. For that matter, not *just* that Michael Sessa was promoted in the crew *just* because his older brother rose up the ranks.

"It wasn't just me; no one respected Michael," Carmine says. "I remember Bobby Zam telling me how ridiculous it was that a jerkoff like Michael could even be *made*, let alone bumped up to captain."

Sure, Carmine Imbriale had reasons for why he flipped.

Not *just* that those closest to him in the life tried to murder him. Not *just* that his entire crew turned on him and neglected to tell their consigliere, who was in hiding and later flipped himself.

Not *just* that his mentor, Joe Brewster, was murdered, betrayed by those closest to him; and not for anything he did, but for what he *might* do, following decades of loyalty and millions in earnings.

Not *just* that a *made* member of his own crew, Michael Sessa, hit on his wife during a wedding reception. (Carmine only learned of that years later. His wife, Janet, was wise enough to keep it from him, realizing she'd be a widow, because, you know, that's how it works when the other guy is *made*, even though he ignores the so-called code he swore to live and die by.)

Sure, those were all reasons. But there's more.

Carmine is the first to tell you he picked the wrong crew. The Colombos were notorious for their volatility and violence. Carmine should've thrown in with the Genovese Family. Jimmy Ida would have welcomed him with open arms. Now there was a captain Carmine respected.

Instead, Carmine got sucked into the one of the most dysfunctional crews ever. The Colombos on 13th Avenue were a mess. All that crap about *Omertà* and codes of honor were no longer part of the Colombo playbook.

But even then, it goes deeper.

When Carmine was 12 years old, his sister Joanne was courted by Robert "Bucky" DiLeonardo. Like Joanne, Bucky came from an old-school Italian Brooklyn family.

Bucky was third-generation Italian-American, his grandfather from Bisacquino, in Palermo, Sicily. For Italians from the north, like Carmine's family, Sicilians were backwater hillbillies. Some of this stems from early waves of immigration. The poorer Sicilians were less likely to afford admission, so more snuck in, labeled as WOPs, for Without Papers. Sicily was also the birthplace of La Cosa Nostra, with different Italian offshoots on the mainland, though its American ranks were filled by all breeds of Italians.

After immigrating to America in the early 20th century, Vincenzo DiLeonardo became a soldier in the Brooklyn faction of a New York Crime Family run by Salvatore D'Aquila. The D'Aquila Family was the forerunner to the Gambinos. [53]

Bucky's father and uncles were not associated with organized crime. Bucky threw in with the Colombos in Bensonhurst, while his younger brother, Michael "Mikey Scars" DiLeonardo, rose high with the Gambinos. Mikey Scars got his nickname as a teen after he was attacked by a dog that marred his face. A third brother, James, was not involved in the Brooklyn rackets.

The DiLeonardos lived nearby the Gambino's Veterans & Friends Social Club on 86th Street. Mikey Scars ran errands for mobsters at the club.

More than thirty years later, after rising to capo (due to his close friendship with John Gotti Jr.), Scars flipped, helping imprison more than 80 members of organized crime.[54]

Yet back in the early '70s, the DiLeonardo boys were young hellraisers in Bensonhurst, and Bucky was not the type of boyfriend Carmine's father envisioned for his daughter. Carmine's father hated the wiseguys and the

---

53. "United States of America v. John A. Gotti Jr., Defendant DiLeonardo Testimony (04 CR 00690 SAS-1) District Judge Shira A. Scheindlin, United States District Court, Southern District of New York New York, NY, February 22, 2006

54. "The Star 'Scar' Witness; Turncoat vs. 'Junior' Gotti Ready to be Mafia's Next 'Sammy Bull'," by Brad Hamilton, *New York Post*, August 7, 2005

hustlers. But as they say, the heart wants what the heart wants. Joanne and Bucky fell in love.

"My father was a pretty good judge of character, and he knew what Bucky was all about," Carmine says. "It's sad because my father and my sister were close. He told her to think like a man and don't take any shit from no one, and she didn't. That was one tough Brooklyn girl, believe me."

Bucky approached Carmine's father to ask for her hand in marriage. He arrived at the Imbriale home in the early afternoon on a Sunday.

"In an Italian family, Sunday dinners are special, and my father cooked; he was a great chef for the entire family," Carmine remembers. "Joanne dating Bucky never sat right with my father, and he was stewing over it, because I think he sensed what was coming. So Bucky, he rings the doorbell, his arms full of wine and flowers. My father comes and opens the door. He starts to ask what he's gotta ask, and my father sees it coming, and right away punches Bucky down the stairs, and slams the door."

Joanne heard the commotion. "My sister comes out, asked who it was. My father shrugs and says, 'Nobody, just some Jehovah's Witnesses.'"

The headstrong teenagers ran away to Virginia to elope. That's where you went back in the day, when the state ran its "Virginia is for Lovers" television post in the 70s.[55] Bucky's cousin, Joe Brewster, Colombo soldier and later mentor for Carmine, stood as best man.

The news hit Bensonhurst like an M80 in the coin slot of a corner payphone. "After that, my father told Joanne she was out of the family. He was so angry. My father wouldn't talk to them, at all. Wanted nothing to do with them."

Joanne and Bucky settled into a small apartment on 13th Avenue, just blocks from the Imbriale home. The

---

55. "Virginia is for Lovers: On Madison Avenue Advertising Walk of Fame," Tourism Website for the State of Virginia

cold war between father and daughter turned from weeks into months; nearly three years passed without any contact between them.

That all changed when Carmine's father discovered he was a grandfather.

"My father grabs me and a stepladder, and we get in his car," Carmine remembers. "We go over there to their apartment. My father knocks on the door and Bucky answers. My father said to Bucky, 'I'm not here to fight, but you're not stopping me from seeing my granddaughter.'" Bucky gave way, and Carmine and his father painted the baby's room.

"Then my father held that baby and rocked her for a bit. When we're leaving, he says to Bucky, 'I'll come any time I want to see my granddaughter.' My brother-in-law laughed, said he wasn't going to stop him, and that was that. They came to an understanding. He could've been a little nicer about it, you know, but that was his way."

Carmine and Bucky had a great relationship until Bucky and his brother later robbed Carmine's apartment and cleaned out his roommate, PeeWee.

Bucky was likeable, an outgoing guy, and an operator in the local rackets. Carmine admired Bucky, who was older. And Carmine was close with his sister, so he'd go over their apartment to hang out all the time.

One evening, Bucky got a call to fill in on a bank robbery job with Joe Brewster. They pulled off the score, and Brewster handed Bucky a suitcase with about $190,000 in cash.

That weekend, Bucky asked Carmine to take a trip with him. Carmine agreed and the two flew down to Miami Beach, where they met with Bucky's father. Bucky handed over $50,000 in cash, part of his cut from the bank job, as payment for a home on 17th Avenue in Bensonhurst.

Carmine says he personally witnessed the transaction. "I saw Bucky put the money in that small suitcase that never left his side for the entire time we flew down to Florida. The father had a house down there, and I was in the room and I saw, again, with my own eyes, Bucky hand over that suitcase."

There was no receipt cut for the sale.

"I even told Bucky to get some kind of paperwork on the house," Carmine says. "He didn't want to hear none of that. He trusted him. Who'd think your own family would rip you off."

A few days later, Carmine helped Bucky move his young family into that home, a growing brood that now included two daughters. It was a happier time for the Imbriales, with an outside chance of a full reconciliation between Joanne and her father.

But there's no such thing as happily ever after for the boys of 13th Avenue.

On the evening of July 16, 1981, Robert "Bucky" DiLeonardo was murdered in a mob-related shooting. The decomposing body was found next to a field on Staten Island, a popular murder site for gangland killings.[58]

"They found his body right across from the old Russo's diner, where all the wiseguys used to hang out," Carmine remembers. "They pulled into someone's driveway, shot him, left him there. They didn't hide it. When you murder someone like that, you want them to be found, to send a message. But they were smart. They threw a bunch of pills and drug shit in the car, an old trick to throw off the cops, make it look like it's a drug deal gone wrong, not a hit. Sure enough, next day, it's all over the papers that he was some junkie in a drug deal gone south. But that's not how it went down."

Carmine was there when Bucky got the call that lured him to his death. "I was at my sister's and Bucky gets a beep, makes a call, gets all serious and says he got to go, and says to tell my sister he had to take care of something and he'd be back later. Didn't tell me where he was going or who he was meeting. I offered to go, but he said no, that it'd be better for him to go alone. I thought he was just handling his business. If I would've gone, I'd've been killed with him. They found him slumped over the wheel, like he was surprised, like he was trying to get out."

Bucky's brother Mikey Scars says he wanted to seek revenge, but was muzzled by Gambino Boss Paul Castellano. The word was that Bucky's murder was internal Colombo Family business, some housecleaning. Castellano warned his captains that any retaliation would be met harshly, as he sought to avoid an inter-Family war.

Meanwhile, a grieving Joanne's woes were just beginning.

"Soon after my brother-in-law got killed, we hear that the father is selling my sister's house," Carmine says. "My sister said, 'How can you do that? We paid you.' They didn't want to hear nothing." Bucky never got the title to the house transferred before he died.

Then, DiLeonardo actually sold the house. "They gave her a date to get out," Carmine says. "Then, they hired a moving company and they just took all of her stuff out, and my sister and her girls had nowhere to go. She had to move in with my parents. Can you imagine that? She couldn't even fit all of her stuff and had to put all this furniture in storage for a couple years.

"When she came home, it was like nothing ever happened. My father took care of them, and I respected that. He didn't say nothing about it, didn't want a pat on the shoulder. Didn't rub her nose in it. No *I told you so*. He was an iceberg. But I tell you, those girls, they really did something to him. He took care of them, and with that, he showed me what a real man does. After two years, she got her own apartment."

Carmine was enraged, but this was a delicate situation. Carmine was a low-level street associate. Mikey Scars was a *made* man, running with John Gotti Jr.'s crew. Gambino Captain Paul "Paulie Zac" Zaccaria agreed to a mediate a sit-down to broker a resolution.

"At the sit-down, the father said Bucky never gave him that 50k," Carmine remembers. "Lied right in front of me, even though I was in the room when he gave him the money. I was fuming. I was with Joe Russo, at the sit-down with Paulie, across from Scars and his father. The father says he didn't care, he didn't need to see his granddaughters. He threw my sister and her daughters in the street and sold the home." Carmine says the home was sold to Genovese Captain Salvatore "Sally Dogs" Lombardi.

Carmine was escorted out of the room midway through the sit-down. There was no resolution, no compromise. When they sold the home, likely at a premium as the real estate market mushroomed in the area, not a cent of the proceeds went to Carmine's sister.

"Broke my heart," Carmine says. "Must've thought they made a big score off my poor sister."

Not long after that sit-down, Greg Scarpa visited Joanne. Carmine was there, helping to move in a new refrigerator. "Greg told my sister he'd be giving her $400 a week, and I said no, we don't need none of your money. Greg didn't like hearing that, said he wasn't offering it to me, and I told him anything he had to say to my sister, he should say to me."

Scarpa backed off, and later that day, Joe Brewster gave Carmine a warning. "You just don't talk to Greg like that, but I was beyond angry," Carmine remembers. "It was a bad move on my part. From that day forward, things weren't the same between me and Greg. He already didn't like me for the other shit. But now, I knew I made an enemy."

In the years since, a cottage industry sprang up as hundreds of Mafia-related books, films, and documentaries were released. Carmine's familiar with many of these men and their crimes. "Half the time, they're full of shit and the other half, they're leaving shit out," Carmine scoffed. Yet nothing prepared Carmine for a 2015 televised interview showing Mikey Scars standing over the gravesite of Carmine's sister, Joanne.

The interview was conducted by Sir Trevor McDonald, the famed Trinidadian-British newsreader and journalist. McDonald was knighted in 1999 for his services to journalism. *The Mafia with Trevor McDonald* was a two-part examination of life in Cosa Nostra.[56]

Stern-faced Trevor lobs softball questions, nods thoughtfully at cavalier responses. Reviewer Ellen E. Jones of *The Independent* wrote of the ham-fisted series, "These interviews were full of lines that were either nicked from the script for Scorsese's last gangster flick or ought to be written into his next one."[57]

The promo for the show caught Carmine's attention, ominously stating: "Michael DiLeonardo—better known as Mikey Scars—who fears he'll be executed after testifying against members of the Gambino Crime Family in court, leading to 80 successful convictions..."

"Singlehandedly, he has inflicted more damage on the Mafia than anyone else in recent times," McDonald says in the episode. "After months of persuasion, Mikey agreed to meet us in Miami. Scars lives in permanent fear of attack and has, until recently, been in the government's witness protection program."

McDonald also says, "There's all this mumbo jumbo about the Mafia being an entirely secret organization. But

---

56. *The Mafia with Trevor McDonald*, ITV, March 23, 2015

57. "*The Mafia with Trevor McDonald*, Review: Nice guy Trevor just isn't cut out for the mean streets," by Ellen E. Jones, *The Independent*, March 24, 2015

this supposedly loyal Family didn't look after their own and broke its codes."

Lines like that had deeper meaning for Carmine and the Imbriale family.

Then came the cemetery scene with Scars standing over the graves of Carmine's sister and Bucky, on the anniversary of Bucky's murder no less, July 16, 1981.

McDonald asked about his first reaction to the news of his brother's death. DiLeonardo responded, "Devastation; your mind runs a hundred miles an hour and you want to go load up so you can kill the people I think killed him, my mother, his wife, his kids; how to deal with all of that."

"Yeah, he should've asked him how long it took his father to throw my sister out in the street," Carmine says. "They're standing over the graves talking about my sister. But he left out how the father stole the house and turned his back on her and the kids."

In the bleak backdrop of the cemetery, McDonald pumped DiLeonardo for more pithy quotes of soldiering on.

"My sister was out in the street, her husband dead, and here he is, parading around, saying how he loved my sister," Carmine says. "Him and his family, they turned their backs and didn't lift a finger for my sister. It was a disgrace."

Carmine wants to know what Mikey Scars thinks his brother would have thought of that interview. "I was there, in Florida. I told Bucky to get something in writing, and he said, 'Come on, Carmine, it's my father; I can trust him.' Scars knew. Always said I wanted to know when he was *made* so I could put in a complaint. How can he be loyal to this Family when he can't even be loyal to his real family?

"Make no mistake, guys like Mikey Scars and Greg Scarpa and his son and the Sessa brothers are the reason why the mob fell apart in Brooklyn," Carmine says. "There was no longer any code, any honor, and anyone who says different is either lying are wasn't there."

Too bad that back in 1984, Carmine didn't realize how bad things were getting.

The Credit Card Bandit
of Bensonhurst

Did you know the credit card was born in Brooklyn?

Kind of.

In 1946, a Brooklyn banker devised a physical card for his local Flatbush merchants to allow their customers to pay with plastic. Flatbush National Bank President John Biggins' "Charg-It" card was a hit.[58] [59]

Diners Club came along in 1950, American Express in 1958, though both cards were limited to certain markets, could only be used for travel or entertainment, and the full balance had to be paid off each month. Then came Bank of America with the first general purpose credit card in 1966, the BankAmericard, a precursor to the Visa and MasterCard networks.[60] [61]

By 1970, nationwide, more than 1,400 banks promoted credit card programs. With 100 million cards in circulation, consumer credit mushroomed to $105 billion ($748.5 billion today, adjusted for inflation). The 1980s saw a further

58. "The Origins of the Credit Card Trace Back to a Flatbush Bank," by Hannah Frishberg, Brownstoner, March 24, 2016

59. "The Beginning of the Credit Card," by Sydney Vaccaro, *Chargeback*, November 13, 2017

60. *Credit Card Nation The Consequences Of America's Addiction To Credit*, by Robert D. Manning, Basic Books, December 25, 2000

61. "The History of Credit Cards," by Jay MacDonald and Jason Steele, CreditCards.com, May 24, 2021

explosion in card programs. Banks blanketed the airwaves with commercials. Billboards urged consumers to "just put it on the card."[64]

The boys on 13th Avenue took notice.

To modern-day hackers, security on credit cards from back then seems laughable. Merchants used what were called "knuckle-busters," handheld devices set next to registers. Cashiers made carbon-copy impressions of the embossed digits on the cards directly onto receipts. Customers signed the slips. The merchants then mailed (or faxed) the receipts to processing companies.[62]

That's about it for security. Kind of like the honor system.

The card companies provided no electronic system to verify the customer present at their register was the actual cardholder, and not, say... Carmine from 13th Avenue. With a stack of cards, a guy like Carmine could go from shop to shop, neighborhood to neighborhood, banging out cards without detection. The banks didn't receive the receipts for days, if not weeks.

"I hit furniture stores, jewelry stores, clothing shops, electronics, all of them," Carmine says. "We'd steal stacks of blue cards from hospitals, put numbers on them, even made up the numbers. Didn't matter. Sometimes you had a guy who had plates and could make them. It was all a total scam and took forever for them to catch on."

Knuckle-busters were used well into the late 1990s.

Card companies did issue a printed book, published monthly, listing cancelled cards. A suspicious cashier *could* check that book. The cashier *could* request a driver's license or some other form of ID. But cashiers were busy, or lazy. For a smooth-talking hustler like Carmine, cashiers were easy to get over on, or he just moved on.

---

62. "What is a Knuckle Buster," Investopedia

The system incentivized merchants to look the other way. Credit cards helped them accept more payments, make more sales. And there was no real financial consequence for the store. Until the liability shift of 2015, the banks and credit card companies ate the cost of fraud, not the merchant. (As of October 2015, all US merchants still accepting cards *without* chips are now on the hook for card-fraud losses.)[63]

"The banks didn't want to stop it," Carmine says. "Even with the fraud, everyone was making so much money. The more the cards were used, the better. They could've used PINs or pictures, but they didn't. If they really wanted to kill all the fraud, they should've hired us as consultants."

In the mid-80s, banks added magnetic strips, but for data storage, not data encryption. Banks could not even alert merchants when a card exceeded its limit.[64] The only safeguard card issuers put in place was indemnifying losses up to a certain per-item value. Otherwise, guys like Carmine would've been banging out cards buying cars and boats.

With each purchase, Carmine fine-tuned his scam as it became his leading source of income.

Carmine obtained cards in various ways. Postal theft was one, as cards were mailed to customers at home in envelopes easy to identify. Rarely did he personally raid mailboxes. He established a network of accomplices to scour the area for cards in the mail. This also helped Carmine obtain the cardholder's key info: name, address, phone number. Then Carmine took out additional cards in that cardholder's name.

Carmine also paid bounties to "dumpster divers" to raid back alleys of department stores and grab the knuckle-buster carbon copies casually tossed out every night.

"It was a gold rush and you could get away with so much, if you were smart," Carmine remembers. "I had this

---

63. About EMVCo, EMVCO.com

64. "The rise and fall of the credit card magnetic stripe," by Marcia Frellick, CreditCards.com, June 14, 2011

major connect for cards, Rocco Barone, and he'd warn me, 'Don't use these in the neighborhood.' And I didn't. But I was surprised by all these jackasses who used stolen cards on the Avenue. Sloppy and stupid."

There were new card programs coming out all the time, and so many ways to scam them. "Every day, I'd come up with a new hustle, a new source for cards, a new spot to use them, a new connection. Have someone who owes your book? Get their card, bang it out. Someone needs cash fast? Get their card, bang it out. Someone loses big on the Mets? Get their card, bang it out. Bang, bang, bang, all day long. Shops didn't care. They just reported it later, still got paid."

Carmine worked hard on his scam. "I start printing them myself, getting numbers from a dozen different guys. Nothing like it is today. Sure, there were risks, and it's all this running around, but the stores didn't turn you away. I had a very good run with the cards. A lot of guys on 13th Avenue did back then."

Carmine bought lavish gifts, outfitted his home with luxuries. Like a pair of four-foot-high, cast-concrete stone lion sculptures. "I'm driving by this landscaping company in Staten Island and see these two massive lions, and had to have them," Carmine recalls. It took Carmine and four friends to transport the lions, each weighing several hundred pounds. He placed them at the entrance of the driveway in his Staten Island home, beside his new ornate mailbox, also purchased with a stolen card.

After not more than a week, Carmine arrived home, pulled into his driveway, and sensed something wasn't right. It took him a moment to realize the lions were gone. And they didn't run off by themselves. Carmine couldn't report the theft to the police. So he let it go.

A few months later, Carmine's watching *Geraldo,* the daytime television talk show hosted by Geraldo Rivera that aired from September 7, 1987, to June 12, 1998. Rivera did a segment on juvenile delinquents on Staten Island.

Relaxing on his couch with his wife, Carmine bolted upright as Rivera interviewed two teen girls from Tottenville High School, describing how they and some friends stole two four-foot-high stone lions as a goof.

That night, in a van with a couple of his boys, Carmine drove around Tottenville, found the house, got out, tied ropes around the lions, which were anchored in the ground, ripped them out, and loaded them into the van. The whole time Carmine eyed the home, hoping for someone, anyone, to please come out and give him a hard time. Fortunately for them, Carmine left without incident.

Over the years with the cards, as Carmine helped himself, he helped others in the neighborhood. "One time, I told all the single mothers with kids, 'Give me a list of things you need,' and I went around shopping for them with the cards," Carmine says. "It gave me a good feeling."

Not all were fans of Carmine's largesse. "I remember one of the old Italian ladies said, 'What do you think, you're a big shot? I can afford this, I don't need you, *disgrazia.*'" Carmine laughs. "She was very prideful. But that was rare. I had fun giving to the people in the neighborhood who didn't have. I was like Robin Hood with those credit cards: helped fixed up houses, got stuff for local kids for Christmas and graduations. Yeah, I had a ball with those cards. And of course, I made a ton of cash for myself."

One day, Carmine came across a large semi rig with North Carolina plates. Back in the '80s, truckers from the southern United States would travel up the East Coast with full loads of stolen furniture, then set up in parking lots or curbside on major commercial strips to sell the furniture at deep discounts.

"So I see this truck on 65th and 11th, outside one of those big apartment buildings across from the Dust Bowl, so I pull over and ask the trucker if he takes credit cards," Carmine says.

The driver whipped out his own knuckle-buster.

"I bought the whole load," Carmine says. "Told him just unload it by the curb, said I was waxing all the floors inside, so couldn't move the furniture in yet. He didn't care. I even gave him a $200 tip on the card and he thanked me up and down."

Carmine gave away a couple sofas and wall units to some of the local mothers walking by. He then called in some of his friends with trucks and big-trunk sedans to caravan the rest of the furniture to the sidewalk outside Neddy's Bar.

"What a spectacle on the avenue that afternoon," Carmine says. "I clogged the whole sidewalk with that furniture. Neddy comes out and laughs but says it just better be gone by the end of the day. I didn't even need two hours. One guy tells another guy, tells another guy, tells another guy, and before you know it, I got a crowd. I practically gave all that shit away, but it was all profit. I made a few bucks, made a lot of people happy. That was a great day on 13th Avenue."

Apparently not for the North Carolina trucker. But that's what you get when you try to get over in South Brooklyn, where they invented the phase for things "falling off the truck."

Carmine became so active with credit card scams, it limited his activities in other areas.

During this time, from 1974, when Carmine was 17, through 1984, Carmine worked off and on at the notorious Hunts Point Market. Built in 1962, Hunts Point Market was the world's largest wholesale food distribution center, pulling in more than $2 billion in revenue every year. By the early 1980s, the facility sprawled across 60 acres, spanning 700,000 square feet of refrigerated space.

However, for much of its history, Hunts Point was plagued by corruption. When Carmine worked in Hunts Point, employed by various companies, the market was dominated by organized crime lords who sucked hundreds of millions of dollars out of it every year.

Carmine secured union cards with the Local 174 of the United Food and Commercial Workers, which was representing 800 employees at the Hunts Point and the Gansevoort Markets, and the Local 202 of the International Brotherhood of Teamsters, which posted 1,400 members at Hunts Point.

"I worked loading and unloading trucks, doing deliveries, and the bosses loved me," Carmine says. "The problem was, I couldn't always be reliable. I had so many different things going on with the cards, sometimes I couldn't go, and I'd lose my spot, and it kept me from getting bumped up. No matter how much they liked me, you gotta be there to actually run something."

Behind the scenes, Carmine did more than unload trucks and make deliveries. "Everybody had a racket over there, so many ways to make money; it was easy for a guy like me. Someone would line me up, tell me to go in back of a truck and give a guy a beating. So I gave the guy a beating. One guy owed $320k and wasn't paying. I gave him such a beating, and he started paying. I did a lot of favors like that. But I was also shylocking, taking bets, and had a good sideline with my football sheets."

Privately operated, hundreds of millions of dollars flowing through it, Hunts Point was rife with shady opportunities. "Government inspectors would check a load and say it was no good, say tape it up, which meant they had to toss it," Carmine says. "But they were too picky and lazy, so maybe a few batches were bad, but most of it was good. So now you could sell it under the table at a huge discount. Let's say you got big strawberries, that's $60 a box. After they taped up the load, you sell them $10 a box, but pure profit. Wiseguys would say to me, 'Go in the back and work with the guy,' and I did, because there's a way to do it, and they only trusted certain guys to do it right."

One of his Hunts Points supervisors, an owner named Al Wilder, even offered to make Carmine a foreman. "Sad, because I had to turn him down. I could've made serious money as a foreman, but I was making even more money on the street, and I had so many things going on, I couldn't commit."

By this time, Carmine was in demand as his loansharking took off. His customers included James S., a foreman on a massive multi-year construction project. What many didn't know, however, was that James S. had a gambling addiction and was into Carmine for thousands of dollars.

"Jimmy was having a hard time, up and down, and I liked Jimmy, but still; you owe, you gotta pay, one way or the other, so we had to figure this thing out," Carmine says. "Then I learn he's the foreman on this big job."

In exchange for Carmine reducing the debt to a manageable level, James S. awarded Carmine a "no-show" job on the project. "No-show" jobs are a staple of organized crime—paid positions where the employee is required to perform little, if any, actual work and may not even require regular attendance.

"I even got Jimmy to give Mike Bolino a no-show on the same job," Carmine says. "We're pulling down $700 a week on this job alone, for a couple years, good money in the 80s, especially when you don't gotta do nothing."

Well, not nothing. Carmine and Bolino did have to show up at the job site occasionally. "Me and Mike, we're sitting around, and they bring us two sledgehammers, tell us we gotta go knock down some walls," Carmine says. "Guy leaves, we break the handles, go back to doing whatever we were doing."

A short while later, the assistant foreman returned to check their progress. Once Carmine showed him the broken handles, he stepped away and returned with replacements. "So then we break those handles too," Carmine says. "We turn those back in and I say, 'Must be a bad batch.'"

They didn't assign any further work for Carmine and Mikey Bolino.

No-show jobs and Hunts Point hustles generated steady income for Carmine, but the real money was in credit cards. By then, it seemed like every hood on 13th Avenue either had a pocket full of plastic or was trying to get in on the action.

One day, Carmine tipped off Joey Ambrosino and Larry Fiorenza about a guy selling stolen cards. They laid out the cash, picked up some cards, then hatched a scheme to impersonate police officers and use the cards to buy six high-end bicycles.

"It was a Chinese guy who had this bike shop on 3rd Avenue, so they bring a van, and Joey and Larry go into the shop and say they're undercover cops," Carmine recalls. "They're loading the bikes into the van as the guy runs the cards, but he also calls them in, which they almost never did. One card comes back cancelled. So, this Chinese guy, now he's wise, and it all goes south. He jumps on Larry's back, gets knocked off. Then he jumps on Joey in the van as Larry's gunning the engine, so now it's an abduction. They throw the guy what a beating and take off, but come back empty-handed."

Police interviewed the shop owner, who declined to cooperate.

"I remember Tommy [Detective Thomas Dades] got the call," Carmine says. "When he was rushing down there, he said he was convinced it was me."

Ambrosino was angry he was out the cash he put up for the cards. "So later, I'm making fun of Joey, telling the story of the Chinese guy hanging on his back, the two of them rolling around in the back of the van fighting. Joey's pissed, says the place was no good. Then he says I got to give him $7k, because that's what he spent on the cards and it was my tip. I says, 'I'm not giving you shit. Go tell Carmine [Sessa] you got beat up by one little Chinese guy and see where that gets you. Not my fault you were posing as a detective and hit the wrong shop.'"

Carmine had other beefs with crew members over credit cards. For instance, he had an agreement with the owner of a large lighting company on Staten Island. Carmine supplied stolen cards. The owner ran them through his merchant account on bogus sales. They split the proceeds.

"Then one day he calls me to stop by. When I get there, he tells me Michael Sessa dropped in and wanted him to run some cards. Asshole was trying to jump my claim. I went right to Carmine [Sessa] to get Michael to back off. And it wasn't the first or last time Michael tried to screw me."

Despite conflict and confrontations, the credit card scam was a lucrative racket for Carmine.

"I'm with two of my boys from 13th Avenue and it's Christmastime, and all the wives want fur coats, so we told them we couldn't afford them," Carmine says. "But that's because we wanted to surprise them. We figured, why not? We had the cards."

Carmine targeted a furrier in Manhattan run by a Jewish consortium. "It was the kind of shop with the security cage at the door, where they gotta buzz you in. I didn't like the set-up from the start. I had this card that said Dr. Rodman. I'll never forget; it was crazy because we're going in there and my guy is using that card, but he don't look like no doctor. He looked like what he was: a 13th Avenue hood."

The shop was long, narrow, lined by multiple levels of racks displaying hundreds of furs and leather coats, as fluorescent light tubes buzzed overhead. Not many were overly concerned for the ethical treatment of animals back then. It was early evening. There are half a dozen shoppers, clerks bustling around. Carmine and his co-conspirators enter the shop through the security cage.

"We're supposed to go in there, nice and easy, be inconspicuous, pick out some furs, not get too crazy, pay with the cards, and leave," Carmine says. "That was the plan."

Instead, "Dr. Rodman" strikes up a conversation with one of the furriers, which takes a left turn into a bizarre consultation with a hands-on examination.

"He not only introduces himself as Dr. Rodman, but, God knows why, says he's a veterinarian," Carmine says. "So the two of them get into talking about dogs. With one eye I'm picking through the coats on the racks. With the other, I'm watching this mess, getting a bad, bad feeling."

The furrier asks "Dr. Rodman" to examine his Doberman pincher. He's got him in the back, says the poor guy is old, not doing too well. "Hold on, one sec," he says, rushing into the back of the shop. Moments later, he emerges cradling an elderly Dobie with a pitiful hangdog look.

"So my idiot friend, he's opening the dog's mouth, looking up his ass, looking in his ears," Carmine recalls. "I'm flashing him *let's go* looks, but he's talking all this dog bullshit, saying how this breed has a brain too big for its skull and other crap he's making up as he goes along."

"Dr. Rodman" completes his examination, steps back, folds his arms, gets real serious, turns to the furrier, places a comforting arm on his shoulder, shakes his head, sighs loudly, and delivers his prognosis. "I'm sorry to tell you this, Abe," Dr. Rodman says. "But you see, unfortunately, your dog's only got a few weeks to live, tops."

No. Say it ain't so, Doc. Must be something you can do.

"Jeez, so this nut job not only keeps us in there for way too long, but he goes and makes shit up and tells the guy his poor dog is about to die. Of course, the guy gets all upset. They go on and on, back and forth. Is there nothing to do? Can't I take him nowhere? Nope, nope, sorry. Lost cause. Took forever to get out of there. I'm surprised we didn't get pinched then and there. And I'll tell you another thing, now this guy was definitely gonna be able to pick us outta a lineup, even with one eye tied behind his back. That's the point of trying to be inconspicuous."

They picked up three nice fur coats, putting several thousand dollars on a stolen card, but not enough to trigger a call to the card company. The furrier even gave his new friend, Dr. Rodman, a discount, waiving the tax.

Carmine had a great run with the cards, which seemed like it would never end. Until one evening not long after the furrier episode, Carmine went shopping. Just a regular errand.

Joining Carmine was Michael Sessa and Carmine' longtime friend, Robert. "I didn't invite them or have a plan or anything like that; they just came along, to do their own shopping," Carmine says. Robert was never involved in organized crime. Just a regular, blue-collar Brooklyn guy. Carmine and Robert grew up together on 13th Avenue, and they were close.

"One time, Robert's mother's apartment got robbed," Carmine says. "I found out who robbed her, some tough kid, and he came to me when he heard I was looking for him. He didn't respect too many people, but he respected me. I got him to bring all the stolen stuff back. And I was so happy to do that for Robert. We went everywhere together."

Robert had four brothers, including an older brother Dewey, a large kid.

"I remember Dewey was a tough kid, and he had a fist fight with Allie Persico on 11th Avenue, where the two of them just went to war at each other. Allie was a tough kid too, and he took his lumps. And to his credit, he didn't go after Dewey after the fight. It was done and no hard feelings. I had a lot of respect for that."

Fast forward to 1984 and Carmine, Michael, and Robert are in line at a department store in the Ceasar's Bay Bazaar shopping center on an old pier where Bay Parkway runs out of road and empties into Gravesend Bay. The store was mobbed, lines were long. So Carmine is standing there for some time, easily distracted, easily noticed, as they step up at the register for their turn to pay.

Carmine finished paying with a stolen card, was being handed the receipt when he casually looked to his left, and...

... *damn.*

"I see two detectives from the 6-2, off duty, a few feet away, couple lines over," Carmine says. "And these two had major hard-ons for me. Hated me. I can't believe I didn't notice them, but the place was jammed. And I'm standing there holding the card and receipt. If I'd only seen them before I pulled out the card, before I paid."

"Well, look who it is," one of the officers said while closing in.

"We take off with the bags," Carmine says. "Robert was heavier and slower, so he doesn't get too far before he says, 'Fuck this,' and they arrest him. Me and Michael got away. But didn't matter. They didn't even have to run. They knew me. They had the video at the register, the card receipt, everything." Police arrested Carmine the following day.

Sure enough, the eyewitness testimony of the two off-duty officers, store security camera footage, and a handwriting analysis from the credit card slip provided damaging evidence against Carmine.

As Robert accompanied Carmine to make the illegal purchase, he was jailed, convicted, and served several years in prison for credit card fraud.

"Robert just assumed it was my fault, that I said something, and he blamed me," Carmine says. "Before that, we went everywhere together. After that, he wouldn't even pick up the phone when I called. I was shocked. I feel terrible what happened, but I didn't say nothing. He didn't say nothing. Just bad luck all around."

In a bizarre courtroom scene, Carmine invited the mothers he helped in the neighborhood to come down. When the judge saw the parade of Bensonhurst moms march into his courtroom, he quipped, "You missed your calling, Carmine. You should've been a priest, such a good man you are."

Investigators also linked Carmine to the "Dr. Rodman" furrier job through handwriting analysis. When it came time to review that count, the furrier declined to testify. "I told the judge, 'I really didn't hurt no one,'" Carmine says. "He said, 'What about Dr. Rodman?' I said, 'He's insured.' The judge said, 'That's not how it works, Carmine.'"

The judge sentenced Carmine to 36 months in prison and sent him to the Federal Correctional Institution, Danbury, in Connecticut.

Carmine and The Horse

In the summer of 1985, Carmine Imbriale entered federal prison in Danbury, Connecticut.

By this time, Carmine and Janet had been married seven years and had three children, so Carmine being in prison away from Brooklyn was a hardship. Still, Janet made the arduous trek to Connecticut to visit. "Seeing my wife and kids in prison, coming to visit me, made me hopeful, reminding me that I was going to get out," Carmine recalls.

For the time being, Carmine focused on his situation to ensure release as soon as possible. "When I was in prison, none of the wiseguys helped my family," Carmine remembers bitterly. "It was my family and my real friends who stopped by and helped. I thought someone would've done something, but nothing. It's not like you see in the movies."

The prison corralled gangsters from all five New York Mafia Families. One aging incarcerated mobster who took a shine to Carmine was Matthew Joseph "Matty the Horse" Ianniello, who rose to acting boss of the Genovese Crime Family.[65]

During the 1960s and 1970s, Ianniello dominated the adult-entertainment rackets in Times Square, when it was a center of vice in Manhattan. During that era, more than 2,300 crimes were committed annually in the one-block radius of

---

65. "Matthew Ianniello, the Mafia Boss Known as 'Matty the Horse,' Dies at 92," by Paul Vitello, *New York Times*, August 22, 2012

42nd Street between Seventh and Eighth Avenues.[66] *The New York Times* labeled it "the worst block in town."[67]

According to the *New York Times*, Ianniello extorted "protection money from bar owners, pornography peddlers and topless dancers during a half-century career that, among other highlights, helped transform Times Square into the dingy world capital of peep shows in the 1960s and '70s."[65]

The notorious 42nd Street area, flush with XXX-rated theaters, burlesque clubs, and peep shows, was known as "The Deuce," an area patrolled by nearly a thousand sex workers.

The Mafia's dominance of Times Square is the setting of the HBO hit series *The Deuce*, starring James Franco. In that production, actor Garry Pastore portrays Ianniello.[68] Pastore is also a veteran of another HBO hit, *The Sopranos*, playing mob captain Jerry Basile.[69, 70] *The Deuce* features one scene where the fearsome Genovese capo muscles in on a Midtown bar. In real life, years before Carmine's imprisonment, he crossed paths with Ianniello in a scene that could have been used for *The Deuce*.

"The joints in the city were easier marks for using the cards," Carmine remembers. "They were busier, more going on, so cashiers were distracted, less likely to look hard at your card."

The scam was simple. Carmine hit a busy strip club, used his credit card to cover a couple hundred dollars in singles. But instead of tipping the talent, he'd have a drink,

---

66. "Shocking Vintage Photos Show Time Square At The Peak Of Its Depravity In The 1970s and 1980s," ByGonely.com

67. "Life on W. 42nd St. a study in decay," *New York Times*, March 14, 1960

68. *The Deuce*, HBO, 2017-2019

69. "HBO'S *The Deuce* Returns for a Second Season With the Mob in Control," by Larry Henry, The Mob Museum, 2019

70. "A Look Back At The Real *Deuce*: Times Square In The 1970s," by Jen Carlson, *The Gothamist*, September 8, 2017

pocket the cash, slip out the side. He'd also hit Manhattan shops, then a club, grab something to eat after his spree.

One day, Carmine strolled into SPQR, a restaurant the Genovese captain owned. The Horse saw him coming from a Brooklyn mile.

Carmine waited on his change as Ianniello emerged from the back room. He sized up Carmine, introduced himself. Carmine recognized the name. Ianniello informed Carmine of his controlling interest in the establishment, then warned Carmine to take his scam elsewhere. Carmine explained he had no idea the place was protected, apologizing for the indiscretion. They parted ways on a positive note.

Fast forward several years. Within weeks of Carmine entering prison, Ianniello was assigned to the same unit, sentenced to six years on a racketeering charge for embezzling more than $2 million from New York City bars and restaurants, including Umberto's Clam House, the Peppermint Lounge, and the Mardi Gras.[71]

At one point, as a captain for the Genovese, Ianniello controlled more than 80 establishments in Manhattan, from porn palaces and gay bars (he owned The Stonewall Inn during the 1969 riots) to restaurants and discos. Authorities captured Ianniello on wiretaps extorting millions of dollars in skim from sex-industry establishments.[71]

When Carmine spotted Ianniello stepping onto the prison tier, he warned his fellow inmates, "Don't screw around with that guy."

Ianniello earned his nickname as a youth in Little Italy, Manhattan. During a baseball game, an older, larger player hit one of his teammates in the face. In the ensuing brawl, Ianniello beat down his taller opponent, inspiring a witness to declare, "That boy is as strong as a horse." By the time he

---

71. "Ianniello Is Sentenced In Racketeering Trial," *New York Times*, February 16, 1986

entered prison, Ianniello was in his mid-sixties, doing time on multiple convictions, but still physically imposing.

Known as much for his short temper and rough demeanor as for his cunning and intelligence, Ianniello developed a soft spot for Carmine, who recklessly tormented the Genovese captain with practical jokes. Anyone else would have been shanked, or at least beaten. Somehow, Ianniello laughed it off.

"Matty was a gentleman and I highly respected him, and I showed him that respect," Carmine recalls. "I remember when he first came to prison. He comes into the day room. Now, he's a big guy, sticks out when he enters a room. So he's looking around the day room, spots me—we're playing cards—then he points to me, calls me over."

"What's up?" Carmine shot back from across the room, not disrespectfully, but he *was* in the middle of a hand.

"I yelled at you once, don't make me do it again," Ianniello barked. Carmine folded his cards and walked over. Ianniello then commanded Carmine to go secure him a God damn cell, and make sure it was located close to the day room.

"So I threw one guy out of his cell, but left the other guy in there." Carmine laughs. "But I didn't tell Matty." The other guy happened to be a flamboyant crossdresser.

Really?

"Matty didn't realize what I'd done at first, until he walked into the cell, and when he did, boy, did he yell! 'Carmine, you got me!'" he remembers.

So they shared a laugh.

"Okay, enough's enough," Ianniello said. "Now throw him the fuck out and no more jokes."

"Of course, I went right in and I threw the other guy out." Carmine laughs. "You gotta admit, though, that's funny."

In another episode, Ianniello decided to get a prison job to help reduce his sentence. This puzzled Carmine. While in prison in 1986, already having served six years on the extortion case, Ianniello was acquitted on racketeering charges in the garbage industry, only to be slammed two years later with 13 years for bid rigging—the case that also snared boss Anthony "Fat Tony" Salerno.[72]

"I said, 'Matty, you're 65 years old and looking at all this time; I don't think you're getting out on a reduced sentence.' But he wanted to try and get years cut off, and help pass the time."

Carmine had just the job. "I said to Matty, 'I got a great job for you.' I gave him this fireman hat, and I said, 'They're always doing these fire drills and need someone on the tier to step up. If the fire alarm goes off, you wear that fire hat, hold the door open and yell FIRE! loud as you can, and you hold that door open. Remember, lives are at stake with this thing.'" Carmine told Ianniello this job would double the hours he knocked off his sentence. The Horse agreed, even thanked Carmine.

"Two nights later, I rang a fake fire alarm," Carmine remembers. "So as I sound the alarm, Matty runs out with the hat on, shouting, but the guard says, 'Ianniello, what are you dressed for, Halloween?' For a second, he don't get it. Then Matty realized what I'd done, and says, 'Damn it, Carmine, you got me again.'"

Ianniello liked Carmine, looked out for him in prison, and took him into his confidence. "I remember me and Matty'd talk for hours, and he told me many things. Like, he thought John Gotti was an asshole for bringing his kid into this thing, not in the right frame of mind, said he should've kept his kid far away from it.

"Matty was very good to me, he liked me," Carmine remembers. "He'd send my wife money, even paid for her

---

72. "U.S. Attorney Reports Indictment of Ianniello," *New York Times*, May 16, 1986

and my kids to come see me in prison, and I wasn't even in his crew on the outside."

Ianniello was not the only senior-level Mafioso imprisoned at that facility. "You had other guys in there, like Nicky Frap and Buster [Genovese Captain John Ardito], but Matty made it clear: keep quiet, do your bid, no problems."

Later, a captain from the Kansas City mob entered the prison. "This guy was such a loudmouth, I thought Matty was gonna kill him." Carmine laughs. "One day, Matty had enough, blew up on him, set him straight in front of the entire tier. After, he says to me, 'What a joke, that guy. Bet my daughter could run the Kansas City mob.'"

Carmine enjoyed these moments. Yet friendship only gets you so far in federal prison, especially when large sums of money are involved.

Passing time was a challenge. Handball was a popular diversion.

Handball is a popular New York sport. Brooklyn is more known for stickball, but handball was just as popular in the borough later in the 70s and 80s, but not the four-wall version of the game played elsewhere. Starting in the early 1900s, a one-wall version had taken hold as byproduct of Depression-era public works projects. Thousands of these ancient walls still stand across the parks and beaches of New York City.[73]

By the time Carmine was growing up, the game exploded across South Brooklyn. And unlike other games, you didn't need a stick or a bat: just a ball and a wall. That worked better than stickball for prisons, which have nothing but walls, and administrators who prefer not to hand out bats to inmates.

Carmine's competitive nature—and skill—put him in the middle of the action. Carmine became a top competitor

---

73. "The History of Handball," by Tom O'Connor, The United States Handball Association

in high-stakes prison handball, in competitions divided along racial lines. Ianniello bet thousands of dollars on Carmine's matches; more than ten thousand dollars on the championships alone, in fact. This was no fun and games. The gambling pitted the prison gangs against each other in screaming matches. Carmine used every tactic available to him, competing physically and psychologically.

"Two years in a row, I made it to the championships facing this Black gangster called Eyes," Carmine recalls. "He was called Eyes because he was cross-eyed. He was a big, mean son of a bitch, and those eyes made him look like even more of a crazy bastard."

Eyes was an enforcer for a drug gang, locked up for attempted murder, assault, and other violent crimes.

Didn't matter. Carmine, being Carmine, just had to stick the thumb in the eye, as they say back in the neighborhood. (Or, in this case, the Eyes.)

"It's the championship, everything's on the line, so of course I talked trash," Carmine says. "I'd say, 'Eyes, you looking at me? Because if you're looking at me, I'm over here. Nope, Eyes, not over there. C'mon, focus, Eyes, focus, I'm over here.' So I keep it up and I got everybody laughing. Everybody... but not Eyes and not his boys."

On Carmine's side of the divided crowd, they're laughing their asses off. On the other, Eyes' boys are pissed at Carmine, pissed at the frickin' Italians, and pissed at Eyes because they see he's losing his shit. Only reason a full-scale riot didn't erupt was the armed prison guards keeping the two sides at bay.

Carmine kept it up, antagonizing Eyes, ridiculing him, playing to the audience, amping up the intensity. "There's yelling and laughing and hollering, and we're in the middle of this serious high-stakes game, in a federal prison," Carmine remembers. "Matty's out front, laughing, shouting, saying what a ball-breaker his kid is. I tell you, I was so bad; Eyes was getting so mad, threatens to quit if I didn't cut it out, but we both knew that was bullshit. He knew, no matter what, he couldn't quit with all that money on the line, because his own guys would've killed him."

No referees. No one to call timeout and reprimand Carmine for unsportsmanlike conduct. No handing out fines or suspensions.

They played on. Trading insults, trading points. Game was razor close.

"He was a great player, no doubt, but I got inside his head, and remember, I was a great player too. The difference? I was mentally stronger. You couldn't shake me, no matter what you did. I been through too much. The shit I've seen, trash talking don't work on me. He's yelling at me to serve the ball and stop talking about his eyes, but of course, I'm laying it on even thicker about his eyes."

Final point, Carmine up one, served, sending a sharp, low-bounce, left-side shot that Eyes had no chance to return, diving, crashing, rolling into a ball of rage as Carmine and the Italians exploded in victory.

"Of course I beat him and Matty made a ton of money off me, which to his credit, he shared with me," Carmine says. "And I not only beat Eyes that year, but the next year, same scene, and the third year, I beat some Indian guy. Sure, the trash talking helped. But I was really good at handball too."

Released in 1987, Carmine headed back to Brooklyn.

Ianniello gained release eventually. Then, when Genovese Boss Vincent "The Chin" Gigante was finally sent to prison, Ianniello was elevated to acting boss, with Jimmy Ida as one of his top captains and consigliere for a time. "Again, it's a shame I went with Carmine [Sessa]," Carmine regrets. "Who knows how my life woulda been different had I gone with Jimmy all those years ago, under Matty. I never saw Matty again after prison."

The Horse pled guilty on racketeering charges in 2005, returning to prison to serve 18-month and two-year sentences, to run concurrently at the Federal Correctional Complex in Butner, North Carolina.

Matthew Joseph "Matty the Horse" Ianniello passed away at home in Old Westbury in Long Island, New York, on August 15, 2012, of health issues stemming from various heart ailments and other illnesses, including prostate cancer.[65]

Beef with the Mad Hatter

Over the years, Carmine endeared himself to many Brooklyn gangsters.

Greg Scarpa Sr. ain't one of them.

In 1953, Scarpa murdered his first victim, on the orders of a local Mafia captain, earning membership into the Profaci Family, the forerunner to the Colombos. In the '60s, he played a role in the Colombo Family insurrection led by Joseph "Crazy Joe" Gallo, as a soldier alongside Carmine Persico.[74]

Officially, Scarpa Sr. never rose above the rank of solider. The 13th Avenue crew was under Colombo Captain Anthony "Scappy" Scarpati, then later Anthony "Chickie" Russo.

"See, where some get it wrong about Scarpa is they say he was a captain," explains former NYPD Detective Thomas Dades. "Scarpa was never a captain. Greg was always a solider, but of course much more than a soldier."

From his base in the Wimpy Boys Social Club, Scarpa Sr. was the de facto ruler over a violent crew involved in illegal gambling, securities fraud, loansharking, extortion, hijacking, counterfeit credit cards, assault, narcotics trafficking, and other crimes. Anything that went down on 13th Avenue, Scarpa Sr. got his piece. Or else.

---

74. *Deal with the Devil: The FBI's Secret Thirty-Year Relationship with a Mafia Killer,* by Peter Lance

"Make no mistake, Greg Scarpa was a feared man on 13th Avenue," Dades says. "He was the true power on 13th Avenue, and for good reason."

When Colombo Boss Carmine Persico wanted someone to suffer, he sent "the Beast," who didn't just kill people. Scarpa Sr. murdered his victims in many ways—decapitating, dismembering, gunning down, garroting with piano wire, beating, blowtorching, bathing them in acid.

"Greg Scarpa had people petrified because of all the murders, the beatings, just a vicious animal," Dades says. "Greg carried himself like a tough guy, and he had no problem killing people for the smallest things. He even shot them to death right in his club."

Usually as most wiseguys consolidate power, they delegate their dirty work to insulate themselves from prosecution. But Scarpa Sr. got dirty, personally involving himself in violence and murder. He even had his murder van customized with secret compartments to hide firearms.

Yet that's not the only thing that made him different. Greg Scarpa Sr. had a secret.

In March 1962, police busted the up-and-coming wiseguy for a hijacking. To avoid prosecution, he agreed to cooperate with the feds, serving as an undercover informant for the FBI for two long stretches of his criminal career. That deal with the South Brooklyn devil lasted three decades, fueling Scarpa's bloody rise to power. In fact, that was the title of a fascinating deep dive into Scarpa's relationship with the government written by investigative reporter Peter Lance: *Deal with the Devil: The FBI's Secret Thirty-Year Relationship with a Mafia Killer*.[74] This is a highly recommended read.

In painstaking detail, Lance unravels decades of deception and duplicity, revealing how Scarpa Sr. played a hand in so many major Mafia milestones, including supplying information justifying the wiretaps that led to lifelong imprisonment for his own boss, Carmine Persico.

For decades, in fact, even before Joe Valachi testified before US Congress, Scarpa Sr. funneled information to the FBI. His briefings were even must reads for FBI Director J. Edgar Hoover. He fed the feds tips that eliminated rivals, within and outside his crime Family. His intel provided the justification for wiretaps on dozens of high-profile cases, including the epic Commission Case.[74]

And here comes Carmine Imbriale, rumbling down 13th Avenue, ready to rub Greg Scarpa the wrong way from their very first encounter.

"I first met Greg outside Wimpy Boys, after I beat the hell out of this neighborhood guy, across the street from Mona Lisa," Carmine remembers.

Sure, some prefer the pastries at Villabate on 18th Avenue, especially after it absorbed Alba in 2004. Others swear by the *sfogliatella* at Mazzola's in Carrol Gardens, or the piping-hot bread at Caputo's in Cobble Hill. But for Dyker Heights regulars, there was never a reason to leave 13th Avenue.

The focaccia and fresh-baked semolina, the grain pies, the seven-layer rainbow Neapolitans. The handmade biscotti, the lard bread, the almond cookies. The trays of Italian perfection confection racked up like a cannoli candy store, shelf after shelf overflowing with espresso Florentines, pignolis, pizzelles, orange-ricotta cookies.

No wonder that at Mona Lisa, there were always lines. And earlier that day, a local guy crossed one of them.

Carmine was visiting his sister's apartment down 13th Avenue when his teenage niece burst in, crying. "She was hysterical, very upset, hard to understand, hard to calm her down, to find out this guy had grabbed her ass and put his hands on her, shoved her," Carmine remembers. "When she finally got it out, my sister tried to grab me, but I was off and running. My sister's yelling down the stairs for me to not do nothing stupid, but all I saw was red."

Carmine raced down into a crowded Mona Lisa, dragged the guy out, and threw him into the street. Carmine beat the guy so badly, he drew a crowd, stopping traffic. All the wiseguys poured out of Wimpy Boys to watch the fight.

Wiseguys like Greg Scarpa Sr. don't appreciate unwanted attention right outside their social clubs. "I told the guy, 'You ever come near my niece again, I'll cut your hands off,'" Carmine says. "I was definitely in the right. But Greg didn't like that at all. You don't act like that with a guy like Greg, right in front of his club."

Fortunately for Carmine, Joseph "Joe Brewster" DeDomenico, was on the scene, put in a word for him and the episode blew over. Twelve years Carmine's senior, Joe Brewster was a *made* man in the Colombo Family who also reported to Scarpati. Brewster came up with Scarpa Sr. and the two were close, so much so Scarpa Sr. referred to Brewster as his "second son."[74] And Brewster was a cousin of Carmine's brother-in-law, Bucky DiLeonardo.

"I got close with Joe," Carmine remembers. In fact, the bond between the two became so strong, Joe Brewster encouraged Carmine to tell people the two were cousins.

"Joe was always getting his driver's license taken away, so I drove him around. I picked him up in Fort Lee, out in New Jersey. I had an all-white leather Buick Impala convertible. I'd get to Joe's house, top down, he'd refuse to get in the car. Didn't want to mess up his hair. I told him no problem, was heading back home, and he gave up and got in. But then he made me drop him off at the barber's once we hit Brooklyn. We had a lot of laughs. Just a great guy."

Joe Brewster was a straight-up gangster, an armed robber, and a cold-blooded murderer.

One afternoon, Carmine had an epic street fight on 13th Avenue with a neighborhood guy, Danny.

"That was some fight," Carmine recalls. "I had two black eyes, my mouth was busted up. I went on my collections like that the next day. And I got looks from my customers, but they were too afraid to ask what happened."

After making his rounds, Carmine met Joe Brewster for lunch. "Joe loved watching me fight, couldn't get enough of it," Carmine says. "So next day, we sit down to eat, and he says to me, 'Every time I see you, you got marks on you.' Then, he asks me to take down my sunglasses." Carmine removed his glasses, revealing a severely bruised face.

"Joe wasn't smiling no more. Gets serious, asks me if I'm ready to put some work in on this guy, Danny." Carmine understood Joe Brewster's deadly proposition.

"Over a fight?" Carmine responded. "Nah, c'mon, Joe. I'm not about to kill someone over something like that."

Joe Brewster sat back, smiling as he said, "I knew you'd say that."

Brewster was about as deep in the 13th Avenue rackets as a wiseguy could get. He was an active member of two major bank-robbery rings, one run by Scarpa Sr. and the other by notorious gangster Gaspipe Casso, both known for their ability to "bypass" security systems. They raked in millions of dollars over the years.[74, 75, 76]

Joe Brewster was also popular on 13th Avenue. As a teenager, he ran with Carmine Sessa, also a Scarpa Sr. protégé, as well as Robert "Bobby Zam" Zambardi.

Brewster may have been successful robbing banks, but he was terrible at managing money. "Joe would get his money and spend it as fast as he could, on eating, drinking, partying, his friends," Carmine recalls. "He'd walk away with hundreds of thousands of dollars on a job, and a month later, he's borrowing money off me. He wasn't a gambler. He just went through money like it was nothing. And I was always with him."

---

75. *Gaspipe: Confessions of a Mafia Boss*, by Philip Carlo, William Morrow, June 23, 2009

76. "14 Are Charged In 7 Burglaries By Skilled Ring," by Arnold H. Lubasch, *New York Times*, November 15, 1990

Before long, Brewster was crashing at Carmine's house on Staten Island or at Carmine's sister's apartment on 13th Avenue.

"He had a wife in Fort Lee and a model he put up in Manhattan, but I never saw either of them and he never really spoke about them. We became close. He looked out for me and he was a stand-up guy who had balls and who I trusted. Joe Brewster was a real popular guy on the Avenue."

One day, Brewster asked Scarpa Sr. if Carmine could come in on a bank job. "Greg said no, didn't give a reason, just a flat no... but he did let Bucky go," Carmine says. "So I knew for sure then, Greg didn't like me. But I didn't care."

Maybe he should have. Because Scarpa *really* didn't like Carmine Imbriale. But there was no avoiding Scarpa on 13th Avenue. "He was always sitting out front of his club, with one of those silly sun visors in the summer, acting like he was king. Greg was the opposite of low key. He was a gangster all the way through. Dressed like it, acted like it, talked like it, wanted everyone to bow down. He had an ego and a half and made everybody on the Avenue feel it."

Scarpa Sr. also had one of the largest numbers rackets in the city. Back then, the backrooms of Brooklyn's bakeries and cafes were not just card rooms and dice pits, but numbers houses. It was the Italian street lottery, dating all the way back to the 1920s.

You pick three numbers, either straight or combo (combo means you get paid when those numbers come out in random order, and paid less than if you play them straight). Because no one trusted gang bosses like Scarpa to not rig the numbers, the Mafia used impartial sources. Some crews used the last three digits of the pari-mutuel handle at the Big A (basically, the total combined take of the betting pool at Aqueduct Racetrack for that day). Another crew would use the closing Dow, another number they couldn't fix.

"Everybody and their mother played the numbers," Carmine says. "Not kidding, even the grandmothers. Even the priests." They saw numbers in everything, everywhere. Stepped on a scale, play your weight. Visit someone in the hospital, play the room number. Grocery bill, play the total. And everyone had some creepy story of how so-and-so's aunt had a premonition, or such-and-such's grandmother dreamt a number.

Of course those numbers hit.

Started out as nickels, but those nickels—and later quarters and dollars—added up. By 1980, the New York numbers rackets generated between $800 million to $1.5 billion a year for organized crime ($2.7 billion to $5 billion, adjusted for inflation).[77]

Scarpa Sr. raked in thousands every week and the wiseguys in general made nice money on those numbers... until, in 1967, New York State started muscling in on the action, launching a legal lottery. At first, it was a six-number game. It wasn't until 1980 that lawmakers in Albany created a daily pick-three lottery, and that doomed Scarpa Sr.'s illicit business.[77]

Want to laugh? The gangsters took 20 or 30 percent off the top when you won.

The Albany shysters? Fifty percent.

However, thick-necked 13th Avenue wiseguys couldn't compete with the convenience of convenience stores and candy shops when they started installing lotto machines. Let's just say Scarpa Sr. didn't take the news well.

"Pete Rizzo had a drugstore on 13th Avenue, and his store was the first in the neighborhood to get one of those lottery machines," Carmine remembers.

Word spread fast on the Avenue. "When Greg heard, he goes nuts. But Greg didn't send no one. He went right to Pete Rizzo's drugstore himself, screamed at Pete to rip out the machine. Pete said he couldn't do it 'cause he had

---

77. "The Daily Lottery Was Originally a Harlem Game. Then Albany Wanted In," by Bridgett M. Davis, *New York Times*, February 27, 2019

a contract with the state. He didn't own the machine, so that'd be like destroying state property, like blowing up a mailbox."

Wrong answer. "Greg stormed out of Pete's shop, then comes right back and drove an 18-wheeler right through the front door in broad daylight, destroying it. It's a miracle no one was killed, not that Greg gave a shit. He probably wanted to kill Pete, send a message to the other shop owners."

Carmine always suspected Scarpa Sr. had a hand in the murder of his brother-in-law Bucky. Bucky was a soldier in the Colombo Family, and he participated in bank robberies with Scarpa Sr.'s crew.

After Bucky's murder, Scarpa was at the sit-down about the dispute with Scars over the home. "So, I'm at the sit-down with Paulie Zac, Joe Brewster, Greg's there, and again, he brings up this bullshit again about how he was going to give my sister $400 a week," Carmine recalls. "I said, 'I don't want your money, fuck that, I'll take care of it,' which sounded disrespectful. But I was angry. Paulie Zac pulled me to the side, said for me to reconsider what I said, saying, 'You don't mean the way you said it,' saying, 'Greg just means that he will support your sister himself.' I asked Paulie, 'Why? What the fuck does Greg have to do with any of this?' Paulie said saying it the way I said it sounded like maybe someone is going to go to the cops. And he said, 'I know you didn't mean that.'"

Scarpa took offense, but let it lie. Still, it was one more bad taste Carmine left in the Grim Reaper's mouth.

It's baffling how Colombo Family members, mistrustful by nature, weren't waving red flags all over 13th Avenue on Scarpa Sr. Again, read Peter Lance exceptional reporting in *Deal with the Devil* to see the warning signs were all over the place.[74]

For decades, one of the Colombo's most active and violent enforcers avoided prosecution, even as he racked up arrests. From the 1950s through the 1980s, police arrested

Scarpa Sr. 10 times (unlicensed firearms, bookmaking, loansharking, fencing stolen property, assault). All charges were dismissed or resulted in minor fines and/or probation, with the exception of a lone 30-day sentence in 1976 for bribing police officers (and that occurred during the period after his status as an informant was closed, before he was reactivated by the bureau).

Many quietly suspected, but none outwardly accused, Scarpa Sr. of cooperating with authorities; or as he liked to called it in private, his "insurance policy."

Carmine had good reason to suspect Scarpa Sr. was cooperating. Both were heavily involved with credit card fraud. Both were arrested. But Carmine, a low-level associate, got busted with three credit cards, resulting in his 36-month sentence in federal prison.

Scarpa Sr., a much higher-profile target of law enforcement operating in a major crew in the most violent of the New York Mafia Crime Families, was caught with hundreds more credit cards than Carmine. In fact, the Secret Service embedded a mole in the Wimpy Boys Club who sold Scarpa three hundred blank MasterCard and Visa cards.

The Brooklyn Organized Crime Strike Force indicted Scarpa. He pled guilty. While the strike force urged the judge to deny bail, FBI Special Agent R. Lindley "Mr. Organized Crime" DeVecchio, with Scarpa in tow, met with the judge. Scarpa received a $10,000 fine and five years' probation.[74]

Carmine brought it up during dinner with Carmine Sessa.

"I get pinched with just three credit cards and do time," Carmine says. "I get out. I'm eating dinner with Carmine [Sessa]. I ask him, 'How the hell did Greg get caught with hundreds of cards *and* testimony from a Secret Service agent, and *nothing* happens? Come on now.'"

Sessa shut the conversation down. "He stopped me cold, warned me to never, ever say anything like that about Greg to anyone unless I could prove it, and even then, I was better off keeping my mouth shut. *Or else.*"

And just what did "*or else*" mean on 13th Avenue when it came to Greg Scarpa Sr.?

In the mid-80s, while Carmine was in federal lockup, Scarpa Sr. told DeVecchio he suspected that Joe Brewster committed burglaries unsanctioned by the mob and heavily abused drugs.

> Linda Schiro told us, "Joe Brewster had started getting a little stupid." She recalled a visit by DeDomenico to the couple's home. "He was kind of drooling," she said. "He was starting to use coke." Schiro told us that Scarpa was also disturbed because he had asked his friend to "do something"—an unspecified crime—and been refused by DeDomenico, who said he was becoming a born-again Christian, an awkward creed for a mobster.[78]

Tension was brewing between Scarpa and Brewster for some time. Brewster worked heists with other crews, including Lucchese associates Sal Fusco and Frank Smith. He did not report those jobs to Scarpa or share any of the proceeds. Then, Brewster gifted a pair a diamond earrings to Scarpa's daughter.

Still, Scarpa was best man at Brewster's wedding, and Brewster stood as godfather to Scarpa's daughter. But on 13th Avenue, business is business. Joe Brewster was not falling into line. He was also a threat based on his participation in numerous murders and scores of robberies committed by Scarpa Sr., Scarpa's son, also named Greg, and other crew members, enough to put them all away for life.

78. "Tall Tales of a Mafia Mistress," By Tom Robbins, *The Village Voice*, October 23, 2007

Those crimes included the December 3, 1980, murder of Eliezer Shkolnik, an abortion doctor in Forest Hills, Queens. Shkolnik was jealous of an affair Scarpa carried on with Shkolnik's clinic partner and former girlfriend, Lilani Dajani, a former Miss Israel beauty pageant winner. *New Yorker* journalist Frederic Dannen reported in a 1996 article that Scarpa Sr. ran off with Dajani to get married in Las Vegas, even though he was still married to his first wife *and* had taken up with Linda Schiro, to start a second family.[79] Police found Shkolnik shot to death in the vestibule of an apartment building in Queens. This was the first murder committed by his son, Greg Scarpa Jr.

According to a report in *The New York Sun* by famed Mafia reporter Jerry Capeci, "DeVecchio allegedly told Scarpa that mobster Joseph (Joe Brewster) DeDomenico had 'found God' and was prepared to tell the truth if subpoenaed, and that Patrick Porco, a young drug-dealing buddy of Scarpa's son Joseph, was talking to police, sources said."[80]

Confidential informant Mario Parlagreco later testified to accompanying Scarpa Sr. on two trips to visit Colombo Capo Anthony "Scappy" Scarpati in prison, seeking sanction to murder Brewster.[81]

"Joe was never under Greg, but a *made* guy who, like Greg, reported up to Scappy, so Greg needed permission," Carmine says. "And Joe was real popular, so that's another reason Greg knew he needed permission to make his move."

According to testimony by Parlagreco, Scarpa Sr. gave Scarpati two reasons. The first, Brewster refused a "piece of work" assigned by the Family. Second, Brewster was

79. "Mole's New Slay Shocker – 5th 'Rap' on FBI Man in 'Miss Israel' Triangle," by Alex Ginsberg, *New York Post*, April 28, 2006

80. "Ex-FBI Agent Probed for Aiding Mob Hits," by Jerry Capeci, *New York Sun*, January 12, 2006

81. *We're Going to Win This Thing: The Shocking Frame-up of a Mafia Crime Buster*, by Lin DeVecchio and Charles Brandt, Berkeley, 2012

dating a born-again Christian and his loyalty was now questionable, at best. Scarpa also played up Brewster's cocaine use; appallingly hypocritical, considering how he himself was flooding South Brooklyn with drugs.

"That was all bullshit," Carmine says. "Greg was a greedy pig and suspected Joe was not sharing from some of his robberies. But again, Joe didn't report to Greg; they both reported to Scappy. So Greg couldn't complain about that or then maybe he gets in trouble for doing shit he's not supposed to be doing. But what he said on the record about the drugs and possibly ratting them all out was enough."

On the second prison trip, according to Parlagreco, Scappy passed along an approval from Carmine Persico condemning DeDomenico, supposedly stating, "If he found God, it's time for him to join God."[74]

Carmine remembers when Joe Brewster told him he was called in by Scarpa Sr. "At the end, he said to me, they called him in, told him it was a big meeting with all the *made* guys to discuss Family business, to make sure he wore a suit, but Joe said something was wrong, said he knew he wouldn't be coming back. He asked me... that if anything happened to him, to help take care of Belinda. I asked him, 'Why the hell are you going then?' I didn't get it. But with Joe, his balls were bigger than his brains. He walked in to get slaughtered, to show them that he wasn't afraid."

Joe Brewster then revealed something rarely ever seen on 13th Avenue.

A conscience.

"Joe told me the reason he found God was he felt bad about all the murders. They haunted him. He was never a born-again Christian like they said, but he did start back at church, even made a shrine in his house, with saints and candles. Joe never cooperated and never would've cooperated. He was the most stand-up wiseguy you'd ever want to meet. But he was a threat to Greg because he wouldn't bow down. And he knew enough to bury Scarpa and the entire Wimpy Boys crew ten times over; not just with the feds, but with the Persicos."

Joseph "Joe Brewster" DeDomenico was found murdered on September 17, 1987. He was shot four times in the backseat of his parked white Buick Regal. The car's motor was still running. Parlagreco testified in court later that on that day, Greg Scarpa Jr. arrived at his garage in Bensonhurst with driver Joseph "Joe Sap" Saponaro. DeDomenico was already slumped dead in the backseat. They pulled the car into Parlagreco's garage, wiped it clean of evidence, then dumped the vehicle with DeDomenico's body still inside.

Greg Scarpa Jr. was the godfather of DeDomenico's daughter.

At the separate trial of ex-FBI Agent Roy Lindley DeVecchio, accused of providing Greg Scarpa Sr. with tips that resulted in the deaths of four victims, Dr. Melissa Pasquale-Styles, a forensic pathologist, testified that DeDomenico died from three gunshots to the head and one to the left side of his chest. She also testified that on the night he was murdered, DeDomenico had been drinking heavily. DeVecchio was acquitted at trial of any charges.[82]

Carmine read about Brewster's assassination in the newspapers. He remembers feeling overwhelmed by sadness, helplessness... and clarity. "I said to myself, when I get that call, like Joe did, I'm not going in like he did," Carmine remembers. "And if I had no choice, then I'm going in with two guns blazing, like Lucky [Luciano]. I'll worry about the consequences after the smoke clears. I swore I'm not going out like that. No way. No how. Not me."

Carmine likens Joe Brewster's decision to the scene in *Donnie Brasco*, the Hollywood film about a federal agent who infiltrated the mob, where Bonanno Solider Benjamin

82. "Examiner testifies in trial of accused mob informant," by Anthony M. Destafano, *New York Newsday*, October 22, 2007

"Lefty Two Guns" Ruggiero willingly went to his death. In real life, in April 1993, Ruggiero, plagued by lung and testicular cancer, was released from prison after serving almost 11 years. He died on November 24, 1994.

"But that scene, where Lefty gets dressed in his best suit, leaves his jewelry behind, the money clip, and goes in knowing he's going to be whacked, was exactly what happened with Joe Brewster," Carmine says. "That's how brainwashed they are, still wanting to live, and die, by that code. But really, he was killed though treachery and deceit."

The murder of DeDomenico reverberated down 13th Avenue and throughout South Brooklyn.

"I can't say enough how Joe Brewster was so well liked and respected all around. This wasn't just another killing. Joe was a *made* guy, did a lot of work with a lot of people all over. After that, Carmine Sessa didn't want nothing to do with Greg, and Carmine came up with Greg. But Sessa and Brewster were close since they were kids. We all loved Joe. It was a sin."

During his testimony years later, Carmine Sessa reiterated his hatred for Scarpa Sr. for the DeDomenico murder, saying, "I was very upset about the murder of Joey Brewster."[52]

"It hit Bobby Zam just as hard because they were also very close coming up, and Bobby was beyond fed up with all the bullshit on the Avenue," Carmine remembers. "Of course, nobody could do nothing about it. It came down all the way from on top, from Carmine Persico. But we knew Greg made it happen, and it was fucked up the way he did it. This murder stuck with a lot of guys; like, what's happening to this thing if a stand-up guy like Joe Brewster could get killed over nothing? You had all the shit that came later, but I think that murder, Joe Brewster, was a turning point for a lot of guys on the Avenue."

As Sessa elevated, he provided some protection to Carmine, insulating him from Scarpa Sr. "When Carmine

[Sessa] became consigliere, I was thrilled," Carmine says. "Another time, there's this guy who bothered my niece who I wanted to hurt. Greg said we didn't need the heat. I went to Carmine, and he gave me the green light. I fucked that guy up like he deserved. And then I had a nice big smile for Greg. I didn't hide it and Greg couldn't say nothing because I got permission from Carmine, another *made* guy. But that was just one more thing between me and Greg."

Little did Carmine know the extent of the jeopardy he was in with the Mad Hatter.

Swimming with Sharks

By 1987, from 13th Avenue to Mulberry Street, there was blood in the water. The ties binding the Five New York Crime Families of the Italian-American Mafia together since 1931, forming one of the most powerful criminal syndicates this nation has ever known, were fraying.

Family hierarchies that endured generations were crumbling. Leadership was either incarcerated or incapacitated. The rank and file infiltrated. *That thing of theirs* was wounded.

Federal prosecutors scored stunning victories in the Commission Trial, sending the heads of four of the Five Families to prison for decades, along with other high-ranking mobsters. The convictions included three bosses—Anthony "Tony Ducks" Corallo (Lucchese), Anthony "Fat Tony" Salerno (Genovese), and Carmine "the Snake" Persico (Colombo). Also convicted were Christopher "Christie Tick" Furnari (Lucchese Consigliere), Salvatore "Tom Mix" Santoro (Lucchese Underboss), Gennaro "Gerry Lang" Langella (Colombo Acting Boss), Ralph Scopo (top Colombo labor racketeer), and Anthony "Bruno" Indelicato (Bonanno hitman).[42]

Meanwhile, high-profile trials against John Gotti, Philip Rastelli, and Carmine Persico dealt blow after blow, crippling each borgata.

''This has been the Mafia's worst year,'' Rudolph W. Giuliani, US Attorney for the Southern District of New

York, stated in a press conference and quoted widely in the media. Giuliani's prosecution of the Mafia helped propel him to the mayoralty of New York City by 1994. ''We keep making gains and they keep getting moved backward,'' Giuliani crowed. "If we take back the labor unions, the legitimate businesses, eventually they become just another street gang. Spiritually, psychologically, they've always been just a street gang."[83]

Not quite. However, the rot set in long before Giuliani came along. During his 1962 testimony before a US Senate subcommittee, turncoat Genovese mobster Joseph Valachi revealed how the Commission, the ruling body of the Mafia, closed its membership books in 1957 in the wake of the arrests of high-ranking gangsters, including his boss, Vito Genovese. Prior to Valachi's defection, Genovese marked him for assassination.[84]

Then, in 1976, the Commission agreed to "open the books," permitting each Family to induct 10 new members. They had to be strong earners, loyal, and not facing legal problems. Carmine Galante, the Bonanno boss recently released from prison, championed the about-face in membership policy. Galante, and the bosses who sided with him, argued that the Families needed fresh blood.

Carlo Gambino disagreed, but was overruled. He correctly predicted that adding so many so fast would draw future informers into their midst. Investigators reported that Gambino sought to dissolve some, if not all, of the weaker Families and consolidate into a single super-Family under

83. "The Mafia of the 1980's: Divided and Under Siege," by Robert D. McFadden, *New York Times*, March 11, 1987

84. *The Valachi Papers* by Peter Maas, Harper Perennial, 1968

his leadership.[85] As a compromise, they agreed on the 10 new-member per-Family limit. [86]

The 4-1 vote was captured in an FBI memo sent to FBI Director Clarence Kelley on February 17, 1976.[87]

That was the same year FBI Agent Joseph Pistone infiltrated the Bonanno Family as low-level jewel thief Donnie Brasco.[88] It was also the same year that Salvatore "Sammy the Bull" Gravano was inducted into the Gambino Family.[10]

Then, on October 15, 1976, Carlo Gambino died at his home in Massapequa in Long Island, New York, removing the final obstacle to new inductions.[89]

"Looking back, that's when this thing started to turn, when they started handing out buttons to all the wrong guys," Carmine remembers. "Used to be you had to earn your stripes. Now that's not the case. I can't believe some of the clowns that got *made* back then, just because their father was this guy or their brother was that guy. And some of these jerkoffs, even if they weren't *made*, they acted like it just because of who they were related to."

One night, Carmine visited the 2020, a club on 86th Street off 20th Avenue owned Sammy Gravano. Gravano later confessed to his involvement in 19 murders and hundreds of assaults as part of his testimony as underboss

85. "Gambino Believed Seeking Single Mafia Family Here," by Nicholas Gage, *New York Times*, December 8, 1972

86. "Five Mafia Families Open Rosters to New Members," by Nicholas Gage, *New York Times,* March 21, 1976

87. "Fateful 1976 NYC mob Commission vote to admit new members marked a Mafia turning point in retrospect," by Larry McShane, *New York Daily News*, May 31, 2020

88. *Donnie Brasco: My Undercover Life in the Mafia - A True Story by FBI Agent Joseph D. Pistone* by Joseph D. Pistone, Dutton Books, 1988

89. "Carlo Gambino, a Mafia Leader, Dies in His Long Island Home at 74," by Nicholas Gage, *New York Times*, October 16, 1976

of the Gambino Family in the trial that brought down John "the Teflon Don" Gotti.

Carmine and his friends were drinking in Gravano's lounge in the early morning after partying at Pastels. His group included Lawrence "Larry" Persico, the second oldest of Carmine Persico's three sons. At the time, the Colombo Family Boss was wrapping up an eight-year sentence for loansharking and hijacking.[6]

"I never got along with Larry because of how he carried himself," Carmine says. "So we go in and we hit the 2020. Larry orders drinks. Acting like a jerkoff, gets rude, tells the girl to put it on his tab. Then he slams his gun down on top of the bar."

Bad move. The 2020 was a popular spot, and even though it was late, there was still a crowd. Not just wiseguys, but also civilians. Many took notice. And the gun sat there. Didn't take long for Sammy to come charging out of the back room to confront Persico.

"I tell you, when I saw Sammy coming out from the back, I was shitting myself," Carmine says. "Everybody knew Sammy, what he's capable of, and this is his joint. Sammy comes out, goes right at Larry, shouts at him in front of the entire bar, says, 'I don't give a fuck who you are, I'll shove that gun right up your ass.' Of course, Larry put his gun away."

Sammy later had choice words for Carmine. "Sammy knew me from the neighborhood and he liked me, and we got along great, so he pulls me to the side and gives me shit for hanging out with Larry." Carmine laughs. "Sammy knew what happens when you hang out with a guy like that, looking for respect he'll never earn. He told me to 'stay away from him. Sooner or later, you'll get caught up in all his bullshit. But he can always run to his daddy. Who the fuck are you gonna run to, Carmine?'"

Rank and file, like Carmine, grinded it out on the street. Guys like Larry—the sons, the cousins, the nephews of the underworld elite—coasted on their last names.

To make matters worse, for the wiseguys at least, the United States government passed the RICO (Racketeer Influenced and Corrupt Organizations) Act, arming law enforcement with a powerful weapon. Before, a gangster had to be directly involved in committing a crime to be convicted. Now, they only needed to order or assist in the act.[90] So prosecutors could bring greater pressure on any member of the enterprise. This new legal weapon coincided with the nepotism and favoritism enabling more sure-to-fold-under-questioning members to be *made.*

Around this time, Carmine ran with a gambler known on the street as Joe Utt, for his mild stutter. Joe Utt was the son of Dominick "Baldy Dom" Canterino, a top captain for Vincent "The Chin" Gigante, boss of the Genovese Family.[91] [92]

Baldy Dom was a fixture at the Triangle Club in Greenwich Village, where he ran a powerful crew.[93] Canterino sometimes strolled the streets with the super-secretive Gigante, dubbed "The Oddfather" by the tabloids for wandering Little Italy in bed clothes to appear mentally disturbed. The ruse worked. Chin avoided prosecution for decades. However, in a plea deal in 2003, Gigante admitted to the charade. Already serving a 12-year sentence for

90. "Criminal RICO (Racketeer Influenced and Corrupt Organizations Act)," Excerpt from Trial, Volume: 22, Issue: 9, Pages: 40-47, By J F Lawless and LR Jacobs, The US Department of Justice, Office of Justice Programs; September 1986

91. "Vincent 'The Chin' Gigante, 'Oddfather' Mob Boss, 77," *The Washington Post*, December 20, 2005

92. "N.Y. crime boss admits he faked mental illness," by Anthony M. DeStefano, *The Baltimore Sun*, April 8, 2003

93. *Chin: The Life and Crimes of Mafia Boss Vincent Gigante*, by Larry McShane, Citadel Press, 2016

racketeering, Gigante dodged an additional decade in prison, but a judge still tacked on three more years. Gigante died at the Medical Center for Federal Prisoners in Springfield, Missouri, on December 19, 2005.

Baldy Dom was a major player. In 1988, Canterino was convicted of conspiring to extort $1.25 million from a record producer and sentenced to 12 years in federal prison. Two years later, he was convicted as a defendant in the sweeping Windows Case. The investigation snared members of four of the five New York Families for extorting nearly $150 million from 1978 to 1990, rigging bids on window contracts for the New York City Housing Authority.

Carmine knew Joe Utt from the neighborhood. The Canterinos hailed from Bensonhurst.

Joe Utt was trouble. "The word went out and all the bookies were told, 'Don't take Joe Utt's bets,'" Carmine says. "He got into jam after jam, lost crazy amounts of money, and he'd always run to his family to bail him out. Anyone else, you'd find them in a barrel out in the Narrows."

Joe Utt parlayed his connection to his father and Gigante to pressure bookies, even claiming the Genovese don was his uncle. "No matter how many times he got jammed up, Utt found someone to gamble with. He was one of those guys who had no problem saying, 'Don't you know who my father is?'"

Time after time, an embarrassed (and enraged) Canterino settled his son's bets, then dispatched him to some mob-controlled joint to work off the debt, including a high-class Midtown Manhattan restaurant. Utt hated waiting tables, felt it was beneath him.

One night, Carmine and a couple of the 13th Avenue guys met up at the restaurant. "We're waiting at a table, couple of drinks, watching Utt half-assing it, itching to get off," Carmine remembers. "He hated that job, hated any job. And we're breaking his chops, so he's getting pissed."

"Excuse me, sir, there's a hair in my soup," an annoyed customer complained to Utt, their waiter.

"So what?" Joe Utt quipped. "One hair? What do you want for $14? The full fucking wig? Go fuck yourself." And just like that, this high-end Midtown Manhattan restaurant was short one waiter for the rest of the shift.

"You sure, Joe?" Carmine warned as they walked out. "Your dad's gonna be pissed."

"Sure I'm sure," he said. "I'd rather kill myself than work here another minute. Let's get the fuck outta here."

You'd think Joe Utt would've laid low for a bit. But then you didn't know Joe Utt like Carmine knew Joe Utt. "Gamblers gotta gamble, it's a sickness," Carmine says. "Word was out on the street that anyone who lent Joe a dime or took as much as a football sheet off him would be disrespecting The Chin. But Joe didn't care. He actually went on a tear."

Carmine wouldn't take Joe's action. Utt respected his refusal. But not all wiseguys on 13th Avenue were as wise. "Joe went to Greg Junior first, and didn't have to try hard to get him to take his bet," Carmine says. "Greg Junior was a cocky fuck who thought he'd get away anything because of his father.

"So you had a Colombo soldier's kid taking a bet he shouldn't be taking from a Genovese captain's kid, and both of these guys didn't give two shits about the rules. Anyone else gets hurt for stuff like this. But these two guys? Nothing. Turning this thing into a joke."

Not only did Joe Utt lose $10,000 with Scarpa Jr., but he convinced Bobby Zambardi to provide the $10,000 loan.

"So Joe loses with Greg Junior, borrows from Bobby, and that's on top of who knows how many tens of thousands of dollars he placed with bookmakers and loan sharks all over the city," Carmine says. "Utt's a frickin' maniac, all over the place. Now, they're all in trouble, but see, Bobby

Zam is in a worse spot because he's the one guy in this whole thing who can't run to his daddy for cover."

Joe Utt went into hiding.

At Carmine's apartment.

"Joe's smoking a cigarette, looking out the window—apartment's on the third floor—and he gets all wide-eyed and can't get out the window fast enough. Broke the screen," Carmine remembers. "Not even a minute later, Baldy Dom and these two goons kick in my door. They tear through the apartment, look out the window, see Joe running down the block like his ass is on fire, and they climb out after him, down the fire escape. *Really*. And even after all that, Joe don't stop."

There were *some* consequences.

"I helped Bobby Zam get straight with that. Bobby was a good guy, one of the best, so I had no problem talking to Joe Utt to help keep things quiet. As for Greg Junior, Jimmy Ida slapped him around in Sirico's, but that was nothing. So now, the rules apply to some guys but not to others. Things like this were happening more and more, and we're all just watching this thing turn to shit."

Later, Zambardi was elevated to captain of Carmine Sessa's crew, when Sessa was named to consigliere by Carmine Persico, under Acting Boss Vic Orena. However, legal trouble derailed Zam from rising further in the rackets.

According to testimony by Joseph Ambrosino in the federal trial against Michael Sessa, "in 1991, petitioner was promoted to acting captain for Robert Zambardi, who was facing a parole violation charge at that time, and acted as the head of a crew that included as members Ambrosino, Larry Fiorenza, Richie Brady, Mike DeMatteo, Louie Ganoli, Carmine Imbriale, Michael Bolino, Anthony Coluccio,

Frankie 'Steel' Pontillo and Anthony 'the Arab' Sayegh."[94] Zambardi died in federal prison in 2014.[95]

Where Carmine flourished under Carmine Sessa, he struggled when the crew's leadership passed to the younger Sessa. "Carmine [Sessa] wasn't greedy like some of the other captains, who always had their hands in your pocket," he says. "I was always into something. Like I'd get a haul of VCRs and I'd just take one out of my trunk and give it to him. Another time, when I was working in Hunt's Point, shaking this guy down, I asked Carmine what he wanted from what I took."

Instead, Sessa told Carmine to give Bonanno Solider Benjamin "Lefty Two Guns" Ruggiero $350 a week. "Lefty was in a bad way, and I liked Lefty anyway. Carmine was smart, and like I said, he wasn't greedy. But his brother, Michael, he was a pig."

Michael Sessa was insecure, handed a position he didn't earn, and not respected by his reports, especially Carmine. Yet it didn't matter. Carmine had to abide by the rules.

The animosity between Carmine and Michael began years earlier. In 1975, at 18, Carmine was not yet a Colombo associate, but he was a Neddy's regular. Carmine was also a top stickball player, when they still ran large neighborhood tournaments. Michael Sessa sponsored a team. One Saturday, there was a grudge match scheduled between Sessa's team, the 69th Street Boys, and a team from Bath Beach.

Stickball was serious business in South Brooklyn back then, from trash talking and bragging rights to heavy wagering. "So Michael puts together this big rivalry game; he knows I'm one of the best stickball players around, so he insists I play," Carmine says. "I didn't like Michael from the

94. "United Stated vs. Michael Sessa 92-CR-351 (ARR), 97-CV-2079 (ARR)," January 25, 2011

95. "Fat Larry Released from Prison: Promises to Go Legit," The Colombo Crime Family

start. I didn't commit, but did say I'd try to make it, which was true. I did try."

There was a popular hair salon called Rosie's on 13th Avenue between 77th and 78th Streets, across from Neddy's Bar. Carmine was friendly with the family that ran the shop, and he conducted business from the location. Whenever he entered, he was greeted by the family pet, one of those small white fluffy dogs. The afternoon before the stickball tournament, the shop's side door was open. The pooch ran out and was creamed by a delivery truck, leaving a bloody gash in the street right outside the shop. The owner was distraught. Carmine, an animal lover, felt compelled to do something.

"That Saturday morning, I told my friend Billy I had to go to the pet store."

"You know you got to play in the game for Michael," Billy warned.

"Fuck the game," Carmine responded.

Carmine went dog shopping. However, finding that same type of dog took most of the day. When he brought the dog to the salon as a gift, the owner was overjoyed. It gave Carmine a good feeling.

"Next day, Michael's pissed because, of course, they lost," Carmine says. "He wanted to know where I was, why I wasn't at the tournament. I said I was busy."

Carmine couldn't care less what Michael Sessa thought. "I was just thrilled to get free haircuts from then on," Carmine says. "But I *always* left a big tip."

As both Sessa brothers rose, Carmine ran into more trouble with the duplicitousness of dysfunctional Family business, like when Michael Bolino headed to prison.

In 1988, a federal judge sentenced Alphonse "Allie Boy" Persico to 25 years in prison for a 1980 conviction, the same case where Bolino received a five-year sentence. Persico jumped bail before sentencing, went on the lam for seven years before he was captured in West Hartford,

Connecticut. Persico had good reason to flee. Having previously served 17 years of a 20-year sentence, he knew he faced hard time.[96, 97] Bolino was Allie Boy's bodyguard and chauffeur when Persico stepped in as acting street boss, with his brother incarcerated.

Colombo turncoat Joseph Cantalupo captured 15 months of incriminating conversations with Bolino and Persico on a body mic and his wiretapped Lincoln. The son of a Brooklyn real estate dealer, Cantalupo had a gambling addiction that got him into deep trouble with the Colombos.[98] One recording captured Allie Boy beating Cantalupo over a $10,000 debt. Cantalupo later penned a Mafia tell-all in 1990, *Body Mike: An Unsparing Expose by the Mafia Insider Who Turned on the Mob*.[99]

Carmine and Bolino were longtime friends on 13th Avenue, even went in together on a string of armed robberies. "Mike used to rob banks, dressed up in a wig and high heels," Carmine says. "I always asked him to let me know when the next job was, and he let me in on a few jobs with him."

Bolino was also a loan shark with lot of Colombo money on the street when he went away. With Bolino sidelined with prison, his collections needed collecting, deadbeats needed deadbeating. So Michael Sessa assigned Bolino's book to one of his most promising earners.

96. United States v. Persico, 853 F.2d 134 (1988) No. 988, Docket 87-1545. United States Court of Appeals, Second Circuit. Argued April 19, 1988. Decided August 4, 1988

97. "Judge Sentences Reputed Mob Figure To 25 Years," by Vera Haller, The Associated Press, December 19, 1987

98. "United States vs. Alphonse Persico, No. 988, Docket 87-1545," Argued April 19, 1988

99. *Body Mike: An Unsparing Expose by the Mafia Insider Who Turned on the Mob*, by Joseph Cantalupo and Thomas C. Renner, St. Martin Press, 1991

Unfortunately for Carmine, Bolino's book was a disaster. "I knew Mike's book was fucked up, but I didn't know just how bad things were when I took it over," he remembers. "But Michael Sessa says, 'You're taking over Mike's shylock book,' and I had no choice. I had a lot of my own money on the street to deal with. What a headache."

Before Bolino reported to prison, Carmine insisted he introduce him to his customers.

"That's when Mike broke down, admitting most of the customers were phony. Mike begged me not to tell. Half those guys didn't even exist. They were actually Mike's own debts. But you could get killed over something like that. We're talking a lot of money. I had to cover all this for Mike while he was away. Basically, I got screwed."

Carmine tried to refuse the assignment. "I said, 'I got a hundred grand of my own on the street and enough problems,' but Michael didn't want to hear it. So I got stuck and had to keep Mike's book going."

Carmine collected what he could and made up the difference, handing in $3,500 a week to Sessa on Mike's book alone. "I couldn't give Mike up, he was a good friend, and he was a *made* guy," Carmine says. "The whole time, Michael Sessa keeps asking me how I liked the extra money. If he only knew the truth. But if I said anything, Mike [Bolino] would've been killed. I *had* to keep it going."

If Carmine needed any reminder of what was at stake for Bolino, he got it shortly after the loan shark reported to prison.

Mike Bolino's brother Anthony was a muscled-up local kid with an attitude. "Tony used to come around 13th Avenue and talk shit to everyone," Carmine remembers. "But for some reason, he *really* didn't like Carmine [Sessa], and he gave Carmine a lot of shit.

"Tony would call Carmine [Sessa] a fake tough guy, shit like that. I pulled him to the side and told him to stop. I even got word to Mike in prison to try and get him to get his brother to cut it out. But Tony kept it up. Only now, Mike wasn't there to deal with it."

Anthony Bolino, 24 years old, was murdered on the corner of 13th Avenue and 78th Street in May 1988, by a single gunshot wound to the head. Another Bolino cousin had been murdered earlier, just a few doors down from the crime scene. Anthony Bolino's case remained unsolved, though detectives suspected it was a mob hit. Carmine Sessa later confessed to the murder.[100] Yet at the time, he covered it up. Carmine did not learn of the deception for years.

"I later heard that Carmine personally shot Tony in that hallway, and wanted to cut off his hands and almost did, but cops passing by surprised him," Carmine says. "He copped to it when he flipped. But back when it happened, he blamed it on the Luccheses. So now, we're arguing with them over this thing, and Carmine Sessa got us all convinced it was them. People coulda gotten killed over that bullshit. To find out all those years later that he did it, that just blew me away. He didn't have to kill him, you know. That's when I realized what an evil piece of shit he was."

Another time, Carmine Sessa put out an all-hands-on-deck call for the Neddy's crew to rush out to Staten Island.

"Carmine Sessa's other brother, Anthony, owned a scrap yard," Carmine remembers. "He had words with a guy who owned the car dealership across the street, who spit in Anthony's face. So they go in with like 30 guys over this shit, and they shoot the guy. This is a regular guy, a civilian, with like four kids. Even if you can't settle it with hands, that's what you do? Run in there like cowboys shooting? There's a right way to do things, and then the stupid-ass way. It really was getting to be grown men acting like kids, only with guns, and your best friend could be the one who kills you."

---

100. "A mobster's trail of bodies," by Dave Goldiner, *New York Daily News*, September 29, 2000

Things got worse for Carmine under Michael Sessa, especially when his captain started charging him an unfair rate. "I built up my own shylock book from nothing to more than 100 grand," Carmine says. "Then Michael says to me everybody now got to pay two points; but I didn't know everyone else in the crew is actually only paying one."

Carmine, like other members in Sessa's crew, should have been able to borrow money at an interest rate of one percent. Then, depending on who he was lending to, he'd provide loans at between five and seven percent. Those are *weekly* interest rates, hence why these are called usurious loans (or unethical, immoral, at ridiculously exorbitant rates) and therefore illegal.

In court testimony, Joey Ambrosino corroborated the underhanded treatment. "Imbriale confirmed that [Michael Sessa] loaned him approximately $90,000 at two percent interest per week and that Imbriale would occasionally make the payments to Ambrosino."

In fact, when Carmine complained to Ambrosino about the high interest rate, Ambrosino revealed Michael Sessa's treachery. "I thought we were all getting ripped off by Michael, but Joey slipped and told me that I was the only one getting charged the two points," Carmine remembers. "I'm laying my life on the line and my captain's ripping me off? What the fuck? All these other jerkoffs are paying one percent. And Joey knew he screwed up by telling me, so then he tells me to not tell Michael how I found out. But after I argued about it with Michael, the second he got off the phone, he called Joey and gave him crap over it. Joey denied it, but Michael knew."

Remember, even if Carmine couldn't collect, he was still responsible for the interest. "I had to swallow it, and it wasn't right. But even at two points, I was still taking home $4,700 a week just on my own book. Sure, I'm spending it as fast as I'm pulling it in. Then, I get stuck with Mikey

Bolino's book and paying off his loans, so that cuts my take-home in half."

Too bad Carmine never had a mob captain for a father, uncle, or brother.

Going to War

One late morning in June 1991, Carmine made his rounds in Brooklyn. Picked up a couple of collections. Took a few bets. Checked up on some of this, handled some of that. Nothing memorable.

Then Carmine strolled into Neddy's Bar a bit after noon.

Carmine saw troubled expressions, hands being run through hair, ashtrays overflowing with chain-smoked cigarette butts. Something was going down.

Carmine Sessa ordered him to turn around, rush home to Staten Island, throw on a suit, and get his ass back to Neddy's, soon as possible. No fucking around, Carmine. This is serious.

A sit-down was set out in Long Island later that afternoon. Sessa wanted Carmine by his side.

That high-stakes summit would determine the fate of the Colombo Crime Family, one of the largest criminal organizations in America at the time. The Colombos were on the brink of civil war, the third such conflict for the dysfunctional crime family since the 1950s. Its hundreds of members and street associates were aligning into two factions.

The storm had been brewing since the early 1980s, following a period of relative calm for the Colombos. In the early 1970s, the Family fell under the control of Carmine "The Snake" Persico and Underboss Gennaro "Gerry Lang" Langella. Unlike other Mafia dons who enjoyed more lengthy careers outside prison walls, Persico was beset by a litany of legal disasters from early in his reign.[6]

By 1985, Persico stewed in federal lockup on racketeering convictions, in part due to wiretaps justified by information Greg Scarpa Sr. funneled to federal investigators.[74] At trial in '86, Persico racked up 39 more years of incarceration; Langella was hit with 65 years. Those convictions paled in comparison to the Mafia Commission Trial in '97, slamming key members from the Five Families with massive sentences. Persico and Langella each received 100 years in prison.[101]

Whereas most of the other Mafioso convicted in the Commission Case were aging wiseguys, Persico was in his prime. However, the Snake never again slithered outside a federal prison.[102] Yet Persico stubbornly insisted on keeping the Colombos firmly in the hands of himself and his bloodline, including brothers, sons, and cousins.

To manage the Family's day-to-day street operations, Persico tapped his brother, Alphonse "Allie Boy" as acting boss, only to see the feds take him off the streets in a loansharking conviction.

More convictions followed for the Family. Four captains (John "Sonny" Franzese, Anthony "Scappy" Scarpati, John "Jackie" DeRoss, and Dominick "Donny Shacks" Montemarano) and various soldiers and associates were imprisoned.

Persico named a three-man panel to run the Family, tapping Vittorio "Vic" Orena, Joseph Russo, and Benedetto

101. "Judge Sentences 8 Mafia Leaders to Prison Terms," by Arnold H. Lubasch, *New York Times*, January 14, 1987

102. "Carmine Persico's 'Commission' case sentencing a miscarriage of justice, insured Colombo family boss' death behind bars: lawyer," by Larry McShane, *The New York Daily News*, March 31, 2019

Aloi.[103] Persico later dissolved the panel and Orena was named sole acting street boss in 1987.

Initially, Orena seemed a solid choice to stand in as acting boss. He owed his success to Carmine. Persico not only named him captain, but *made* him when the Colombos opened the books. Alphonse Persico even sponsored Orena for membership.

Orena wasn't a cowboy. A remarkable earner, he built a powerbase throughout Queens, Long Island, and New Jersey, mostly in labor racketeering, loansharking, gambling, and more. Orena dressed well and projected an aura of confidence.

The narrative picked up in the media had Orena orchestrating a palace coup. He supposedly chafed under Persico's iron grip, frustrated with an imprisoned mob boss slow to make decisions, hindering the Family's ability to grow.

According to federal case files for Orena's 1997 trial, "in early 1991 Carmine Persico announced that Allie Boy, upon his anticipated release from prison in June 1993, would become boss of the Colombos. The announcement raised tensions between Family members loyal to Orena and those loyal to Persico."[103]

The actual sequence of events does not support that clean a narrative of usurper attempting to seize the throne. Prior to the outbreak of hostilities, in the late 1980s, as acting boss, Orena began inducting new Colombo members, but only those on his side of the Family, creating unrest throughout the borgata in Brooklyn. Orena was also bumping up soldiers to captains, but again, favoring those closer to him. The power was shifting away from South Brooklyn out to Queens.

---

103. Orena v. United States, US District Court for the Eastern District of New York - 956 F. Supp. 1071 (E.D.N.Y. 1997) March 10, 1997

As the power struggle engulfed the Family, Colombo Consigliere Vincent "Jimmy" Angelino was found murdered, on the orders of Orena. Carmine Sessa shot Angelino in a basement in Kenilworth, New Jersey. Following the hit, Vic Orena appointed Carmine Sessa as consigliere in recognition of Sessa's loyalty. Sessa had been spending more time in Queens and Long Island, and had increased his loansharking and other Family business activities with Orena.

Orena then instructed Sessa to poll the captains in the Family to gauge who would support his bid for the throne. In a fateful meeting, Scarpa Sr. warned Sessa how the captains, especially the Persicos, would react to such a poll.

There are conflicting accounts about how the situation deteriorated after that meeting. In testimony and interviews, such as with Scarpa Sr. underling Larry Mazza, Sessa supposedly panicked. Other accounts, as with Colombo Captain Michael Franzese (imprisoned on a parole violation at the outbreak of the shooting war), maintain Sessa went directly to Theodore "Teddy" Persico to report Orena's treasonous request to poll the captains. Teddy got word to his brother in prison, who ordered a hit on Orena.

Whatever the story, Sessa assembled a hit team, including Henry "Hank the Bank" Smurra and John Pate, and headed to Long Island to ambush Orena on June 21, 1991. The attempt failed when Orena, returning home, spotted the assassins and fled the scene.[103]

Had Sessa succeeded, there never would have been a Third Colombo War. (Note, there were two preceding conflicts, the First Colombo War in the early 1950s, when Captain Joseph "Crazy Joe" Gallo failed in an attempt to unseat then boss Joseph Profaci. The Second Colombo War broke out in 1971, when Gallo was released from prison and launched a second coup, also unsuccessful and leading to Gallo's murder.[104])

As things stood in 1991, the Colombo Family entered a tense period of uncertainty, as nearly 90 *made* members aligned under Orena and up to 30 inducted members sided with Carmine Persico, including Persico blood relations. It was during this standoff that Sessa barked at Carmine to run home and put on a suit.

Sessa's handpicked crew was heading to Long Island. This was one of several meetings held to broker terms for peace. Long Island made sense for the sit-down. No way was Orena coming down to 13th Avenue. Long Island was safer. Dozens of ranking Colombos, mostly aligned with Orena, had migrated out to Nassau and Suffolk Counties during the 1980s.

The meet was set for Stella's Restaurant in Floral Park, an Italian restaurant owned by Tommy Petrizzo, a Colombo captain elevated by Orena. A prosecutor later labeled Petrizzo a "liaison for the Colombo Family on the organized-crime construction panel that has a stranglehold on the New York City-area construction industry." Petrizzo was involved in multimillion dollar bid rigging. (Despite the fact that one of Petrizzo's daughters, Joanne, married Carmine Persico's son, Michael, the captain sided with Orena. The couple separated in 1991.)[105]

Stella's was one of two primary Long Island restaurants Orena used to conduct Family business. The other was The Manor Restaurant in Merrick, owned by Tommy Ocera, a Colombo solider. According to testimony, Orena had been using The Manor on Monday evenings up until the fall of 1989, when Suffolk County Police staged a raid and confiscated Ocera's loansharking records.

---

104. "Colombo Family – The Youngest of the 'Five Families'," American Mafia History, October 19, 2015

105. "Double Portrait of a Man on Trial Astounds Friends," by Selwyn Raab, *New York Times*, April 11, 1995

This was a disaster or Ocera. Now the feds had evidence implicating Orena. Vic already suspected Ocera of skimming proceeds of the loansharking and gambling operations. Ocera also murdered Greg Reiter, the son of a close associate of Gambino Boss John Gotti. Sammy Gravano later testified how Gotti revealed that "they whacked Tommy Ocera." Ocera was murdered by Greg Scarpa Sr. on November 13, 1989, on the orders of Orena, killed in the home of Colombo Captain Pasquale Amato and dumped in a shallow grave. Orena was later convicted of conspiracy to murder Ocera, and the hit was a precursor of the Third Colombo War.[103]

Also accompanying Carmine Sessa to the sit-down at Stella's was Michael Sessa, Robert Zambardi, who by then had taken over Sessa's crew, and Lawrence "Larry Tattoo" Fiorenza. Carmine and Larry were the only attendees accompanying Sessa who were not *made* members of the Mafia.

"This was a big honor, for me to be invited by Carmine to something like that with Vic," Carmine recalls. "Carmine Sessa said to us, 'Don't talk unless I ask you something.' They agreed on no guns, which was even more of a reason to have guys like me and Larry on hand."

Not everyone was elated with Carmine's good fortune. Joey Ambrosino was miffed he'd been passed over for this important meeting. Like Carmine, Ambrosino was a Colombo Family associate, and the two were frequent confederates on crimes. Joey Brains got his nickname from an incident when a NYPD officer chased him through the streets of Bensonhurst, according to 2007 testimony by mob informant Larry Mazza. With the cop right behind him, Ambrosino ducked into a door of a club on 13th Avenue: The Wimpy Boys Social Club.

"Right away, Joe Brains was upset he was not invited. But Carmine picked Larry because he was a big guy, and he picked me because he knew me better, trusted me, and I could handle myself if something went wrong.

"We took one car, all of us, went to Long Island to this mom-and-pop restaurant, where we met in a private back room," Carmine remembers. "Vic came with his two sons and Petrizzo."

They sat facing each other across the table. Food was served. They shared small talk about minor Colombo Family business, common acquaintances. "One of the things that came up was Bobby Zam sharing how we just lost a good guy in Joe Brewster. When Bobby brought up Joe Brewster, Vic said he knew the name, and asked Bobby about Joe. Bobby turned to me, told Vic how me and Joe were close, and I could tell him all about Joe. I told Vic I loved the guy, how he was a role model for what a wiseguy should be, and he was a mastermind at robbing banks."

Carmine Sessa grew agitated at the mention of Joe Brewster. "Carmine wanted to move on 'cause he didn't take the news of Joe's murder lightly," Carmine recalls. "It bothered him a lot, with him and Joe so close. Not just Family business, but friends. Carmine [Sessa] didn't want nothing to do with Greg [Scarpa] after that murder."

Orena said one more thing to Carmine. "Vic turned to me and Larry and said, 'So you're the two guys getting your mustaches shaved soon; good for you,'" Carmine remembers. "Vic meant we were going to be *made*, which was a surprise. But it was exciting, especially to hear it from him."

That revelation would be bittersweet. "Who knows what would have been. But what happened was, Michael [Sessa] took over the crew when Bobby got jammed up, I was stuck under him, and then the war started."

The conversation turned to the purpose of the meeting. Orena slyly recounted the many Colombo Family woes with having a boss incarcerated. Too many things couldn't get done. Decisions were not being made. Beefs were lingering unresolved.

No offense, but the time had come for change.

"Vic asked [Sessa] if they could work together, meaning to move [Persico] aside," Carmine recalls. "Carmine refused him flat, told Vic that he had his orders. Carmine asked Vic what he was willing to do, if he was willing to step down, step aside. Vic refused. They went back and forth, neither willing to give in on anything. The only thing they did agree on was there should be no shooting, and we all know how that turned out."

As the discussion wound down, Orena offered to show the Brooklyn Colombos around the area. They declined, shook hands, and parted, again agreeing there would be no shooting.

The Orena faction broke the peace first. On November 18, 1991, William "Wild Bill" Cutolo organized a hit on Greg Scarpa Sr. as a preemptive strike to take out the biggest threat on the Persico side. Assassins wearing ski masks ambushed Scarpa outside his home while he was with his wife and daughter. They escaped. Yet that set the murderous Scarpa Sr. off on a rampage.

Larry Mazza later testified that immediately after the attempted hit, he joined Scarpa Sr. to report to Anthony Russo, who agreed to contact Sessa, Joseph Russo, and others to let them know that "the shooting started." At a summit of Colombo captains and soldiers at the Brooklyn home of Russo's grandmother, the Persico faction laid plans to strike back. Carmine and Ambrosino later corroborated the events for federal investigators.[106]

---

106. United States vs. Monteleone, United States Court of Appeals, Second Circuit, July 20, 2001

Less than a week later, Persico soldier Henry "Hank the Bank" Smurra was shot to death while parked in front of a Brooklyn Dunkin' Donuts.[107]

In a flurry of ensuing body blows, Genovese member Gaetano "Tommy Scars" was murdered in an attack on Colombo Associate Joey Tolino (December 2); Persico Soldier Rosario "Black Sam" Nastasi was gunned down inside his Belvedere Social Club in Brooklyn (December 5); and Scarpa Sr. shot to death Orena loyalist Vincent "Vinnie Venus" Fusaro outside his home in Bath Beach.[108] In the Fusaro hit, Scarpa Sr. rolled down his car window, stuck out his rifle, and picked the man off with three shots.

"Vinny Venus wasn't even a soldier," Carmine says. "Vinny's crime was he owed Billy Cutolo money, plain and simple. Greg shot him just because he saw him *with* Wild Bill. But Vinny wasn't a shooter. He was only making loan payments."

Below is an account of the murder that ran in the *New York Post*, from testimony given by Larry Mazza at trial in 2012:

> We were passing by the social clubs where Vic's guys would hang out. This day we were on Bath Avenue and spotted Vinnie's car, so we came around the block again. He was in his driveway, hanging Christmas lights on the garage. He never seen us. He was facing the garage.
>
> Greg had an Army type of rifle, an M52. He says, "Don't even get out." He rolls down the window and hit him right behind the ear. It was a hell of a

107. "The 1990s Colombo Mob War Murder Timeline: NYC Mafia Clan In Chaos As Jailed Don Fought Off Insurgence," by Scott Burnstein, The Gangster Report, June 6, 2017

108. "Organized Crime: A Gang That Still Can't Shoot Straight," by Richard Behar, *Time Magazine*, June 24, 2001

shot. Guy went down like a sack of potatoes. But he shot him two more times—once in the neck and once in the body.[109]

After the Fusaro hit, Scarpa Sr. paged his consigliere with his signature satanic code (666) to report a fresh kill.[110]

The bodies were dropping fast and everyone was running for cover through December 1991.

Yet the worst was to come for the Colombo Family— and Carmine Imbriale.

---

109. "My life as a Colombo hit man," by Brad Hamilton, *New York Post*, March 4, 2012

110. "The G-man and the Hit Man," by Fredric Dannen, *The New Yorker*, December 8, 1996

Out of Hand

Can you be considered suicidal if you know you're dying?

Barreling into December 1991, the Third Colombo War in full swing, Persico's top button man, sixty-three-year-old Greg Scarpa Sr., was seriously ill.

Five years before, in 1986, Scarpa Sr. was rushed to Victory Memorial Hospital on 92nd Street in Fort Hamilton for a hiatal hernia operation. The procedure required a blood transfusion. Scarpa Sr. rejected stores from the hospital blood bank, preferring blood donated from a family member or friend. A quick search found a match with Paul "Paulie Pumps" Mele.

Mele was not the most popular guy on 13th Avenue.

"Paulie Pumps was a piece of shit," Carmine says. "He was a hanger-on, always lurking around, a slimy, sleazy scumbag that no one liked and no one respected. Always running his mouth, then running away. But he was Greg's boy. Greg fed off guys like that, always up his ass. That made Paulie just about untouchable."

Years earlier, Carmine's out at a night club with a bunch of the 13th Avenue crew, when Mele became involved in an altercation. "Paulie's drunk, loud, gets in an argument over some stupid shit, dancing like a clown, bumps into some guy," Carmine recalls. "Paulie don't know it, but the guy's a wiseguy. This guy's by himself, with his girl. He leaves, comes back with a gun. Paulie shits himself, can't run away fast enough, climbing over people. Joe Brewster steps in between them. Joe gets shot, twice, BANG, in the chest no less."

The flashes of the gun and loud blasts cleared the dance floor. Club emptied out in a stampede. Brewster survived the shooting, declined to comment to police. No video surveillance. No witnesses. The police had no one to arrest. But Brewster did catch up with the shooter down the line.

"We're out and about a couple months later, and Joe goes to the bathroom and runs right into the guy," Carmine recalls. "The guy's taking a piss. Joe's got the drop on him. Just the two of them. It's not a large bathroom, no room to move around. This guy's trapped, looks up, thinks he's about to get blown away. Joe tells him, 'Relax.' Guy finishes up, he's apologetic, even thanks Joe for not making an issue. Not with the cops. With the wiseguys. Like the stand-up guy he is, Joe accepts the apology. Joe knew the rules, knew what would happen. They're both *made*, and this guy broke the rules. You gotta get permission. That could've started something big, and it was all caused by that little weasel, Paulie Pumps."

While Brewster gave a pass to the guy who shot him, he held a grudge against Mele. But not much he could do, with Mele under Scarpa's wing. Moreover, Mele was in debt to the 13th Avenue crew for thousands of dollars they'd lose if he was found floating off the 69th Street Pier.

The best Brewster could do was antagonize Mele. "We'd be driving on the Avenue, see Paulie, Joe'd make me fly up on him like it was a hit, or roll up real slow, surprise him, break his balls, ask him to come for a ride with us to the Staten Island dump, stuff like that." Carmine laughs. "Paulie'd run off scared, right back to Greg, and tell on Joe. Then Joe'd get called in to Wimpy Boys. He'd go in, tell Greg, sure, he won't touch Paulie, but Greg can't stop him from breaking Paulie's balls. I mean, come on now."

With Scarpa Sr. scheduled for surgery, Paulie Pumps was more than willing to donate his blood. However,

Mele didn't know he was HIV-positive. The testers did not screen for the disease. Mele, an intravenous-steroid-using bodybuilder, contracted HIV from an infected needle and passed it to Scarpa in the transfusion.[111]

"But what they didn't report in the papers later was that Greg wasn't the only one Paulie infected. He made a lot of guys on 13th Avenue sick with those dirty needles. They all died miserable deaths. What a nightmare for all those poor families."

Scarpa's body shriveled from a muscular two hundred and twenty-five pounds to a gaunt one-fifty. His stomach had to be removed, and he digested his food with pancreatic-enzyme pills. Yet his trigger finger worked just fine. During the war, Scarpa drove through Brooklyn, hunting, usually with underling Larry Mazza, scouting social clubs and bars where Orena loyalists frequented.[112]

"We're at war, but life went on for the Families," Carmine says. "So you still had to make your stops, meet people, do business. But now maybe you didn't stay long, you didn't have that espresso or that beer. Because you never knew who was going to make a call and if maybe you'd be walking out into an ambush."

One high-profile target was William "Wild Bill" Cutolo, who orchestrated the failed attempt on Scarpa that prompted the shooting war. One evening, Michael Sessa summoned Carmine and other members of the crew, including Joey Brains, to Robert Montano's home on Staten Island to plan Cutolo's murder. They planned to drive to Cutolo's girlfriend's home off of Richmond Hill Road, where Cutolo was spotted with a group of Orena members, and "try to grab him, try to shoot him, kill him." However, by the time

---

111. "Settlement in Lawsuit on H.I.V.-Tainted Blood," by Mary B. W. Tabor, *New York Times*, August 30, 1992

112. *The Life: A True Story About A Brooklyn Boy Seduced Into The Dark World Of The Mafia*, by Larry Mazza

the crew arrived, each carrying a gun, Cutolo had already left.[94]

Michael Sessa ordered the hit squad to regroup the following Friday for a second attempt on Cutolo on Thanksgiving Day. Ambrosino testified that he, Michael Sessa, and Larry Fiorenza "were going to dress up as Hasidic Jews in costumes and murder [Cutolo] in front of his girlfriend's grandmother's home in Brooklyn, [at] 60th Street and 13th Avenue." As the "neighborhood that [Cutolo] was going to was a Hasidic neighborhood, [M. Sessa, Ambrosino, and Fiorenza] figured [they] could blend in with the crowd."[94]

Michael Sessa instructed Ambrosino to give six hundred dollars to crew member Anthony "the Arab" Sayegh to purchase the disguises, which were stored at Fiorenza's girlfriend's home, where she testified to seeing them.

However, on Thanksgiving morning, a *New York Post* article implicated Scarpa Sr. as a government informant, and fearing that Greg "knew about the plan and if he was cooperating, he would tell the law what [they] were going to do," Michael Sessa called off the murder.[94]

Next came an opportunity to take out Orena and several captains. In November 1991, Carmine Sessa beeped both his brother and Ambrosino, informing them Orena, Scopo, Petrizzo, and other targets were spotted in Ozone Park, Queens. The Sessa squad met at a diner on Rockaway Parkway. By the time they made it to the club in Ozone Park, Orena and Petrizzo were gone, leaving only Scopo, playing cards with a group of Gambinos. Carmine Sessa called off the hit.[94]

Soon after, according to court filings and testimony at Michael Sessa's trial, a team—including Michael Sessa, Joseph Ambrosino, and Carmine Imbriale—rushed out to Staten Island to hit Michael "Spat" Spataro, a member of Cutolo's crew. They met at a pizzeria off Huguenot Avenue before driving to Spataro's home on Amboy Road.[94]

The armed group drove past Spataro's home in a white rental car. Discovering Spataro not home, they patrolled Amboy Road for an hour before intercepting a police bulletin responding to a crime committed in the area by men driving a similar white vehicle. The group abandoned the hit.[94]

Then, the Third Colombo War took a disastrous turn.

At approximately 9 a.m. the morning of December 8, 1991, two gunmen entered Wanna Bagel on 3rd Avenue near 89th Street in Bay Ridge, and shot to death 18-year-old Matteo Speranza.[113]

The bagel shop was owned by two Colombo associates, but Speranza was not involved in organized crime, confirmed by Deputy Chief Emil A. Ciccotelli, commander of Brooklyn Detectives, at a press conference at the 68th Precinct. He was just a kid working toward a high-school equivalency degree. He wasn't even scheduled to work that morning, filling in at the last minute for a co-worker. He got the job two months earlier with the help of his mother, who knew one of the owners.[123]

The Speranza killing exploded in the media.

"When Mateo Speranza got killed, it really turned up the pressure," recalls NYPD Detective Thomas Dades, who was working out of the 68th Precinct during the Colombo War, covering Bay Ridge and Dyker Heights. "That's when we got involved very deeply as a conduit to the FBI, because we had extensive knowledge of the players. Billy Cutolo was in our precinct. Greg Scarpa lived in the 6-8, and then you had all the 13th Avenue clubs. Black Sam was also killed in the 6-8, and of course, Wanna Bagel, where Speranza was killed, was in our precinct.

"We recovered a can of soda one of the killers brought to the counter and that led us to the Liberatores, father and

---

113. "Killing Is Tied To Mafia War In Brooklyn," by George James, *New York Times*, December 9, 1991

son, who were supposed to kill the owners, and instead shot that kid," Dades says. "When we went to the Liberatores' home to arrest them, I was with Detective John DiCarlo, may he rest in peace. The mother laughed in our faces. Later, we took a door down with a ram on 99th and 4th. Chris Liberatore was in the apartment, had a pistol-grip shotgun in his hands he tried to dump. We collared him, and later, both Liberatores wound up cooperating."

Speranza was the fourth person killed within six days at the height of the war, but this was the hit that blew it open.[123] "When they killed that poor kid, everybody knew it was a mistake, all a big mix up," Carmine recalls. "But that one shooting really put the heat on. It was embarrassing. What are we now, like in the ghetto, we're pulling drive-bys, jumping out and shooting kids?

"That's when things started going downhill fast," Carmine says. "It's already in a tailspin, but after that shooting, on the street, back at Neddy's, it started to feel like things were falling apart, like it was every man for himself. It was all over the news. I felt bad for the kid's family. This wasn't mob business. This was out of bounds, a civilian, like when Gotti's son was run over. That also was an accident. So when they killed the guy who ran over Gotti's kid by accident, the papers ran with it forever. This shooting was even worse for us."

With public pressure mounting, on December 17, the Brooklyn District Attorney's Office issued 90 subpoenas, served 41, and dragged in 28 members and associates of the Colombos—from both factions—to State Supreme Court in Brooklyn. By then, key leaders on both sides were either imprisoned or on the run (Carmine Sessa and Vic Orena were already in hiding).[114]

---

114. "Brooklyn's Mob War Interrupted With a Quiet Day in Court," by Robert D. McFadden, *New York Times*, December 17, 1991

Brooklyn DA Charles Hynes was interviewed for a segment on Greg Scarpa Sr. entitled "Bad Blood" on *Street Stories with Ed Bradley,* a CBS television news program. "I have no problem letting these folks blow each other away," Hynes stated. "I think it's good for us, ultimately. The problem is, most of them don't get annual firing practice, so they started shooting at each other, they begin to miss, and they end up killing innocent people."[115]

None of the subpoenaed gangsters cooperated. Yet. Despite the pressure from media and law enforcement, the war raged on.

In January 1992, Carmine Sessa ordered members of the Neddy's crew to murder Frank "Frankie Notch" Iannaci, Carmine's childhood friend. Carmine was part of that hit squad, also including Michael Sessa, Ambrosino, and others. Iannaci, a Colombo associate, aligned with the Orena Faction as a member of Cutolo's crew.[122]

The group sat on Iannaci's apartment building in the Hamilton Houses on the corner of 101st Street and 4th Avenue for an hour. When a Hamilton House security guard appeared and took notice, they fled.[94]

"I knew Frankie wasn't there, but I went along for the ride," Carmine says. "In fact, I didn't tell Carmine Sessa, Michael, or any of the others about all the other times I ran across Frankie or other guys on the other side. I wasn't going to run and tell. Listen, these guys were not as hard to find as you'd think. Just look at how many of them Greg killed during the war."

One night, Carmine entered the bathroom of a Bay Ridge club on 3rd Avenue and faced Joseph Iannaci, surprising the father of Frankie Notch. Joseph was a longtime Colombo solider in his own right. "All right, let's get it over with," Carmine recalls the elder wiseguy saying, convinced he was about to be shot.

---

115. "Street Stories With Ed Bradley," *CBS News,* November 12, 1992

"I told Joe, 'Don't worry about it, go where you gotta go,'" Carmine remembers. "I didn't even know what side Joe Notch was on, but by how he reacted, I knew he was with Vic. But still, I couldn't whack Joe Notch in a bathroom taking a leak 'cause then I'd have to face Frankie down the line on it."

Next, Michael Sessa, Joey Ambrosino, Carmine, and others set their sights on Joseph "Joe Campi" Campanella. They targeted him at his home on Stillwell Avenue in Brooklyn, but when they did not see his vehicle in the driveway, they left. On another occasion, the hit crew attempted to locate Campanella at his shop on 16th Avenue between 63rd and 64th Streets in Brooklyn, but were unsuccessful.[94]

Many other attempts failed, but the reason was not captured in court records.

"Of course we never found Joe Camp, or Frankie Notch, or Billy Cutolo, or any of those guys, because that idiot Michael [Sessa] had us out driving around in the middle of the night," Carmine remembers. "You're not gonna find gangsters hanging out on street corners at three in the morning. But in a way, Michael's stupidity was God looking out for me. It was good thing we never found those guys. I didn't want to kill nobody. Not over all that stupid shit."

With every attempted assassination, near miss, and confirmed kill, tensions rose on both sides of the Colombo divide.

"I changed up my routines and habits during the war," Carmine says. "I used to have money dropped off at the florist, so then, instead, I had it dropped off at the butcher shop. The next week, I'd change it up. Everyone's nervous. Everyone's changing things up. You knew it wasn't smart to be sitting in one place for too long."

This was the 1990s before smartphones. They used electronic pagers and payphones.

"I had multiple beepers and different payphones I used, when the phones still called back," Carmine says. "If I had to go meet someone, I tried to bring someone else with me. You had to be smart, careful, aware of your surroundings. You didn't know, maybe you walk into a bar, and you run into the wrong guy. Maybe someone sees you. Maybe you see someone first. Or maybe you see each other at the same time."

Around every corner, someone could be waiting.

"In the middle of all this mess, Joe Sap passed away," Carmine remembers, referring to longtime Colombo Solider Joseph Saponaro. "Joe Sap and John Sap were with Greg, always outside Wimpy Boys, so of course we all had to go and pay our respects."

The wake was held at a funeral home in Bay Ridge. Carmine arrived to a viewing area jammed with dozens of Colombos. "We're all at this wake, and suddenly, the beepers start going off, beeping and buzzing all over the room, and that meant we had to go outside, all at the same time," Carmine says. "So there's like 20 of us huddled together like a pack of penguins. Car's there, window rolls down, we get called over. Carmine Sessa gets out of the car, and we have to walk him in. So, he's in the middle of all us, we're like his human shields, expecting any second to hear the gunfire. The feds are across the street snapping pictures. When I got arrested later, they pulled out those pictures and wanted to know who was in the middle of the huddle."

Not long after, Carmine strolled into a Brooklyn barber shop, there's about three customers ahead of him. He grabbed the paper, about to sit down, glanced at the mirror, and saw, in the chair getting a shave, Colombo Soldier Vincent "Chickie" DeMartino.

They froze.

Right before the war broke out, DeMartino was released from prison, after serving time for a bank robbery. Chickie was on the Orena side, definitely a shooter, so likely armed.

But here, he was tilted back in the barber chair facing the mirror, his back to Carmine, the barber cape wrapped around him.

"We're staring at each other through the mirror, and Chickie knew that no way he'd be able to draw in time," Carmine recalls. "But I didn't make a move. We just stared at each other."

The barber instinctively took a step back.

"We good here?" Chickie asked.

"I said, 'Yeah, we're good,' and I left," Carmine says. "I liked Chickie. Never had a problem with him. When Chickie said he was on Wild Bill's side, we were all shocked, but it made sense after what happened to Bird."

When DeMartino left prison, he joined William Cutolo's crew, aligned with Orena. That crew also included Joseph Petillo, Dominick Dionisio, Michael Spataro, Ralph Guccione, Michael Donato, and the captain's son, William Cutolo Jr. DeMartino participated in the first failed attempt on Scarpa Sr.[103]

Chickie was one of a slew of Colombos Orena *made* as the acting boss consolidated his power. But Chickie didn't start his career on that side of the Family.

"I thought Chickie would have come with us, but he wanted a shot at Carmine and Michael [Sessa], to get back at them over Bird." Anthony "Bird" Coluccio, a well-liked associate of the Colombo Family, and a member of the Neddy's crew, was murdered in May of 1989 by Michael Sessa and Joey Ambrosino.[103]

"A couple months back, we robbed a jewelry store in Staten Island off Arthur Kill Road," Carmine says. "Michael sets it up, says to meet at six in the morning. He picked two guys to go into the store, but when we got there, for whatever reasons, they didn't want to go in."

The next day, again, early morning, Michael picks two different guys to go in, and then these two didn't want to go in.

"Bird's fed up, says he's not coming down at six in the morning no more, unless I was the one going in with him, so that was the plan," Carmine says.

Next morning, Carmine and Bird don masks, enter the store, and hold it up at gunpoint. Henry "Hank the Bank" Smurra was assigned to drive the getaway car. Michael Bolino and Joseph Ambrosino were on standby in a crash car, half a block away.

"So, now it's the third day, six in the morning again, we go in, me and Bird, beat the shit outta the owner, rob the place," Carmine says. "We come running out and there's no car. I don't know what spooked Hank, but he took off. He's gone. No cops, no alarms, nothing. Not even no one walking a dog. What a jerkoff. He just left us there. I don't know what Joey was waiting for, but finally, he rips out of the spot, screeches up, we pile in the crash car. Michael's on the radio screaming, just a mess."

The robbery crew drove to Carmine Sessa's home. Smurra arrived minutes later.

"I'm pissed, so when Hank comes in, I pull my gun on him, and they gotta hold me back and calm me down," Carmine says. "Hank leaves. Two weeks later, they straighten him out. I couldn't believe that. This coward. He runs away in the middle of a job, when there's not even a threat. Now, this guy gets *made*, right after that mess? What a joke. Made sense he was the first to get whacked during the war." Months later, the first official casualty of the Third Colombo War, Smurra was gunned down in Sheepshead Bay getting donuts with Mike "Black Mike" Calla, who escaped the ambush. The shooter was Chickie DeMartino.

"I let it go, but not Bird," Carmine says. "He was pissed about the whole thing and went on and on about it." Coluccio put in a complaint to Carmine Sessa, not only about Hank the Bank, but also Michael Sessa and Joseph Ambrosino. But by this time, Coluccio was already on thin ice with the Sessa brothers.

Carmine Sessa ordered his brother and Ambrosino to "kill [Coluccio] in the car and dump him off on Third Avenue under the highway where the Puerto Ricans hang out, in a drug-infested neighborhood; let everybody think that the drug dealers killed him." Michael shot Coluccio three times in the back of the head in a car driven by Joseph Ambrosino on Staten Island, followed by another car driven by Hank Smurra.[103]

The Coluccio murder did not sit well with many of the Colombos. Coluccio was popular with soldiers throughout the Family, with a reputation as a proven earner and loyal associate.

In the months leading up his murder, the story was that Coluccio was dealing drugs, taking drugs, committing armed robberies, and not sharing with the crew. According to court testimony, during a meeting with Michael Sessa, Carmine [Imbriale], Coluccio's wife, and Mike Bolino, Michael Sessa stated, "Bird is up to his old shit again."[103]

Coluccio also participated in murders with Carmine and Michael Sessa. Their cover story had the murder as a preemptive strike, out of fear he'd cooperate if arrested. But that wasn't what really went down.

"For one thing, Michael was having an affair with Bird's wife, and in this thing, you don't do that, ever," Carmine says. "Disgusting. That shows you the kind of man Michael was. Just because you give a man a button, and he takes an oath, don't make him a real man. So when Bird was complaining about Michael, Michael knew he was a threat, so he killed him. It was a sin what they did to Bird."

DeMartino wasn't the only Colombo incensed by the Coluccio murder. Carmine was even approached at a local bar with a proposal. "During the war, Frankie Notch and Chickie reached out to me, made me an offer to set up Michael," Carmine says. "I was giving Michael my shylock money every week, so it would've been real easy for me to set him up."

Carmine admits that the offer sounded attractive. "I hated that piece of shit and he had it coming. But I said, 'I can't do that.' I still liked Carmine at the time. I respected Carmine, but not Michael. So even though I hated him and it was a great idea to end the war, and I would get to keep the money, I never went against them. In a way, I regret it."

After the Third Colombo War, DeMartino was sent back to prison to do four more years on weapons charges.

As the war wore on, with Scarpa Sr. and Mazza racking up even more hits, Michael still had little to show his brother. "Michael's getting all kinds of shit from his brother to go out and look for people," Carmine says. "But still, Carmine don't know we're going out in the middle of the night. I don't know if Michael was scared, or stupid, or whatever. But he gave the orders, and he's the captain."

They say New York is the city that never sleeps. "But out in Brooklyn, at that time of night, all you got is sanitation workers and *Daily News* delivery guys." Carmine laughs. "Night after night, nothing. We'd get home for 5 a.m., say better luck next time. It was a joke."

Then Scarpa Sr. scored a stunning hit on Nicholas "Nicky Black" Grancio. When Grancio stepped outside a social club on McDonald and Avenue U, Scarpa Sr. crept up in his Toyota Land Cruiser SUV and blasted him with a shotgun.

That hit was not in the middle of the night.

Grancio was involved in the earlier attempt on Scarpa Sr. and his family. A vengeful Scarpa Sr. exited his vehicle and shot Nicky Black again, in the face. The brazen hit was later reenacted in the series *I Lived with a Killer* in the episode about Larry Mazza.

Nicky Black's murder was the topic of conversation in every café and social club in Brooklyn. "That's when Carmine found out what his brother was doing," Carmine says. "He comes in the bar, starts yelling at Michael,

'What's with this three-in-the-morning bullshit? Who the fuck is going to be out at that time, so stupid.'"

Michael talks back to Carmine, who's not just his brother, but his boss. "You don't talk back to a boss," Carmine says. "But Michael talks back, and does this is in front of other people. So then Carmine goes after Michael. Michael runs out of the bar. Like a clown show. This is what this thing was coming to, stupidity and bad leadership. But there was nothing we could do but follow orders from these idiots."

Next came the double homicide of Orena Soldier Johnny Minerva and his friend Michael Imbergamo. The pair were gunned down on March 25th while sitting in Minerva's car outside the Broadway Café in North Massapequa.

A reprisal followed two days later.

On March 27, 1992, Thomas Gioeli and other Persico loyalists were ambushed. During a high-speed car chase, Gioeli caught bullets in the shoulder and stomach, earning him the nickname Tommy Shots and a reputation for toughness. In the mid-80s, after his release from prison on robbery counts, Gioeli became a top earner in Orena's crew and was inducted into the Colombos.

As the conflict progressed, "Tommy Shots was just one of many Colombos who switched sides during the war," Thomas Dades says. "That shows you how out of control this thing became. It was a mess. Made no sense and nobody wanted any part of it. But they were all stuck and had to pick sides or switch sides."

Gioeli later rose to the position of boss, before Federal Judge Loretta E. Lynch slammed him with 224 months in prison in 2014 for a slew of murders and racketeering charges spanning the Colombo War in 1991 up through 2008.

Meanwhile, the war provided convenient cover for Scarpa Sr. to settle scores and eliminate threats, and not just DeDomenico and Coluccio. Lorenzo "Larry" Lampasi, an Orena loyalist, was shot-gunned to death while leaving his Brooklyn home to go to work at a school bus company. "Larry Lampasi wasn't killed because of the war but because he was a threat to Greg," Carmine says. "Larry went to Carmine [Sessa] and said he was hearing bad things about Greg on the street. Carmine said to Larry that you better make sure you're right because Greg is not the kind of guy you want to fuck with. Carmine must've said something to Greg, and that got Larry killed. "

On the witness stand, Linda Schiro said, "There was talk on the street" that Scarpa was an informant. "This fucking Larry Lampasi," she quoted Scarpa Sr. as telling DeVecchio, "he started rumors I'm an informer, that I'm a rat."

"Greg was using the war to tie up loose ends, like Bird and Larry," Carmine says.

Little did Carmine know at the time, that he was also one of Greg Scarpa's loose ends.

The Beginning of an End

In the summer of 1992, the Third Colombo War in full swing, NYPD Detective Tommy Dades sat in the squad room of South Brooklyn's 68th Precinct.

Exhausted closing out a double shift, Dades was about to receive a tip that set in motion a series of events, not only helping to end the War, but send dozens of mobsters away for lengthy prison terms.

The mob on 13th Avenue never recovered.

For Detective Dades, it involved a familiar face. Tommy Dades grew up in Sunset Park, and knew Carmine Imbriale well. Years earlier, the two men dated sisters and struck up a friendship.

As an NYPD detective, Dades was not investigating the Colombo War. Organized crime investigations are the jurisdiction of the FBI, at times involving other agencies based on the crimes involved, including the DEA, the ATF, and other entities.

Yet as a homicide detective, Dades often worked with the feds to connect the dots between crimes and criminals in his South Brooklyn precinct (the 6-8 covers Dyker Heights, Bay Ridge, and Fort Hamilton, all traditional Mafia strongholds).

"I was in the office, last to leave, and I'm in the 6-8 squad room. I don't know how the guy got past the front desk, heavyset guy, crying to talk to a detective. It was like two in the morning, and I said, 'Unless it's a dire emergency, we'll get a radio car to take you home.'"

This man insisted, telling Dades he had a trunk full of stolen merchandise. "I asked him why, out of nowhere, was he now in the precinct telling me this," Dades says. "He leans in again and says, 'I don't know if you know what's happening in the street, but there's a war going on out there.'"

Of course Dades knew. Many of the murders during the Colombo War occurred in his precinct. "I was a homicide detective with the 6-8, so not on the taskforce investigating the Colombo War. But I did investigate the murders within the precinct. Also, in the precinct, you had Neddy's and Wimpy Boys, Wild Bill's club, Veterans & Friends, and a hundred other spots. The Persicos, the Scarpas, Christie Tick, Gaspipe, Jimmy Ida, Joe Waverly, the list goes on and on. This was a Mafia stronghold for years with so much of that activity focused in and around 13th Avenue."

Still, Dades was heading home. It'd been another long day, and he was more than ready to refer this potential informant to the front deck. That's when this character mentioned two familiar names.

"He asked me if I knew Carmine Imbriale and Joey Brains Ambrosino," Dades says. That's how it is in South Brooklyn, where everybody is connected by only a couple degrees of separation.

Dades grew up about two miles from Bensonhurst, in Sunset Park. "Sunset Park is not too far from Bensonhurst, but they're two different worlds," Dades says. "Sunset Park was poorer, but more diversified. And where they glorified the gangsters in Bensonhurst, we hated them in Sunset Park. Growing up, we fought those Bensonhurst guys. Back then, every neighborhood had beefs with other neighborhoods, just how it was. But Bensonhurst was close enough that you had this familiarity. I had relatives on 13th Avenue. Michael Sessa was a member of my gym. So it wasn't the same circles, but you knew people, knew faces, knew a lot of the same guys. Same world, small world."

After the relationships with both sisters fell through, Carmine and Tommy remained friendly over the years, as much as a homicide detective and street hustler can.

"Carmine is very funny, a comical guy, make you laugh at the drop of a dime, and I liked him, I think most everyone who met him did," Tommy says. "But early on, before he became affiliated with organized crime, Carmine had a reputation as more of a street guy, a tough guy. Carmine hung around on 13th Avenue with a lot of rough guys, guys like Mikey Bolino. I locked Mikey up a bunch of times, and that guy was just infatuated with that whole 13th Avenue gangster lifestyle."

Tommy knew Carmine was affiliated with the crew from Neddy's Bar. "Those bars on 13th Avenue were dangerous," Tommy recalls. "In Neddy's Bar, the crew was younger. Still a rough crowd, but sometimes—not all the times, but sometimes—you could walk in there on a Sunday afternoon maybe, have a beer, watch a ball game. But in bars like Wimpy Boys and Flipside, you walk in there without knowing someone, they'd hand your ass to you, and that's if you were lucky."

As a homicide detective in the 6-8, Dades had a ringside view to the escalating violence.

"On 13th Avenue, it was all treachery, a lot of murders. They'd kill them in the bars, drag them out, dump them somewhere else. Bodies being dumped all over the place, many we found, but many we never found. They'd come up with different excuses to try and kill you, something you did, or may have done, or may do, or they'd think you' do. You're involved with that scene, like Carmine, it was always a possibility it goes wrong and you get killed in one of those bars and buried in some basement under fresh concrete."

Still, with the War raging and so much criminal activity escalating, Carmine was not on anybody's radar. "Carmine was like half a wiseguy, and there were a hundred guys right there, all doing the same thing Carmine was doing, day in, day out. So, when this guy comes into the precinct that night and says Carmine's name, that definitely got my attention." Dades sat back down, asked this potential informant to tell him more about Imbriale and Ambrosino.

"He said the stuff downstairs was *their* merchandise, and they were forcing him to steal," Dades says. "He said he had five kids and didn't want to get killed, but couldn't keep it up with them. So Carmine and Joey Brains were basically using this guy as a gopher, and I could see it in his eyes; he was afraid for his life."

That evening though, Dades was wiped. "I said, 'It's late, I'll help you, but you got to come back in the morning,' and we exchanged beeper numbers. I went home to shower, change, eat something, came back in, called George Terra— used to be a detective and was now in the DA's office. He did a lot of organized-crime cases, and he was later my boss in the DA's office. I called him, told him the story, and invited him to come down."

Again, Dades could not actively investigate this lead if it crossed into organized-crime territory. "We did the murder investigations that fell in our precinct, but for this we needed to get the DA involved. Also, I knew Carmine prior, so I didn't want to be involved intimately. I had to relay the information. Our office didn't do investigations like that. So George came down, met the kid, and the kid was very informative. Then the FBI got involved and the DA's office goes on to use this informant to take a run at Carmine. I'm out of it at this point, so it's all with the FBI and DA's office."

That conversation changed the trajectory of Carmine's life. "Before that night, no one was really looking at Carmine," Dades says. "But they quickly connected the dots because of his heavy involvement with Sessa's crew in the middle of the war. That really got their attention, and they just jumped all over that lead. Now, Carmine was a definite target for investigation and they threw resources at him."

Dades referred the man, Fat Billy, to federal investigators. "Fat Billy was a delivery driver for Artistic Florist on 13th Avenue, and the fat little pig used me as bait because I was a bigger fish," Carmine says. "He was a bum. Guy was a mess, never had his shit together. I gave him money, helped him out all the time, so I never thought in a million years he'd turn on me."

Fat Billy traded his extensive knowledge of Carmine's criminal activities. Based on the information he provided to investigators and subsequent surveillance, the feds amassed a substantial amount of evidence on Carmine.

"Then Billy sets me up, says he wants me to help arrange a drug buy, some weight, says he has a buyer all ready, so I say okay, seeing an easy score," Carmine says. "But I'm not into drugs. I don't have a connection. I'm just planning on ripping Billy off. But all this other stuff is going on with the war and then my collections. I'm all over the place. But Billy, see, keeps beeping me, calling me, annoying the shit out of me to get this deal done. Now I realize that all along the feds were using Billy, trying to locate me."

Eventually, by June of 1992, Fat Billy helped nail Carmine down to a specific location. The feds rushed to converge on Carmine.

"He's calling and calling and he gets me at home, so I gotta deal with him now, so I says okay. We set up a meet for later that day in Staten Island. I say I got the drugs. But before I hang up the phone, I tell him, 'If you fuck this up, I will kill you.' And that's all the feds needed to hear to move in. On top of all they had, now they got me on tape threatening Fat Billy; and they also think I'm holding the drugs. But there never were any drugs. I was just gonna rob that fat bastard."

As Carmine hung up the phone, he heard the screeching tires and saw the blues and reds bouncing through his window blinds.

"Billy kept me on the phone long enough for the marshals to get there and surround my house, guns drawn, like a movie," Carmine says. "My wife is there, my kids are in bed, so not like I can climb out the back window and leave them to have these guys bust in with guns. I walked out slowly and surrendered."

"They had enough on Carmine to easily get him a 25-to-life sentence," Dades says. "The feds grab him up, and they talk to him, basically telling him the reality of what he's facing. So Carmine knows he's done, plus whatever else the FBI will get him for as the investigations continue."

"When they took me in, I asked what it was about," Carmine recalls. "They wouldn't tell me nothing. But later I learned it was on usury [shylocking], illegal gambling, assault, robbery, and a bunch of other stuff, and that it was also a RICO case, so I'm facing down 25-to-life, and whatever else they'd throw at me."

Until that arrest, Carmine never knew how close the feds were on his heels. Now he was sitting in a federal lockup in Lower Manhattan, his life in the balance. One morning, guards came, cuffed Carmine and led him to an interrogation cell.

"A federal investigator, George, comes in, says he wants me to listen to some tapes," Carmine says. "I got no idea what I'm about to hear, so I'm thinking they're gonna play back a recording of me involved in some things. I already knew they got me cold, so what do I care what they got on tape? Only that's not what they played back."

It was a series of recordings, multiple conversations. There was background noise and the sound quality was rough, but Carmine recognized the voices on the tape. One clip involved Greg Scarpa Sr. and Larry Mazza plotting Carmine's murder, discussing in detail how it needed to be done secretly. In another recording, Michael Sessa ordered Joey Ambrosino to dig the hole.

Up until that point, Carmine was frustrated and disillusioned with his crew, yet did not suspect he was being targeted for murder. "During the war, I could almost put two and two together, but I never knew for sure. When the FBI first approached me to cooperate, made me listen to those tapes, I realized they were not only trying to kill me, but this goes back to '91, and I was arrested in '92. That tape of Michael and Joey Brains saying they had to get rid of me, that just blew me away."

Then the feds confirmed Carmine's suspicion of Greg Scarpa.

"Of course I suspected Greg was cooperating," Carmine says. "But to actually hear it's true, from a federal agent, made me even more angry, realizing I basically never stood a chance out there."

Carmine faced a dilemma. There was the certainty of life in prison, with a high likelihood of being murdered before he even made it to trial. Even if he did survive, he'd spend decades in prison, his family left to fend for themselves without him, without any help.

On the other hand... the once unthinkable.

"In lockup, when they told me about at least two unsanctioned attempted plots on me, I was pissed off. I'm out here laying my life on the line, and they're looking to kill me? I seriously considered the fed's offer when they asked me to cooperate. It's not an easy decision. You got to agree to leave all your relatives and friends, leave everything behind, never come back. But I started to see this as something else—a second chance, for me, my wife, my family. Every time I went out the door, worrying if I would come back, that was wearing on me and my wife. I didn't break the rules. They broke the rules trying to kill me. And now I knew, without a doubt. They wouldn't stop until I was dead."

While in lockup, Carmine thought long and hard on his situation.

"They were trying to flip Carmine when I got involved," says defense attorney Darrell L. Paster, who represented Carmine following his arrest through his agreement to cooperate with the federal government. "I entered at a point where Carmine had done some of his own negotiating. They decided he needed a lawyer, and so the Court called me."

However, Paster was instructed to go to the US Attorney's Office and not the federal court house in Downtown Brooklyn. "That's unusual," Paster says. "Normally, a person arrested is interviewed by the court system, you meet that person in the marshal's office in the federal court house, then he's brought before the magistrate, assigned an attorney, and then a decision is made if bail is to be set. That's not what happened here. With Carmine, they didn't bring him before a magistrate."

Paster immediately assumed involvement with organized crime. "When you're busted in federal court, they give you all these conditions, including travel restrictions. That's one of the reasons the US attorney decided not to bring Carmine in front of the magistrate in federal court, because they didn't want him to have to adhere to all of these restrictions."

They wanted Carmine back on the street.

As a Colombo associate, Carmine was called upon to make trips to other jurisdictions, including Florida. "Carmine was always going to Florida for one reason or another for his mob bosses, whether to courier money or whatever. So if Carmine had to follow these restrictions, and they flipped him, it would make that cooperation difficult, if not impossible, if he could not travel outside the New York area," Paster says. "How would he ever explain that to his mob bosses? See what I mean?"

Paster's assignment was not random. "I was very active in the United States Eastern District Federal Court," Paster says. "I did a lot of work with cooperating witnesses. I just finished a major Gambino case that lasted six months. I knew the judges and clerks and staffs, working with them day in and day out. I knew the rules, that there's a certain element of trust that has to exist. So I got a call from one of the magistrates, someone from their staff actually, and was asked if I would take on this defendant, Carmine Imbriale."

There was urgency; the more time Carmine spent in federal lockup and was a no-show at Neddy's, the more suspicion would grow on 13th Avenue.

Meanwhile, the district attorney wanted more than passive cooperation. Entering the fall of 1992, the height of the Colombo War, they wanted Carmine back on the street, wearing a wire, gathering evidence.

"See, I knew they were trying to kill me, but they didn't know I knew," Carmine says. "They also had to be careful because they had to kill me in a way that didn't lead back to them. And these are the treacherous bastards I'm going back to on the street."

Remember, despite an ongoing Colombo civil war, business was business, and the life had to go on. Payments to crew chiefs were not optional.

"Remember, everyone in Carmine's world was very sophisticated; this is a deadly business," Paster says. "So someone like Carmine cooperating, they have to take certain steps to not be discovered. The wiseguys are so paranoid and suspicious, Carmine really had to be careful. And they're always scheming, very cunning. Carmine was definitely in mortal danger."

Underworld Undercover

At the time Carmine Imbriale was arrested, RICO wasn't the only statute motivating organized crime figures to cooperate with the US government.

In the 1980s, the United States Congress and state legislatures passed a series of tough-on-crime bills that required mandatory minimum sentences be applied to those convicted of specific crimes.

"I'd say at least 90 percent of federal defendants at least *tried* to cooperate because of the mandatory minimum sentencing guidelines," Paster says. "That's just how the system worked back then. Someone could get busted for a low-level crime, even first offense, and face more than a decade in jail."

Paster explained that judges had almost no discretion. "But based on the value of that cooperation, the defendant's sincerity, and other factors, *then* the judge could be flexible and not apply the guidelines," Paster says. "So the system really promoted defendants cooperating with the government, but that meant really delivering true value."

By the fall of 1992, Carmine was delivering such value, operating on the street, without the cover of Carmine Sessa, who was in hiding.

Strict federal guidelines issued by the United States Department of Justice are very clear governing the use of confidential informants, who are "authorized only to engage in the specific conduct set forth in the written authorization" and that "under no circumstance may the CI participate in an act of violence" or commit other illegal offense.

"FBI agents were very experienced dealing with these guys and made accommodations, looking the other way, not hardcore criminal activity, more of what we'd call mischief," Paster says. "So they were probably breaking the law, but not serious crimes."

Not long after agreeing to cooperate, Carmine became embroiled in some of this so-called "mischief."

"There was a big issue early on, after Carmine beat somebody up," Paster says. "Being a former boxer and street fighter makes for a great loan shark, but not so much for a cooperating witness. Once Carmine began cooperating, he was told he could not do that anymore; the government can't have cooperating informants going around beating up people." Carmine was called in for a sit-down, but instead of wiseguys across the table, it was members of the District Attorney's Office about to kill his deal and likely send him to prison for the rest of his life.

"Fortunate for Carmine, he was able to justify the fight and it blew over. But really, that's the kind of thing that can kill your cooperation, which he realized. See, Carmine may have dropped out in high school, but he's bright, charismatic, funny, and above all, shrewd. But he'd have to be to be able to operate on the street."

Technically, Carmine was prohibited from collecting from his loan shark customers. "The FBI would give me a bag of money to pay off Michael," Carmine remembers. "What they didn't know was that I'm still collecting on some of my debts, which I kept quiet."

With Colombo gunmen lurking, an alphabet soup of law enforcement agencies surveilling, conducting business became complicated for Carmine. "When Carmine [Sessa] and Michael had people to meet, they used different spots along the New Jersey Turnpike," Carmine recalls. "So, when I had to turn money over to Michael, it was usually at one of those Bob's Big Boy restaurants."

With at least three Bob's Big Boy restaurants on the NJ Turnpike—at rest stops in Montvale, Cheesequake, and Atlantic City—things got confusing. "They kept switching spots," Carmine says. "So everyone with a book went to a different place on the Jersey Turnpike to turn in their money, to throw off the agents or the wiseguys from the other side."

Not only was Carmine driving out to Jersey every week to make a drop, now he also had to meet with his attorney. To throw off suspicion, they met in secret, late at night, at Paster's Court Street office in Downtown Brooklyn.

"I remember Carmine coming in and pulling out a wad of bills," Paster says. "I don't know if the rest of the bills were fives and singles, but always hundreds on top. All these mob guys did this. Part of their shtick, flashing money. But the court paid my fee."

Yet as time wore on, Paster noticed a change in Carmine. "I felt he wanted to get out of the life. He was still a young guy, wife and kids. Though he never said this directly to me, I got the feeling he was sick of being in the mob. I tried to steer him in a direction where he wouldn't get killed and could please the government enough to get a deal done and escape that life. I sensed a need to break free that, more and more, drove him... changed him."

This high-wire balancing act between violent and mistrustful underworld figures and aggressive, zealous agents had Carmine on edge.

"I shredded everything, didn't want nothing in the house, got rid of all my old shit," Carmine says. "I changed my routines and habits again, and not just because of the war. It was intense."

In a *New York Post* article, Carmine revealed how during this period, three assassination attempts failed, including one where Joey Ambrosino and a hit squad came to his house on multiple occasions. He was only able to avoid murder because he could not leave his home, with his wife and children, due to a migraine headache.

"Joey came into the house and I was on the floor, throwing up," Carmine says. "They couldn't kill me in the house because my wife and kids were there. Remember, Carmine [Sessa] had not sanctioned the hit on me. So killing me was one thing, but not my family. And this was before I helped them plant the bug in Joey's car that led to him cooperating. Joey already killed, so I have no doubt that he would have shot me if he could have gotten me out of the house that night. And on top of Joey and Michael Sessa trying to kill me, then I learn Scarpa had put Larry Mazza on me for a hit."

When the feds asked Carmine to wear a wire, he knew he could not refuse. But he could have some fun with it. "Every time I put on a wire and was preparing to go to meetings, I'd sing Frank Sinatra's 'My Way,'" Carmine says. "So, on every one of my tapes, you hear that. That was my warm-up routine."

The technology for listening devices had come a long way. "They called it a wire, because that's what it was, a wire," Carmine recalls. "Sure, you could find it if you knew what you were looking for. Wasn't much to it. I taped it to my lower back and wasn't worried about it at all. I even played stickball with it on, wore it all over 13th Avenue, in and out of Neddy's Bar and Wimpy Boys, like nothing."

Though a small device, it could still be found on Carmine, and at least one episode nearly proved disastrous. "I'm at Joey Ambrosino's for a party for his daughter. Everyone's there, the whole crew. His daughter spills something all over me. Joey's wife, Lucille, wants to take my shirt and throw it in the dryer. I had to physically push her off me and run outta there. It was a close call. Luckily, no one suspected nothing."

Carmine, wearing a wire, returned to the Ambrosino home a few days later to drop off money, but instead of Joey, he found Lucille. "She just wouldn't shut up," Carmine says. "Not only did she take the money, but she's saying out loud who's getting what, saying this goes to Lefty [Ruggiero], this goes to Carmine Sessa. Then she's writing all this stuff down, keeping records. That was a great tape for the FBI. She was blabbing on and on, giving it all up. I couldn't keep a straight face in her living room."

The feds were not quite ready to make their move. They didn't have enough on Ambrosino. However, Carmine's recordings provided the justification for a warrant to wire Ambrosino's vehicle.

Joey Brains had his fingerprints on so many of the crew's operations, and his car was frequently used to conduct crew business. However, placing the listening device was problematic as Ambrosino was very active, and even when not in his vehicle, it was usually parked in his garage.

"They asked me to help bug Joey's car, and I couldn't refuse," Carmine says. "If Joey or anyone in the crew would've seen me, they would've killed me on sight. But really, what choice did I have? I was in this thing with the feds all the way. Cooperation is more than just answering questions. If I wanted any hope of minimizing jail time, I had to do everything I could to help their investigations."

However, Carmine was not a surveillance technician. Installing a listening device in an automobile requires more than slapping a tape recorder under the dash with some duct tape. Carmine needed to separate Ambrosino from his vehicle for the brief time it took an FBI specialist to bug the car.

An opportunity presented itself. "My Aunt Josie passed and the wake was at Torregrossa's on 13th Avenue," Carmine says. "I borrowed Joey's car, which we did all the time so it wasn't suspicious. I parked it a couple blocks over in the lot of St. Bernadette's."

This afforded an FBI team with the brief window needed to plant the device. "I went about my business, got the beep that they were done, and returned the car to Joey. Joey never had a clue. You'd think they'da been more careful, but that single bug recorded so much shit on them. And on that bug they captured Michael Sessa again saying how they were gonna kill me."

This was a major break for investigators. "Carmine providing probable cause to bug Joey's car was key," Dades says. "So, with the bug in his car, bunch of them go out on a hit, and they mention high-ranking guys—Carmine Sessa, the Persicos—saying they told them to do this and do that, and it just opened everything up. That's what started everything, and when the dust settled, the war was over, more than 40 guys were indicted and they all went away."

"They made Joey listen to the tapes, including the one with Lucille," Carmine says. "Told him his wife was going to be prosecuted as a co-conspirator in this thing, so he spilled his guts." They also had Lucille on a weapons possession conspiracy: tipped off that police were about to raid his home, Ambrosino ordered Lucille to gather up all their guns and put them on the neighbor's porch. Later, Scarpa Sr., the king rat himself, plotted to murder Ambrosino's mother to send a message to potential cooperators. That plot was never carried out.

There were at least four attempts on Carmine's life. "Not by the other side, but by my own crew," Carmine says. "By the grace of God, they never did."

"On one tape, Greg tells Joey [Ambrosino] to go dig the grave for Carmine, and they're good friends at that time, so that tells you all you need to know about that life and those people," Dades says.

Soon after that recording from the bug in his car, the feds grabbed up Ambrosino. "Joey wanted to cooperate, but said it wasn't safe because when Carmine cooperated, an hour later there was a leak, so he wouldn't wear a wire or even go back on the street," Dades reveals. "Joey said he'd never participate in killing Carmine because he liked him and didn't believe he was cooperating. But then Joey's cooperation led to arrests on Michael Sessa on murder, then Carmine Sessa, Teddy Persico, and many others, so that's the end of everything once that starts to happen."

By in the fall of 1992, Carmine's tense relationship with Michael Sessa continued to worsen. "There's other guys in the crew, not even Italian, and Michael's charging them one point, and me two?" Carmine says. "I laid my life on the line for this thing, and he's ripping me off. I'm making $3,500 a week and should've been making eight or nine grand."

In fact, while Carmine was on the street, he was responsible for coughing up the weekly vig on his loans on the street to Michael Sessa, totaling between $6,000 and $7,000.

Carmine's frustration got the better of him. "We're arguing again on a payphone about how he's ripping me off, and I told him I'm going to go over his head and tell his brother," Carmine says. "So now I'm on really bad terms with Michael, a murderer many times over. But I was fed up."

Carmine wore the listening device nearly 50 times, capturing dozens of incriminating conversations with multiple members of the 13th Avenue Colombo crews, many featuring Michael Sessa.

The last night Carmine wore a wire, he captured perhaps the most damning testimony.

The year before Carmine's initial arrest, in January 1991, Orena lieutenant Joel "Joe Waverly" Cacace led a failed attempt on the life of Greg Scarpa Sr. Waverly rolled up on Scarpa in Sheepshead Bay and unloaded several shots, though Scarpa escaped unharmed.

The two rival Colombo enforcers hated each other. Bent on revenge, Scarpa Sr. bided his time until February 26, 1992. At approximately 10 a.m., he poked a rifle from a parked white station wagon and unloaded 14 shots in front of the Party Room Social Club at 2112 East 14th Street near

Avenue U, striking Cacace several times, though not killing him. Scarpa's TEC-9 jammed. Cacace, who returned fire, was seriously injured, enough to require surgery at Kings County Hospital.

The day following the gun battle, Carmine attended a dinner with Scarpa, Carmine Sessa, Michael Sessa, Larry Mazza, Joseph Ambrosino, and Larry Fiorenza. Carmine was wearing a wire throughout that meet.

"We met a diner on Arthur Kill Road, not too far from my house," Carmine recalls. While in the parking lot waiting for Scarpa and Mazza, Carmine Sessa berated his brother. "Greg and Larry were very active, but Michael still had us driving around in the middle of the night, which was ridiculous. It was also embarrassing to Carmine [Sessa], that his brother was such a clown, and he's pissed Greg's crew was doing all the work. Michael was making excuses, and Carmine was so angry, chasing his brother around the car, then we went inside and grabbed a table."

Shortly afterwards, Scarpa arrived with Mazza and started crowing about the Cacace shooting. "Greg gave us a play-by-play of the gun battle, said how Joe fell, got back up, how he put the bullets in him and he still kept shooting back, swore he killed him, and was surprised he survived," Carmine says. "He not only made a toast, but he made us all come outside and check out the five or six bullet holes Joe Waverly put in his car. This was a big deal. Carmine warned Greg, said he should've killed him, because now he'd have his hands full once Joe got out of the hospital."

The group then returned to the table.

"The rest of the dinner, they just spilled so much about the War and the shootings and street business, and they also argued about paying the bill." Carmine laughs. "That's the one thing with these guys, especially the captains. They're the cheapest son of a bitches you ever want to be around. They never put their hands in their pockets. I wound up putting the dinner on a credit card just to shut them up."

Scarpa Sr. basically confessed to a murder conspiracy as a leader in the Persico faction, a RICO offense.

"I'm cooperating, and they're on top of me, all over me, monitoring everything, even down to my collections," Carmine says. "I couldn't do nothing. If I spit on the sidewalk, they'd know. And over there, you got Greg running around shooting people all over Brooklyn, bragging about it, and everybody knew." Likely the only reason Carmine survived that final dinner was the presence of Carmine Sessa.

"At one point, Greg looks at me sideways, like he knows I'm cooperating," Carmine says. "I didn't know Greg knew at the time. And I don't think he even cared, even if I had a wire. He knew he'd never have to serve that time. He was always crazy, in on all those hits. And by then, he was so sick with AIDS, he knew he wasn't surviving, so what did he give a shit."

When another wire captured a plot to take out Carmine the next day, the District Attorney's Office decided it was time to take Carmine off the streets. For good. "They came to my house right away, said it was over, said I did a lot of good work," Carmine says. "And soon after, that's when I learned Greg and Larry were looking to shoot me that night."

Carmine risked his life, wearing a wire dozens of times over the course of 10 months, during the height of the Third Colombo War.

"Through the grapevine, while I was in custody, I knew they were convinced I was already cooperating," Carmine says. "Then I heard Greg was cooperating, but on the tapes, how did he already know I may have been talking?

"At the beginning of my cooperation with the government, the agents said that they would never, never let anyone get my name. And then, Lindley DeVecchio, who later said, 'We're going to win this thing!' was suspected of giving Greg my name. Whatever happened, afterwards, my life was in imminent danger and the agents pulled me out."

Producer David Chase later borrowed the line for his smash hit *The Sopranos*. In a pivotal scene, Special Agent Harris uses the phrase upon learning wiseguy Phil Leotardo was killed. Harris had provided information to series centerpiece mob boss Tony Soprano.

Tommy Dades confirmed to Carmine that Larry Mazza was assigned the hit. Mazza was a soldier, hitman, and protégé of Greg Scarpa. When Mazza was an 18-year-old delivery boy, he was seduced by Scarpa's wife, Linda Schiro, who then encouraged her husband to give him a job. In a bizarre underworld twist, they carried on the affair for years, sanctioned by Scarpa himself. Mazza eventually cooperated with the government, admitting to four murders, and was very active at Scarpa's side during the Colombo War.[110]

"Tommy said Scarpa really put a hit out on me, and asked Larry Mazza 'to make sure Carmine was gone,'" Carmine remembers.

During Carmine's high-risk time on the street as a federal informant, he grew close with Special Agent Jeff Tomlinson, who confirmed what Carmine suspected: Scarpa had been cooperating with the feds.

Carmine was now relocated to a hidden location. He was now an invaluable asset for federal investigators, perhaps more so than he realized, Dades says.

"In my opinion, Carmine Imbriale is the one who initiated the beginning of the end of the Third Colombo War," Dades says. "I don't even know if Carmine knows the chain of events on how he got caught up, and by helping himself, helped the FBI end the war. The evidence he helped gather, and the information and testimony he provided, took down dozens of active mobsters."

"Sure, the feds had plenty of the pieces of the puzzle, but didn't have the whole picture," Carmine says. "I had my hands in everything. They knew half the stuff I told them, but they had no idea about the rest. With the murders, I could tell them why they were hit and who was involved. I could tell them who was with who, who was meeting who, why they were meeting, where they liked to meet. I pointed out the local businesses being extorted, the friendly spots where they used fake credit cards. Then there were all those cold cases, the old unsolved heists, the robberies from years ago, all of it."

Despite the massive trove of information he unleashed, there was one shortcoming. "I'm terrible with dates," Carmine says. "But dates they could figure out. They didn't even need an eyewitness, though that helped. Sometimes, they didn't even know the right questions to ask. They needed to know how it was all put together. They needed details about relationships, who was involved in what crimes. Who got paid. Who had a beef with who. They needed someone to put it together, to build the cases, so it wasn't just taking the stand, but hundreds of hours of work."

Now in federal custody, Carmine ceased all contact with his extended family. He didn't even get to say goodbye.

"Earlier that year, in July, I got a call from Carmine; his voice was very deep, he was obviously upset, said he was going through a lot and I could hear the stress in his voice," Maryellen Imbriale recalls. "Then later, I got a knock on my door from the federal marshals to inform me that Carmine was gone, and not coming back, said the family was gone. It was very abrupt, very upsetting."

"They called us up once, a woman from the District Attorney's Office, saying they wanted us to come down, and get involved," Frank Imbriale says. "We weren't willing to do that."

Carmine's immediate family, his wife and five children, would spend months in safe houses in Pennsylvania as he cooperated with investigators, including shuttling back and forth for dozens of meetings and court hearings.

Their long journey into the abyss had begun.

A War Ends, A New Life Begins

On April 1, 1992, federal agents convened on the Long Island home of Vic Orena's girlfriend and arrested the renegade mob boss. They confiscated four shotguns, a massive cache of ammunition, a bulletproof vest, a suitcase with $55,000 in cash, phone records, and other evidence.[116]

On December 22, 1992, the US government convicted Orena of the 1989 slaying of Tommy Ocera, a preceding casualty of the Third Colombo War, as well as racketeering, and a slew of other charges. A federal judge slammed him with three life sentences, plus 85 years in prison.[117]

By late 2021, a federal judge was still considering a motion to release Orena on compassionate grounds. The wheelchair-bound, 86-year-old gang boss suffers debilitating dementia and reportedly can no longer take care of himself, incarcerated at the Federal Medical Center (FMC) near Devens, Massachusetts. (A 1992 firearms conviction may be tossed on a technicality, triggering a resentencing.) In the autumn of 2021, Orena's attorney claimed that due to the

---

116. Orena v. United States, Judgement, Memorandum, and Order, "Nos. 96 CV 1474, 92 CR" Orena v. U.S., 956 F. Supp. 1071, (E.D.N.Y. 1997), United States District Court, E.D. New York, March 10, 1997

117. "Acting Crime Boss Is Convicted of Murder and Racketeering," by Arnold H. Lubasch, *New York Times*, December 22, 1992

effects of Alzheimer's, his client sometimes thinks he's the president of the United States.[118][119]

Orena's conviction sounded the death knell for the Third Colombo Family War, though the conflict continued for almost a year.

By April of 1993, Colombo Crime Family consigliere Carmine Sessa, in hiding for nine months, secretly met with several other members of the Persico faction outside St. Patrick's Cathedral on Palm Sunday in Midtown Manhattan. Heavily armed investigators lying in wait pounced on Sessa and his confederates, taking them into federal custody.[120]

The Sessa arrest was not nearly as dramatic as anticipated. "When the feds surrounded Carmine at St. Patrick's, he passed out," Carmine says. "Here was a man who killed all these people in the street. He gets surrounded by cops and feds, agents yelling at him, and he passes out. What a joke. I heard it was the easiest arrest they made in the war.

"I couldn't believe it when an agent told me. I said, 'Get out of here. He passed out?' The agent said, 'Yeah, he hit the floor like a sack of potatoes.'"

The image of a crumbling Sessa was in stark contrast to the ruthless crew chief Carmine served for so many years. "This is the guy, who if you gave him the wrong look on the street, he'd kill you and try and cut your hands off, and here he is passing out," Carmine says. "And not only that, he said in the squad car he'd cooperate. Didn't even have to

118. "Ailing ex-Colombo family boss Victor Orena, 86, could be released from prison: lawyer," by Noah Goldberg, *The New York Daily News*, April 29, 2021

119. "Alzheimer's has the former acting boss of Colombo crime family thinking he's president of the United States," by Noah Goldberg and Larry McShane, The New York Daily News, October 13, 2021

120. "Greg Scarpa Sr. talked too much, mobster says," by Scott Shifrel, *The New York Daily News*, October 26, 2007

sweat him in interrogation. He didn't even wait to get to the station."

While cooperating, Carmine had a self-awakening regarding his former mentor. "I remember the day Carmine [Sessa] told me to put on a suit for the big sit-down. I was so proud that he picked me. I wanted to earn that trust, make him proud. But the more I learned, the more I realized what type of animal he was."

Carmine Sessa admitted to murdering four people. He testified at numerous trials over the span of four years, and spent six years in prison for his roles in 13 murders. This included the September 1984 murder of Mary Bari, a former girlfriend of then Colombo Consigliere Alphonse Persico. When Persico went into hiding to avoid an indictment, the Family decided to kill Bari out of concern that she knew Persico's location. Bari was a young, innocent local Bensonhurst girl lured into Sessa's social club, Occasions, on the pretext of a job interview. When Bari arrived, Sessa shot her three times in the head.[121]

"I didn't like Carmine [Sessa], especially after I heard they shot Mary Bari, and that story about Carmine's dog finding her ear later and chewing on, and they're all laughing, it was disgusting," Carmine says. "What the fuck is that? Shooting a young girl? And then all the other stuff that came out. He's a piece of shit, lived by his own rules. Not supposed to kill women or kids. Carmine Sessa is proof that with these wiseguys, when you get to the top, the rules don't apply."

After four years of testifying, Sessa was released on bail in the summer of 1997. "The movie *Goodfellas* explains it well," Sessa said in court, reported in the *New York Post*. "Everybody gets killed by a bunch of animals or so-called

---

121. "From 'Drop-Dead Gorgeous' to DOA," by Jerry Capeci, *New York Sun*, February 16, 2006

'friends' ... This thing I thought I respected as a young man has no respect."[122]

Sessa's cooperation did impact one Colombo mobster who definitely still adhered to a code. "In the middle of the war, Sally Fusco gets arrested, and they give him like 30 years, said he shot this guy five times in the head," Carmine says. "Fusco was a bank guy, an alarm guy. I tried to get in that crew because they used to carry home suitcases full of money. So the guy gets hit with five shots, and even testified it was Sally Fusco, and they gave Sally all that time, and he took it. Just took it like a man, didn't complain, didn't say nothing."

Unbeknownst to federal authorities, they imprisoned the wrong gangster. "Carmine [Sessa] admitted to me that he did it. Then years later, when Carmine went into the program, he told the feds all he knew. Sally was lucky Carmine decided to turn. He woulda been in prison for decades."

In September 1993, Sal Fusco walked out of the Metropolitan Correctional Center in Manhattan a free man. In throwing out the attempted murder and burglary convictions of Fusco and a co-defendant, a federal judge cited illegal witness coaching perpetrated by law enforcement. A defense attorney accused a Nassau County police detective for overzealous behavior investigating Fusco and the burglary ring.[123]

"When Carmine flipped, Sally was all smiles," Carmine says. "He walked right out of prison and got twice the credit, because not only didn't he open his mouth but he did time for someone else's attempted murder. He was always good to me, and Joe Brewster loved Sally. Of course, he moved up the ladder for all that. Quiet kid, never get two words

122. "Murderous Mob Canary Sprung," by Christopher Francescani, *New York Post*, September 29, 2000

123. "Judge Throws Out Convictions Of Two Men in Burglary Case," by Joseph P. Fried, *New York Times*, September, 20, 1993

outta him, one of those guys who never knows nothing. The Fuscos had a good name, Sally and all the uncles."

Sessa was released on bail in the summer of 1997. Within a year, he was re-arrested for gun possession and domestic violence, after beating his wife. "Carmine went berserk, attacked his wife and son and had to be held in a psychiatric ward," Carmine says. "His wife left him and took the son, who had to be about 25 by then. But his wife was a bitch anyway, always saying, 'You know who my husband is?' I didn't like her. Nobody did."

Carmine never again spoke with Sessa. The former consigliere requested release from Witness Protection in 2006, news broken by legendary organized crime reporter Jerry Capeci.

By May 1993, despite the turncoats and chaos, the violence continued. New Jersey soldiers and Orena faction members Salvatore "Tutti" Lombardino, Aurelio "Ray" Cagno, and his brother, Rocco Cagno, killed soldier James "Jimmy Ran" Randazzo. Although they served in the same regime under Salvatore "Jersey Sal" Profaci, Randazzo was suspected of being an informant. Being the son of old-timer Vincenzo Randazzo didn't save him. Randazzo was lured to a parking lot and shot to death.[124]

Then on October 20th came stunning news of the assassination of Orena "co-underboss" Joey Scopo, a major hit for the Persico side. Following dinner, returning to his home in Ozone Park, Queens, Scopo exited the 1993 Nissan Altima driven by his future son-in-law Angelo Barrone when gunmen approached. Attempting to flee, Scopo was shot three times. The crippling blow marked the end of shooting on the streets during Third Colombo Family War.[125]

---

124. State of New Jersey v. Aurelio Ray Cagno, Superior Court of New Jersey, Appellate Division, Argued March 18, 2009

125. "Man Tied to Crime Family Is Shot to Death in Queens," by George James, October 22, New York Times, 1993

An imprisoned Theodore "Teddy" Persico ordered the Scopo murder while attending his grandmother's wake with a contingent of correction officers guarding him. "You've got to kill Joey," Persico whispered to three Colombo cohorts at Scarpaci Funeral Home in Brooklyn's Dyker Heights in August 1993. This is based on the later testimony of Anthony "Big Anthony" Russo.[126]

"He was whispering to us," Russo testified. "He said, 'Get it done.'"

In the 2016 sentencing of Michael Persico, prosecutors provided details of the hit. The feds hold that Michael, through an intermediary referred to as "Smiley," provided the murder weapon, a suppressed Mac-10 recovered at the scene along with the stolen car used in the drive-by. Andrew Russo confessed to participating in the hit, and named Frank Guerra, Eric Curcio, John Sparacino, and John Pappa as members of the hit team.[127]

Pappa, a wannabe wiseguy, was later convicted of racketeering, drug dealing, and four murders, including the Scopo hit. Pappa's father, Gerard Pappa, was a member of the Rampers, the Bensonhurst street gang once led by Sammy the Bull. Pappa was first a Colombo associate, then a Genovese soldier who ran with Anthony "Gaspipe" Casso. Pappa was murdered in 1980 on the orders of Vincent "The Chin" Gigante for committing two off-the-record killings.[128][129]

---

126. "Mob turncoat says shackled Colombo crime big ordered hit while at grandmother's wake," by Mitchel Maddux, *New York Post*, June 14, 2012

127. United States of America v. Michael Persico, United States District Court, Eastern District of New York, Filed July 19, 2017

128. "John Pappa Failed at Shooting His Way into the Mafia," by Ed Scarpo Friday, Cosa Nostra News, February 4, 2011

129. "Colombo hit man John Pappa makes the most of his time cooking and cheering on the Yankees as he's holed up in high-security prison," by John Marzulli, *The New York Daily News*, June 27, 2012

After the hit on Scopo, John Pappa killed co-conspirators John Sparacino and Eric Curcio, supposedly jealous they shared credit for the murder. The judge sentenced the would-be wiseguy to life in prison. Due to Pappa's young age (22 at the time of sentencing in 1997), he has the dubious distinction of perhaps eventually serving one of the longest sentences in US criminal history.

On the run, Pappa was nabbed on the steps of a church in Staten Island while attending a wedding rehearsal in 1997 for the brother of one of his victims, John Sparacino. Tommy Dades was the arresting officer. As Pappa fled, he drew a 9mm handgun on Dades, who didn't flinch in the standoff. Pappa surrendered.

The Third Colombo War brought the Family to the brink of extinction. The entire Colombo hierarchy was indicted for racketeering related to murders during the conflict. For a time, fragments of the Colombos were close to being absorbed by the other Families.

In all, 12 people, including one innocent teenager, died in the gang war and another 14 were wounded.

The FBI, with the assistance of the New York City Police Department, arrested 123 Colombo Family members. More than 80 *made* members and associates from both sides of the Colombo Family were convicted, jailed, or indicted.

While Persico outlasted Orena in the war, Orena outlived his former boss. Having served 33 years of a 139-year sentence, Persico perished on March 7, 2019, at the Duke University Medical Center in Durham, North Carolina.[130]

"In my opinion, and it's the opinion of most people who know what really happened, the Colombo War was a waste of time," Dades says. "It was senseless. So stupid for them, just a disaster. Just look at all the guys switching sides. Or who declared themselves neutral, who stopped paying, guys

130. "Carmine Persico, Colombo Crime Family Boss, Is Dead at 85," by Selwyn Raab, *New York Times*, March 8, 2019

going to jail over this, guys getting hit who didn't deserve it. They gained nothing and lost half a family."

Carmine Imbriale provided evidence used in upwards of 40 convictions. This included testifying in half a dozen cases. "I testified six times, and the first hearing was with Michael Sessa," Carmine recalls. "When I took the stand, he was staring at me hard, then took his glasses off. Thought he could intimidate me. Didn't bother me. He was a joke. Actually made me smile. I never killed nobody, but I woulda killed Michael on the street with my bare hands. He was a punk."

Carmine also testified against Colombo loan shark Robert Donofrio, *made* by the Colombos in 1988. Donofrio served his time quietly. As recent as 2018, multiple Mafia blogs, like Ed Scarpo from *La Cosa Nostra News*, claim Donofrio is now a candidate to lead the Colombo Family. However, others speculate Teddy Persico Jr. as the odds-on candidate for boss.

Carmine also testified against Sessa crew member Richard Alan Brady in a trial also including Frank "Franky Steel" Pontillo, Robert Montano, Michael DeMatteo, and John Pate. Following a three-week trial that included the testimony of three cooperating co-conspirators (Joseph Ambrosino, Carmine Imbriale, and Alan Quattrache), on March 23, 1993, Federal Judge Leo Glaser handed down a conviction on a "six-count superseding indictment, charging them with participating in a conspiracy to commit murder for the purpose of increasing their positions within a criminal enterprise."[131]

"Their testimony revealed the appellants' involvement in various murder plots, particularly the April 1992 attempt

---

131. The United States of America v. Appellee Richard Alan Brady, Frank Pontillo, also known as Franky Steel, Robert Montano, Michael DeMatteo and John Pate, Defendants-Appellants, Nos. 590, 613, 760, 762, 842, Dockets 93-1215, 93-1220, 93-1251, 93-1252, 93-1618, United States Court of Appeals, Second Circuit, Decided May 13, 1994

to murder Louis 'Bo-Bo' Malpeso, a *'made* member' of the Orena faction. Although he missed, Pontillo actually shot at Malpeso. The cooperating witnesses also linked these appellants to a murder plot against William 'Wild Bill' Cutolo."

In all, the cooperating witnesses detailed attempts to locate and murder at least seventeen different individuals. The named defendants in this case were involved in some, but not all, of the murder plots. That list of targets included Carmine, as well as Joseph Amato, Pasquale "Patty" Amato, Joseph Campanella, William "Wild Bill" Cutolo, Alfonse "Funzi D" D'Ambrosio, Vincent "Chickie" DiMartino, Dominick Dionisio, Nicholas "Nicky Black" Grancio, Frank "Frankie Notch" Iannaci, Louis "Bo-Bo" Malpeso, Victor Orena, Joseph Russo, Gabriel Siana, Joseph Scopo, Frank Sparaco, and Michael Spatero.

At trial, defense attorneys for associates, like Pontillo and Brady, attempted to distance their clients from the indictments, claiming that as they were not "*made* members;" they were "non-members" and therefore "had no position within the enterprise to increase or maintain."

In reality, that's not how this thing works. Testimony from former co-conspirators, like Carmine and Joey Brains, debunked that defense, proving the associates and *made* members constituted a criminal enterprise.

Brady's lawyer in particular homed in on Carmine's involvement with Brady.

"Isn't it true that you don't even know my client?" Carmine recalls Richard Brady's lawyer asking him.

"I don't know what that lawyer was thinking, but I had to laugh, and looked over at Jeff [Tomlinson, FBI agent] and other investigators, and saw them shaking their heads," Carmine says. "I knew Rich Brady for years. He was brought into this by Joey [Ambrosino], who destroyed him with testimony. The lawyer asked me to point Rich Brady out in court, and not only did I point him out, I also pointed out his wife."

Carmine testified in cases over the course of a year and a half. "I didn't mind getting on the stand at all. These guys didn't scare me. They had no power over me. The judge, though, did say he gave me credit for providing so much information. I helped put 40 people away. And trust me, they all got what they deserved."

Carmine did preface each court testimony with a key disclaimer. "Every time I testified, I said to the judge, no disrespect, but I'm not good with dates," Carmine recalls. "Jeff Tomlinson said tell them that first, so they're not asking it over and over and it then causes a problem. Sure enough, worked out good."

Jeff Tomlinson became a regular presence in Carmine's life. "They had me stashed in Pennsylvania and I had to keep coming back and forth. Jeff lived in Lancaster and I spent a lot of time with him. He was straight with me. He was a great agent and a credit to the FBI."

Carmine may be a former associate of a major crime family, a loan shark, a bookmaker, and an armed robber. Yet Carmine Imbriale is not a murderer. He never killed anyone, proven by investigators. But he sure did harm a hell of a lot members of the underworld.

"I believe what comes around goes around, and I didn't kill nobody in my life," Carmine says. "Everybody else who killed pretty much got themselves killed."

Carmine's cooperation was not an automatic get-out-of-jail-free card. That's not how it works. The FBI and other government agencies can submit a recommendation to the court, but it is up to the judge's discretion to make a determination of leniency upon sentencing.

Fortunately for Carmine, his cooperation was invaluable in so many cases. Carmine was convicted on multiple counts, sentenced to 10 years in prison, though the judge suspended the sentence due to his cooperation, as well as the strength of many letters of recommendation.

"The judge commended me, said I did a lot for justice, and asked me why I made the decision to change my life and cooperate," Carmine recalls. "I said, 'I had enough.' He said, 'Good for you, good for your family,' and he gave me time served, so I was really happy. But for some time there, my wife didn't know if I was going to prison, coming home, or whatever."

Carmine estimates he left nearly a quarter million dollars on the streets. "But it really wasn't my money, it was Michael's and Carmine's, and they were lost, so there were a lot of happy folks on 13th Avenue when this was all over."

With the Family in a shambles, the 13th Avenue rackets were a mess. However, it wasn't just the Third Colombo War that doomed the South Brooklyn rackets.

In federal court in the 2012 trial of then Colombo boss Thomas "Tommy Shots" Gioeli, former captain Dino "Big Dino" Calabro testified of his involvement in the 1997 ambush murder of NYC police officer Ralph Dols, along with his cousin Dino "Little Dino" Saracino.[132]

Ralph Dols' transgression? He married the former wife of Joseph "Joe Waverly" Cacace.

Cacace, insecure and obsessed with Dols, handed down the death sentence to Gioelli, who dispatched his underlings. Calabro testified how he and his cousin cased Dols for more than a week, but were not aware Dols was a police officer. Both Calabro and Saracino earned their buttons with the Colombos for the hit.[143]

The news of the cowardly assassination hit the media like a bomb.

"When they killed Police Officer Dols, that's when we went in and knocked over every social club and café these

---

132. "Mob turncoat details the 1997 slaying of NYPD cop Ralph Dols," by Mitchel Maddux, *New York Post*, March 27, 2012

guys were in," Dades says. "Most of them never reopened. That was it, they were done. Joey Flowers' club never reopened. Georgie DiCicco's club never opened. All the 13th Avenue clubs. Done. Anthony Spero's Bath Avenue club, we locked him up and shut his club, never reopened. Frankie Lino's club, shut. The list goes on and on, from one end of Brooklyn to the next. There used to have these clubs on every block. And maybe you got a few here or there, but nothing like it was."

And it never will be like that again.

"The Grim Reaper"
Meets his Match

So what happened to Greg Scarpa Sr.?

Investigations in the aftermath of the Third Colombo Family War brought to light Scarpa Sr.'s decades-long duplicitous betrayal. From when he first began cooperating with the FBI in 1962 to avoid prosecution for hijacking, [74] the FBI case file spans more than eleven hundred pages.[133]

In the mid-1970s, the FBI cut ties with Scarpa Sr. Then, following five years of dormancy, Scarpa was reactivated as a TE (top echelon) informant. Before and during the war, R. Lindley DeVecchio, the self-described "Mr. Organized Crime," ran the FBI squad investigating the Colombo Family, became the long-time handler for informant Scarpa Sr. DeVecchio had been with the FBI since the J. Edgar Hoover administration.[74]

Under DeVecchio's watch, Scarpa participated in 26 homicides, the final being the December 1992 slaying of Vincent Fusaro as the Orena loyalist hung Christmas lights.

The district attorney for the Southern District later charged FBI Agent Roy Lindley DeVecchio for allegedly furnishing Scarpa Sr. with Larry Lampasi's work schedule, enabling his assassination.[110]

---

133. "It's not just Whitey Bulger: Meet another Mafia killer aided for decades by the FBI," By Peter Lance, *Salon Magazine*, June 30, 2013

A *Newsweek* profile reported how when, at FBI headquarters, DeVecchio was told of the gangland slaying, he allegedly responded, "We're gonna win this thing," as he slapped his hand on the desk. By "we," some speculated he meant Scarpa Sr.'s branch of the Colombo syndicate. The incident, publicly reported years later as part of an internal FBI investigation into DeVecchio's handling of Scarpa Sr., became the basis for a scene in *The Sopranos* finale.

DeVecchio was also later suspected of tipping off Scarpa that Carmine Imbriale was an FBI informant. However, following a two-year internal investigation, the FBI declined to move forward with charges against DeVecchio, who retired in 1996.

Ten years later, Brooklyn District Attorney Charles Hynes indicted DeVecchio on multiple counts of providing classified information that led to four murders. That case was based largely on testimony from Linda Schiro, Scarpa's girlfriend. However, the conflicting accounts Schiro provided to organized crime reporter Jerry Capeci, also chronicled in a report by journalist Tom Robbins of *The Village Voice*, destroyed the case against DeVecchio.[78] DeVecchio later co-authored a tell-all book refuting the claims.[81]

Regardless who leaked the information to Scarpa Sr. that Carmine Imbriale was an informant, it signed his death warrant on 13th Avenue. "They had to move on me because of Greg," Carmine says. "When I heard my name on those tapes, I knew then that someone told Greg I was cooperating. It had to have come from the other side, because it's not wiseguys tapping your phones or parking surveillance trucks outside your home."

Yet what stunned Carmine was the length of time Scarpa played both sides. "Thirty years. Here they were, giving me money to turn in for my shy every week, and they're worried about me slapping someone. And Greg is out there on the street murdering people. Basically, Greg had a license to kill, and he not only used it, he wore it out."

Scarpa exploited his advantage to the fullest. "Wiseguys like Greg usually get others to do the dirty work, the shootings, the beatings," Carmine says. "But not only is Greg running around killing people, he's feeding the feds information. You're in his way, he either kills you or gets the feds to lock you up. And not just the stuff you read about in the war. Day-to-day stuff, going on for years. Sure, the tips he gave were used to arrest other wiseguys. But at the same time, they helped Greg increase his power on the street."

Carmine regrets he never pushed the issue when he suspected Scarpa of betrayal. "It always bothered me that when Greg got picked up with 60 credit cards in his pocket, nothing happened. You don't beat a case like that. Greg's a big fish for the feds, so he's not getting a pass. Not only does Greg got the feds protecting him, but the guy knows he's dying. So, of course, he's got the biggest balls in neighborhood."

It has never been determined how many victims met their end at the hands of The Grim Reaper.

Larry Mazza testified that his former mentor "stopped counting" after 50 murders. Most of these homicides were committed while Scarpa Sr. cooperated with federal investigators.[133]

On August 30, 1992, he received a $300,000 settlement in civil court from his first surgeon and Victory Hospital for negligence. He'd not live long to enjoy that win.

Scarpa and his relatives told everyone he suffered from cancer to explain his deteriorating appearance. Then, sick with full-blown AIDS, Scarpa was arrested on a firearms charge and later indicted for several murders.[110] Released on a $1.2 million bond and ordered confined to his home except for authorized medical treatment, Scarpa was nearly murdered. The bizarre sequence of events was not even related to the Third Colombo Family War.[134]

Two Lucchese Family mobsters, Michael "Mikey Flattop" DeRosa and Ronald "Messy Marvin" Moran, threatened Joey Scarpa, Gregory's son, over a drug deal. Climbing out of bed, the elder Scarpa drove with Joey to DeRosa's house and shot Mikey Flattop, who survived. In the ensuing gun battle, Moran fired back, shooting out Scarpa's eye. Scarpa fled the scene, returned home, poured himself a whiskey, then went to the hospital, where he underwent surgery. Prosecutors revoked Scarpa's house arrest and sent him to jail.

The shootout splashed across media outlets the next day.

Surgeons at Mount Sinai Hospital in Manhattan removed Scarpa's stomach. Blind in one eye, emaciated, and in poor health, he pled guilty to three murders and conspiracy to murder several others at trial on May 6, 1993. On December 15th, a federal judge sentenced Greg Scarpa Sr. to life in prison. His sentence was later reduced to 10 years due to his poor health, but it didn't matter.

On June 4, 1994, Gregory Scarpa Sr. died in the Federal Medical Center for prisoners in Rochester, Minnesota, from AIDS-related complications.[135]

"You know, we're supposed to take care of our children, give them a better life," Carmine reflects. "If you want to know what an animal Greg was, just look at his son." Scarpa drew his son into organized crime, molded him into a murderous hitman, even orchestrated his elevation to the position of captain. All the while, he cooperated with the federal government.

Think about that.

---

134. "Top Member of Colombo Crime Family Is Ambushed in Brooklyn," by Selwyn Raab, *New York Times*, December 30, 1992

135. "The Mobster Was a Mole for the F.B.I.; Tangled Life of a Mafia Figure Who Died of AIDS Is Exposed," by Selwyn Raab, *New York Times*, November 20, 1994

Junior's reward for following in his father's footsteps? In 1998, while in prison on another charge, Greg Scarpa Jr. was slammed with a multi-count racketeering conviction, including four murders. He received a 40-year sentence and was initially not scheduled for release until 2035.

In November 2020, a judge took pity on Scarpa Junior, granting him early release on compassionate grounds. By then, suffering from late-stage cancer, he had already endured multiple rounds of chemotherapy and radiation treatments.

Surgeries, including one to remove a tumor, left a hole in his throat, and the removal of salivary glands means he chokes regularly on his food.[136] [137]

---

136. "Ailing Brooklyn mobster blamed in 1980s killings wins compassionate release from prison," by Noah Goldberg, *The New York Daily News*, November 11, 2020

137. United States v. Larry Sessa, Gregory Scarpa Jr., United States Court of Appeals, Second Circuit, No. 1363, Docket 96-1631, Decided September 9, 1997

Getting Straightened Out

The Life was over for Carmine.

A new life was beginning.

With high-stakes court hearings behind him, Carmine stepped into the unknown. "People think you go into the program, it's gonna be all smooth sailing, but it's a sentence in itself," Carmine says. "It's like the *Twilight Zone*. You don't know what to expect, except to expect everything will never be the same."

The United States Code, Title 18, Part II, Chapter 224, Section 3521 has governed "witness relocation and protection" since the program's inception.[138] Among the stipulations in this sophisticated document, it states that the attorney general *may*, by regulation, provide suitable documents to enable the person to establish a new identity or otherwise protect the person.

As per the code, the attorney general *may* "provide housing for the person." The attorney general *may* "provide to the person a payment to meet basic living expenses, in a sum established in accordance with regulations issued by the Attorney General." And the attorney general *may* "assist the person in obtaining employment" and also *may* "provide other services necessary to assist the person in becoming self-sustaining."

---

138. The United States Code, Title 18, Part II, Chapter 224, Section 3521

Notice that the code states, repeatedly, the things the attorney general *may* do. Not *must* do.

"You're at the mercy of the government, hoping they come through, but you don't know until you're in it how that plays out," Carmine says. "At the beginning, you're living out of suitcases, moving around. Just so stressful, hoping it'll all work out."

There was some certainty when they left Brooklyn. Carmine and his family *must* relocate from the only home they've ever known to a new life thousands of miles away. Carmine *must* find a way to support a family, despite being a high-school dropout with no formal training or employment history.

And above all, Carmine and his family *must* meticulously follow every rule, to the letter, or be thrown out of the program for breaching protocols.

Carmine says he feels they were treated justly by the US Marshals Service, and the government delivered on its promises.

Most importantly, they were alive and free.

When Carmine walked out of a Brooklyn detention center and into the wind, with his wife and children, they headed to the Midwestern United States.

"My wife was upset," Carmine recalls. "She was happy I was escaping the life, but sad that we left aunts and uncles, and her mother. But she was happy we were together. I get homesick, but don't regret starting things over and saving my life."

Even if Carmine had a profession, the Marshals Service strongly discourages WITSEC participants from resuming their careers. Too easy to cross paths with former acquaintances in that industry.[139, 140] All it would take is one phone call back to 13th Avenue.

By the time Carmine entered Witness Protection, gone were the lucrative stipends and subsidies the federal government provided to backstop businesses.

Carmine had no hidden stash of cash or horde of jewelry. This isn't the movies. The US Marshals don't play. Even the hint of deception triggers an investigation. Federal agents are very thorough in processing program entrants and experienced at rooting out deception. One false move, they'd bounce him out of the program.

Like Gaspipe.

Anthony "Gaspipe" Casso, the homicidal underboss of the Lucchese Crime Family, was suspected in upwards of three dozen murders when he was arrested in 1993. When the Luccheses turned on him, Casso flipped, becoming, at the time, the highest-ranking wiseguy to cooperate with the US government. In accepted a plea deal, he admitting to 70 crimes, including 15 murders. [141]

Casso's cooperation included testimony against the infamous "Mafia Cops," two NYPD detectives, Stephen Caracappa and Louis Eppolito, on the Lucchese payroll. (*Friends of the Family: The Inside Story of the Mafia Cops Case* is the bestseller written by Tommy Dades, former top Brooklyn prosecutor Mike Vecchione, and writer David Fisher.)[142]

---

139. "Inside the witness protection program," by Gabriel Falcon, CNN, February 16, 2013

140. "How the Witness Protection Program Decides Where To Send People," *Popular Mechanics*, February 8, 2019

141. "Mobster Anthony 'Gaspipe' Casso, who murdered dozens and caught COVID-19 behind bars, dead at 78," by Noah Goldberg, *New York Daily News*, December 16, 2020

142. *Friends of the Family: The Inside Story of the Mafia Cops Case*, by Tommy Dades and Mike Vecchione, with David Fisher, William Morrow, May 12, 2009

Yet in 1998, Casso was removed from WITSEC for multiple breaches, including infractions while incarcerated (violence, bribing corrections officers), withholding information from investigators, and making false statements about other wiseguys, including Sammy Gravano.[143]

Not only was Casso thrown out of WITSEC, prosecutors set aside the plea agreement, and a federal judge slammed Gaspipe with a sentence totaling 455 years in prison.[141]

On December 15, 2020, Casso died in prison from myriad ailments (prostate cancer, coronary artery disease, kidney disease, hypertension, bladder disease, and lung disease) exacerbated by contracting COVID-19. He was 78.[144]

Casso is not the only example made by the Marshals Service. Testimony by former New England gangster Francis "Cadillac Frank" Salemme helped convict corrupt FBI Agent John Connolly in 1999. When Salemme left prison in 2003 after serving a reduced sentence, he entered witness protection. Years later, evidence emerged that Salemme orchestrated the murder of Steven A. DiSarro, who was strangled by Salemme's son. Not only was Cadillac Frank expelled from WITSEC, but in 2018, he was convicted for his role in the DiSarro murder. Salemme is currently incarcerated at the federal prison in Hazelton, Virginia.[145]

Even Henry Hill, perhaps the most infamous of Mafia informants, was unceremoniously chucked out of the

143. "Plea Deal Rescinded, Informer May Face Life," by Selwyn Raab, *New York Times,* July 1, 1998

144. "Ex-Lucchese underboss Anthony 'Gaspipe' Casso dies after getting COVID-19 in prison," by Priscilla DeGregory, Larry Celona and Tamar Lapin, *New York Post*, December 16, 2020

145. "Boston mobster known as 'Cadillac Frank' gets life in prison for an old murder," by Taylor Telford, *The Washington Post*, September 14, 2018

program in 1987 upon his conviction of narcotics trafficking in Seattle.[146]

No, Carmine did not want to end up like Gaspipe or Cadillac Frank. Carmine knew how to respect rules.

They were safe. According to the US Marshals Service, of the more than 19,000 people participating in the program over the years, none have been murdered while in WITSEC.[147]

However, earning a living was not going to be easy. For the first six months, the federal government provided housing and a modest monthly stipend, enough to cover basic necessities. After the stipend dried up, Carmine was on his own.

At 42 years of age, Carmine had neither the skills nor temperament to go into retail sales or customer service. He spent a couple years cycling through failed career prospects before he saw a television infomercial advertising a course on how to purchase real estate with no money down. Within weeks, he completed the $3,500 online course.

Soon, Carmine amassed a portfolio of 18 rental properties he managed, mostly multi-family units; some he purchased as foreclosures, others at auction. He was so successful with the real-estate course, the program's producers invited him down to Florida to film a spot for their next infomercial.

There was one catch. "I asked who's paying for the trip," Carmine recalls. "They said they'd provide airfare, but not accommodations. I said then give me back my $3,500. They hung up."

The rental hustle came naturally to Carmine. As his stock rose in the local realty business community, some took notice. "I met this local guy, a contractor," Carmine says. "We became friendly, talking real estate." After a number of

---

146. "Henry Hill, Mobster and Movie Inspiration, Dies at 69," by Margalit Fox, *New York Times*, June 13, 2012

147. US Marshals Service Witness Protection Program Sheet, US Marshals Service

these conversations, the man made an offer for Carmine to buy into a real-estate deal, to build and sell condominiums, for an upfront investment of $120,000.

Carmine soon handed over a cashier's check for the full amount.

"Then I don't hear from this guy for a week. When I track him down, he says, 'Hey, I got some bad news for you,' and I stopped him right there. I said, 'If you're gonna tell me you lost my money, don't even try it.' He said, 'Shit happens.'"

Carmine, being Carmine, hung up the phone, jumped in his car, and sped over to the man's home. "I ran over there like a rocket, said I don't care how you get my money back, but you have three weeks, and I better get it back."

The deadline passed. The man stopped returning Carmine's calls. So now, Carmine sits in his car, waits outside the guy's home, like he did way back in South Brooklyn tracking down deadbeat borrowers.

Carmine is patient when he needs to be. He got up early, real early, to sit in front of this guy's home, 4 a.m. until dawn, hoping to get the drop on him sneaking out. The guy spotted Carmine. Barricaded himself in, refusing to leave his home. The guy tipped off the local police, who arrived on the scene in minutes.

"Cops said, 'What are you doing?' and I said, 'I just want to talk to him, man to man,'" Carmine says. "Cops said, 'This is a civil matter' and I had to leave. But I kept after him. Finally, he agreed to give me money every two weeks to pay down the debt. Said he didn't have it all. He needed more time. I told him, 'Fine, but it's no longer $120k. It's now $130k. And the longer you take to pay, it only goes up.'"

Miraculously, the guy paid—in full—the next day.

Carmine built his portfolio the hard way, earning modest but steady income from multiple properties, and reinvesting. Many of the same skills he possessed on the streets now served him well, brokering deals with his hard-nosed style, collecting from delinquent renters, dealing with unruly customers—many of whom were not his own.

Keep in mind, Carmine does not deal in high-end real estate. Managing rental properties in low-income communities is a grind. Tenants are rough around the edges and often reluctant to pay when the rent is due.

Take Dan: recently unemployed, two months behind on his rent. Every time Carmine visited Dan to collect the overdue rent, the home seemed empty (or more likely, someone was hiding). By law, the owner is not allowed to throw the delinquent tenant out in the street. What do you think this is, 13th Avenue?

In most states, the law is predominantly on the side of the renter. A landlord can only enter the unit with permission or in an emergency, and it better be a real emergency. Then, you likely need a court order, unless the unit is actually on fire or under water. Even if the unit requires maintenance, the tenant must give permission. And if the landlord changes the locks, they must provide the keys or face arrest. And then the tenant can take them to court.[148] [149]

Carmine tracked down Dan. Carmine was firm, but reasonable, empathetic, and offered Dan an extension. Even back in Brooklyn as a loan shark, Carmine sought non-violent solutions to delinquencies. A man with broken thumbs has a harder time paying you back.

So he gave Dan a break with that extension. But unbeknownst to Dan, Carmine's patience has its limits.

"A month goes by after I gave Dan a break, so I call him and say I need my money," Carmine recalls. "He said, 'You call here again, and I'll box your ears.' Who even says things like that?"

148. "Tenants' Rights: Knowing Your Rights as a Tenant," by Brette Sember, J.D., Legal Zoom, September 4, 2020

149. Tenants Rights State-By-State, US Department of Housing and Urban Development

Bad move, Dan. Carmine sprinted out the door, his wife hot on his heels. In his rush, Carmine inadvertently sent her flying into the bushes. After helping poor Janet to her feet, making sure she was not injured, Carmine jumped in his car and raced to settle up with Dan.

"I'm outside the property in minutes, and Dan answers the door, surprised to see me. Just another fake telephone tough guy. I tell Dan, 'I not only want the rent, but first, I want to fight you.' I said, 'Come on, tough guy. You said you were going to box my ears, so box my ears.'"

Carmine was not joking. Dan's wife heard the shouting and came out of the next room. Carmine asked her, politely, for a pen and paper, on which he wrote a promissory note pledging to give Dan and his wife one full year of free rent. In return, all Dan had to do was fight Carmine in the schoolyard directly across the street *and* agree to not call the police.

Dan's wife agreed. Enthusiastically, at first. Then, insistently.

Dan did not. Dan scampered back into the apartment and barricaded himself in a room.

By himself.

Dan's wife did not want to lose the prospect of entire year of free rent. With Carmine smirking in the doorway, Dan's wife hammered on that door, hollering at Dan to be a man.

Dan never did come out of the room that day.

In the weeks ahead, Dan continued to refuse to pay. He would not take Carmine's phone calls. He even climbed in and out of his back window to avoid a lurking Carmine.

Carmine started eviction proceedings at the local civil court, where he learned this was not Dan's first trip to eviction court. At a hearing, the judge recognized him, and gave him two weeks to vacate the premises. "I said to the judge, 'Please don't give him the two weeks, he'll wreck the place,'" Carmine recalls. "He asked if I had a suggestion. I said we could hang him. Judge said, 'Nice try, but the answer is no.'"

Dan eventually left, and didn't completely wreck the unit, as Carmine feared. Carmine got off easy with Dan. In dozens of eviction hearings, things have not always worked out. Low-income rentals come with headaches. But it's the dogs that really get to Carmine—dogs chained to fences, starved, abused, left to endure the weather.

"Lease says no dogs and I mean no dogs," Carmine says. "Terrible, how so many people don't have money for rent, don't have money to feed themselves, can't take care of their kids, but they get all these big dogs and just neglect them. It bothers me like you don't know to see that."

Early one morning, Carmine rented a pickup truck, arrived outside one rental unit, cut the chains on all the dogs and drove them down to a farm and gave them to a farmer, who was glad to have them. "Tenants went around looking, but what could they really do. On the lease it says no dogs."

Another time, a delinquent tenant, a muscular body builder, called Carmine to tell him, "I don't like how you look at my girl," to which Carmine responded, 'I wouldn't ____ her with your ____.' The tenant threatened Carmine, said if he wanted his rent, he needed to come down.

Will these telephone tough guys ever learn? The tenant had not even hung up the phone when Carmine ran out the door in a fury, jumped in his car.

"Door was open on the unit, so I went in, and boy, he was surprised," Carmine said. "So I'm pulling him out the door, trying to get him outside to beat the living crap out of him, and I get up real close in his face and say, 'Kiss your girl goodbye. You're not coming back.'"

The terrified tenant wiggled out of Carmine's grasp, shouting he wasn't going anywhere with him. His girlfriend called the local police. Carmine denied the threat. They all landed in eviction court.

Another time, Carmine was selling one of his multi-unit properties and was onsite with prospective buyers. One tenant let him in, while another tenant, delinquent on the rent, stormed in cursing, yelling, flashing expensive jewelry no less. "You shoulda seen how fast I knocked that baseball cap right off his head," Carmine recalls. He then tackled him and they both went flying down the stairs and out the door, with Carmine choking him into near unconsciousness.

"The real-estate agent and the buyers took off, just as the police arrived. I told the cops he lunged at me, which he did... sort of. Sure enough, this guy has three warrants. They asked me if I wanted to press charges. I declined, said he's got enough of a mess to deal with, with all his warrants."

And once again, another trip down to eviction court.

When not chasing down crooked speculators or scrapping with delinquent tenants, Carmine also engaged in altercations with no less than three contractors. "Like this one guy, as I'm showing houses, I get a call from him, a contractor, yelling into the phone, cursing, calling me a 'slimy, greaseball,'" says Carmine, a fiercely proud Italian American. "I flew down to the site, picked him up, dragged him out into the street, then put my arms behind my back and offered him my chin, the first shot.'"

The contractor declined. Yet he didn't call the cops. Strange, thought Carmine. Unlike on 13th Avenue, here, *everyone* called the cops on Carmine. But for some reason, not this guy.

Months later, federal authorities arrested that contractor, identified as a terrorist on an international watch list, later convicted for laundering money to terrorist organizations in the Middle East. "That sure explained why this clown didn't call the cops. I even got him an office to rent upstairs from my own lawyer. They raided that office, took him away, and now he's doing life in a federal penitentiary."

These days, Carmine knows his way around the courthouse, where they adjudicate evictions, code enforcement, and restraining orders. "Many tenants who don't have money, they'll call code enforcement, so then they buy time as I have to fix everything," Carmine says. "After that, they still don't pay, but at least I can move forward with the evictions."

In one instance, a delinquent tenant brandished a machete. Carmine tried to throw him off a third-floor porch, and almost succeeded. That resulted in a restraining order.

Against Carmine. Not the guy with the machete. "Judge asked me why I threatened him," Carmine said. "I said, 'Who me? I didn't threaten no one. He was the one with the machete, Judge.'"

Then there was the drug dealer, who Carmine warned to cut the crap. "I said, 'I know what you're doing here and I'm not calling the cops, but I'm warning you to stop,'" Carmine says. The next week, robbers burst in and shot the dealer, who survived the attack.

He sued Carmine for operating an unsafe building. A judge dismissed that suit.

By this time, Carmine had been in and out of court so many times, he was recognized on sight by the eye-rolling judges. "I kept going in and out and always told them I didn't remember nothing, I don't know nothing. What are they gonna to do? I'm always in the right. These are all cheats and despicable people and fake tough guys who get called on their bullshit."

But it's not all fake tough guys and drug dealers. More recently, Carmine rented to two young ladies who were behind on the rent. "When I came around to collect the rent, they showed up at the door naked, asking if we could all work things out," says Carmine, fiercely loyal to his wife. "I told them, 'No, thank you.'" Unlike most Brooklyn wiseguys, Carmine has a stable marriage, one of the key factors he credits with saving him.

So here we go again, back to eviction court. "I went to my lawyer to have them evicted," Carmine says. "I told the lawyer what happened, that they were nude and propositioned me. So, I'm in court with my lawyer, and the two girls were called up and the lawyer leaned over to me, asked which one had the better body. I got serious and told him to pay attention to the case before he gets a slap, and I called him a degenerate."

By then, Carmine had a reputation not only in law-enforcement circles, but also among real-estate agents. "Coming from Brooklyn, I know how to collect money, after all the shylocking; except now it was legal collections, but still the same thing.

"I was always honest, always told truth, so no one could say I was lying, and I was known for my honesty. But I was also known for my temper. I don't have a bad temper; I just want answers, direct answers. I think it has more to do with how I need to get my point across."

Soon, other landlords not able to get their points across were asking Carmine to collect on their delinquent renters, offering ten percent of whatever he collected. "Even today, I get calls and I go and collect," Carmine says.

"There was this Italian guy, supposed to be in the mob here, which was a joke. My granddaughter could run a mob here." This guy had a house in foreclosure. "Seemed like a nice guy, so I wanted to help, so I said, 'Instead of bidding on it, sell it to me,'" Carmine remembers. "'I have proof of funds. Give me $5k and I'll put your name on the contract.' He said, 'Are you trying to shake me down?' I said, 'Don't be an asshole, come down to the bar and settle this. Keep $5k down so you and wife don't get thrown out. I'm doing you a favor. I will throw you in the street.' He didn't listen. And he lost the house. Gangster? What a joke."

Then there was Crazy Freddy, the brother of a woman renting from Carmine. "So I kick the sister out and she asks, 'Don't you know who my brother is?'" Carmine remembers. "I said, 'I don't care who your brother is.' Later, I'm not there, he comes around and makes a scene, looking for the landlord. But he knew I wasn't there. On the way out, he stepped on a neighbor's dog and killed it, on purpose."

When Carmine heard, he jumped in his car. With a baseball bat. "I didn't know where this Crazy Freddy jerkoff was, so I went to the local barbershop with my bat. I went in there and asked for Freddy, asked if there was someone who could get in touch with him for me."

Sure enough, someone offered to text Crazy Freddy. "I say, 'Tell him I got a bat and I'm waiting,'" Carmine said. For dramatic effect, Carmine smashed the front door of the barbershop with the bat on the way out. Carmine never heard from Crazy Freddy or the sister again.

Part of Carmine's success is due to an agreement he struck with a local investor. "He was retired, wanted to invest some of his money in real estate," Carmine recalls. "So he'd finance my deals. First deal was $100k on a hand shake. With me, he never lost money, I never paid late, and he never went with nobody else."

The partnership became mutually beneficial in other respects. "One guy screwed him, didn't pay in two years, and I knew this other guy had apartments, so I went to all his buildings and went to all his tenants, said I was his nephew, said I was collecting, and that's just what I did. He called and threatened me, said, 'You don't mess with me.' I said, 'I'm here waiting,' but he didn't show up."

So instead, Carmine went to him. "I went there, wanted him to sign over, make good on his obligations," Carmine says. "I got him [to] sign the papers. Afterwards, my partner said, 'I don't know how you did it.' I got all the money back for him. Felt real good."

Carmine has found God, has a strong support network, attends church regularly, meets with his priest, and even joined the church gardening crew. "It helps, especially when I come home and want to go after someone. I'm blessed."

Going on 43 years of marriage, Carmine credits his adoring wife with saving him, as well as his faith. "To see him back in church is very nice," Maryellen Imbriale says. "He's not over-the-top religious, but does pray and attend church. And now he's even friends with the priest."

"After 22 years in real estate, still doing great, but going to wind it down, especially with the troubled rentals," Carmine says. "I found peace and I attend church regularly. I have a really good priest, much younger than me, real nice, feels like part of another family."

Father Francis doesn't know of Carmine's past, but counsels him on controlling his temper. He told Carmine, when he feels anger come on to make the sign of the cross.

"So next day after mass, I tell Father Francis about this guy who cut me off," Carmine says. "I told him I made the sign of the cross at the guy. The guy still gave me the finger, but I didn't get out and wipe the street with him, so that's a start."

Fish Out of Water

In 2005, a mysterious stranger in a colorful Sergio Tacchini tracksuit and Aviator shades strode into the local taxidermist shop in a sleepy hamlet somewhere lost along the backroads of Middle America.

This is the kind of shop with a shingle that states "We Git R Done," and yes, they sure do. But this was more than just a shop that stuffed dead critters. It's as much town square as taxidermy, where you're sure to find a gaggle of locals shooting the shit about shit they shot. Even doubles as a butcher shop, offering free strips of deer jerky to sample as you mull over the latest in skull dipping and Euro mounting.

This mysterious stranger, proud of his kill, tossed a burlap sack on the counter that landed with a fur-meaty thud. Earlier that day, the stranger borrowed a neighbor boy's BB gun and set off in search of small game that were now the contents of that sack.

Not much ever happens 'round these here parts. So that small sounder of shotgun-rack shack, big-beer-bellied outdoorsmen huddled in the corner paused mid-conversation, and leaned to the left to listen in on what this city slicker had to say.

You see, it wasn't so much *what* this stranger said that had the locals straining their red necks to hear. It was *how* he said what he was saying. Like Damon Runyon lost in the land of Paul Bunyon, here was a character from one of their cable TV crime shows... but... different. His voice was rough, a bit grating, a little gritty. Maybe from *Noo Yawk* or *Bahstahn,* or somewhere else East Coast exotic.

Not so fast there, pardner.

The tentative taxidermist surveyed the sack before quickly sliding it back across the counter, as if it were rotting roadkill, requesting the stranger immediately leave the premises. Hunting small game out of season in this county, without a permit, is a serious offense, punishable by a two thousand-dollar fine and up to six months in the county jail.

The stranger shrugged, thanked the taxidermist. Turned and left.

"You see, my daughter, she loved the *Chipmunks* on TV," Carmine says. "I wanted to get them stuffed, put little sweaters on 'em, for her birthday. Had a green sweater to go on the little fat guy. Small glasses for another. Put the skinny little one blue. But he just asked me to leave."

Carmine Imbriale soon forgot about the conversation. But those in the shop that day did not. That's the thing with sleepy hamlets out in the middle of nowhere. Locals talk. Housewives squawk. And soon everybody and their mother was abuzz about the stranger with his burlap bag of shot-out-of-season squirrels. Apparently, plopping a tracksuit-wearing, thick-accented slice of South Brooklyn smackdab in the middle of Middle America stirs the pot.

Didn't matter. Soon after that little girl celebrated her birthday, sans sack of stuffed squirrels clad as cartoon chipmunks, the nomadic Imbriale family was back on the road again.

Calling Carmine Imbriale a fish out of water during his time in Witness Protection is an understatement. There was that time the US Marshals Service dinged Carmine just for expressing a bit of holiday spirit. C'mon on, guys. Was that *really* necessary? After all, it was a just a little South Brooklyn holiday spirit kind of thing. See, back in the old neighborhood, after the leaves change colors and

Thanksgiving passes, with a nip in the air, the men pull out their ladders and unravel their extension cords.

In Dyker Heights, this annual tradition is now world famous. Even before the turkey clears the table, homeowners itch to rush out to their garages to start lathering their homes in layers of retina-searing bulbs and dancing animatronics to celebrate the holiday season in true "Dyker Lights" fashion.[150] [151]

These over-the-top displays draw thousands, clogging narrow streets with slow-moving herds. There are now guided tours that bring busloads of gawkers down at $20 a head. The local precinct issues tickets to unlicensed sidewalk vendors selling hot cocoa at five dollars a pop. In fact, the blocks from 11th to 13th Avenues, from 83rd to 86th Streets, so inundated with shrieking lights, can be seen from space, so they say.

No longer living in Dyker Heights? No problem. Carmine decided to recreate a bit of that old Brooklyn holiday magic. But looking in the rearview, even Carmine confesses that maybe, just maybe, he could've kept a lower profile.

"Okay, I admit I sometimes had a difficult time with that," Carmine says. "But that Christmas, I wanted to decorate my house for my family, just like we did back in the old neighborhood."

Word spread. Foot traffic was brisk. Eyes widened. Brows raised. Mouths opened. Cars lined up around the block to cruise by this strange blinking home. Just like in the old neighborhood.

Only this ain't the old neighborhood.

"You know, when we made the newspaper *and* the six o'clock news, I knew I was getting a call." Carmine

---

150. "The Dyker Heights Christmas Lights Guide," by Collier Sutter and Jennifer Picht, *Time Out New York*, December 1, 2020

151. "This Brooklyn Neighborhood Is a Con Edison Christmas Wet Dream," by Harmon Leon, *The Observer*, December 23, 2019

chuckles. "Let's just say the marshal was definitely not in the Christmas spirit about all of the news coverage."

This was way before Carmine found traction in real estate. Back then, he had trouble fitting in.

WITSEC typically pays for witness housing in their new region, new furnishings, and a "salary" based on the cost of living in the area. That amount is dependent on local economics and the size of the family. On average, members receive roughly $60,000 from the government for about six months before they're expected to land jobs and become self-supporting.[152]

"But we didn't even get half that, maybe thirty grand," Carmine remembers. And, once that stipend stopped, Carmine struggled. Without a career or even vocational training, Carmine's prospects were bleak.

"I got a job delivering newspapers, it was cold as hell, and I'm earning next to nothing, so that didn't work out. Then I get a job working as a supermarket manager. That worked for about five minutes."

Salaried positions were not suited for Carmine, especially at minimum wage. He's not exactly a work-your-way-up-the-ladder kind of guy, especially in his mid-40s.

Carmine came across an opportunity to buy into a vending-machine route. For $6,000, Carmine purchased the machines already placed in retail businesses like convenience stores, restaurants, and bars.

There are pros and cons of running a vending-machine route. For starters, you're not investing in a physical operation, so it's a modest investment. Still, $6,000 was a sizable nut for Carmine. However, after that, he didn't have to cover large overhead every month. Aside from that initial investment, there was little financial risk. Moreover,

---

152. "Witness protection program faces challenges," The Associated Press, NBC News

there was room to grow modestly without requiring a major injection of more capital.

Unfortunately, those same advantages work against the operator. With a modest investment, your profit potential is limited. And unless you start buying machines, you're more likely to grow slowly, if at all.

The logistics are also a pain in the ass. Operating a vending-machine route means physically covering a broad geography to service the machines and collect the coins on a constant basis.

Then there's the tedium. You need to keep a close eye on what you're vending, make adjustments based on the appetites of your client base. Then there's the haggling with the owners of the establishments where your machines are placed, repairs, and competition to place and keep your machines in prime locations.

"I went and bought these vending machines, had them in all these stores, and they weren't doing too good," Carmine recalls. "I worked hard, tried to make a go of it, but that's a tough business to make money, especially stuck out in the middle of nowhere. If you're in Brooklyn or some city, sure, it's easier. But these were small, dipshit towns. Hard to make money out there with that."

Carmine put his route up for sale. He invested $6,000, so he set the sale price at $15,000. "This guy calls, says he's interested, wants to know where I got 'em placed," he says. "So I invite him to come with me on my collections."

Carmine sweetened the pot.

"The day before, I went down and filled all the machines with coins and the next day, I took him with me on collections and showed how they were doing so much business." That interested party wrote Carmine a check on the spot for the full $15,000.

"Honestly, the machines performed well enough, and someone who put in the time and invested in the business could make it profitable," he says. "But that person wasn't gonna be me. I had to get rid of the route and find something else."

In every place they moved, Carmine struggled with how different things were than they'd been back in Brooklyn. In these places, people didn't hog parking spots. They returned items they borrowed without being threatened. They didn't even need to be reminded. They didn't chain up their bikes, just left them outside. They didn't lock their doors, or put bars on their windows, and left their keys in their cars.

When they took public transportation, they were trusted to pay for a ticket, no turnstiles. They cleaned up after themselves, they looked out for their neighbors, they didn't cheat, they didn't lie, and they didn't connive.

Those must be nice places. But they sure ain't Brooklyn.

For crying out loud, in Brooklyn, they place metal poles side by side outside the supermarkets, to prevent people from stealing the shopping carts. Yeah, they steal shopping carts in Brooklyn. Not sure what they do with them, but they do steal them.

You don't see poles outside supermarkets in Nowhere, USA.

"I went into one grocery store, and they had this crazy system, where you put your groceries in a wagon, you pay, and then you get a number and go around and they put your groceries in your car for you, on like the honor system," Carmine says. "So they did that, and I went around to pick up my groceries. I even tried to tip, but they said no. Couldn't even slip it to them on the sly."

Carmine was baffled, rushed home, and told Janet, who didn't believe him. No way. She had to see for herself. So he took her down to the market.

No shit.

What kind of people are these?

Gave Carmine an idea. "So I went back, bought a few things. Only this time, when I went out back, I loaded up someone else's groceries. Did that a few times, for fun. They were so stupid."

Another time, Carmine was shopping in Kmart. He just closed a purchase on a new house he was planning to convert into a rent-to-own property. Rent-to-owns can be very lucrative. They attract a higher-quality tenant, as opposed to straight rental units. The renter commits to renting the property for a period of time, with an option to purchase that unit before the lease expires. So the chances of getting stiffed on rent and having to cover property damages or eviction-related court fees are minimal.[153]

Carmine shopped that day to make necessary repairs to prepare the property for the new renters. "I have two wagons filled with household stuff, hoses, statues, plants, and as I'm walking by the front counter, a lady working there says, 'Excuse me, is that returns?'" Carmine says.

Guess what he did next? Go ahead. Guess.

"I said, 'Sure, of course these are returns.' She goes through everything in my cart and figures it all out and gives me the cash. Then I went back another time and did the same thing. Couldn't help myself. Too easy."

These were games for Carmine, not schemes. He was smart enough to know, sooner or later, he'd get caught, and that would be a disaster. Humor aside, these episodes hammered home just how far he'd come from Brooklyn—physically, mentally, emotionally.

Maybe it's what they call the "New York State of Mind." Frank Sinatra, Billy Joel, Alicia Keys, every generation sings about it. Those who live it, they brag about it. Those who leave it, lament about it. And it took Carmine Imbriale a long time to shake it, though not all of it. Basically, it's that always-on, aggressive, pushy, cut-the-line, lean-on-the-horn, bite-the-finger, throw-the-hands, get-outta-my-way-or-I'ma-run-your-ass-right-over mentality.

---

153. "How Does Rent-to-Owning Work?" Zillow.com

That's not something a native New Yorker can shut off easily, especially one of the boys from 13th Avenue. Even when it's just a little friendly game.

They don't play handball in Middle America. They don't play stickball, stoopball, punchball, none of that. And they certainly don't play concrete tackle.

But they do play racquetball. Close enough.

Carmine was in his 50s, body banged up, not as fast nor skilled as he was back on the concrete schoolyards of Brooklyn.

Yet Carmine was fitter than most Boomers, and never did lose that do-or-die drive. "I play to win, play hard, no matter what we're playing or playing for," he says. "All my life, I just loved competition. Sure, I take it too far. Some people don't like that. For them, it's like for exercise or for fun. I always wondered what it's like to be like that. That must suck."

One day, a neighbor struck up a conversation with Carmine. He invited him, as a guest, to play racquetball down at the local sports club where he had a membership. Carmine agreed.

Racquetball at a posh downtown gym is not exactly a high-stakes prison handball game in front of bloodthirsty inmates. For one thing, Carmine's opponent wasn't a convicted drug-dealing murderer from a notorious African-American gang with an eye condition. But he was a local optometrist. Still, not really the same.

And instead of a dark, dingy prison gym, they played in a pristine-white-and-glass walled, state-of-the-art upscale racquetball court in a trendy athletic facility.

Didn't matter. Once that small blue ball dropped and the game began, *it was on*. Carmine slipped into his old kill-or-be-killed mindset.

Thing was, though racquetball and handball use the same style ball, the two games are mad different. Racquetball is played with, well, a racquet, and a hollow rubber ball on an indoor court. The strings on the racquet add remarkable velocity, unlike a handball slapped by a palm.

Unlike most racquet sports, say tennis and badminton, in racquetball, there is no net to hit the ball over. Instead, a racquetball court's 20-foot-high white walls, floor, and ceiling are legal playing surfaces; unlike handball, where only a single wall is used.

For novices, the fast pace and confined quarters of racquetball can be disorienting. "Remember, I'm a handball guy, but no one plays handball no more, so I agree to play and we go play," Carmine says. "But I never played. So I'm making bad shots and cursing and banging my racket. Like I said, I'm very competitive."

They weren't wagering thousands of dollars on the outcome. There was no large crowd of rival gangs screaming, no one threatening to break anyone's legs. A ruthless Genovese mob boss who had thousands riding on Carmine was not glaring at him. Carmine's opponent wasn't even talking trash. This was a friendly game.

Fuck him.

"Are you okay?" his neighbor asked, confused as to why Carmine was so agitated. "Take it easy, pal."

Take it easy?

Is this guy kidding me?

Fuck outta here 'fore I give you a slap and a half.

"I'm getting frustrated, angry, so I bite my finger," Carmine says. "You know, it's a Brooklyn Italian thing, just something we do when we're aggravated." Carmine's opponent, though, was neither Italian, nor from Brooklyn, so the finger biting must have seemed bizarre.

"I'm also yelling at him to shut the fuck up and serve the ball." Carmine laughs. "It went like that for a little while, and then gets worse. I couldn't help myself. I was there to win."

After one too many "shut the fuck up"s, Carmine's neighbor called timeout, edged toward the glass door, bent down like he was tying his shoe. Soon as Carmine turned his back, the neighbor took off like a ricochet rabbit, bing-bing-binging right off the court, ran out the front door, jumped in his car, and raced off.

"I called my wife to come pick me up, and told her he just ran away," Carmine says. "She asked me what I did now. I told her nothing. She didn't buy it. She knows me better than anyone."

Carmine ran into this neighbor several times. Sort of. "The guy wouldn't even look at me. I mean, I didn't threaten him or hit him or nothing like that. I was just cursing at myself, angry at myself, and okay, I guess cursing at him. I was just competing as hard as I could. That's the only way I know. But I guess guys like him never seen nothing like that."

Carmine Imbriale has one gear. Full throttle. Whether that's turning a friendly pick-up racquetball game into a death match or cutting a business deal. For a time, Carmine and his family lived in Montana, one of their many stops on the road. While in Big Sky country, Carmine met a man we'll call Chuck. Originally from Seattle, Chuck worked as a contractor when he met Carmine. When Chuck bragged to Carmine about his career as a former college football player, the two struck up a relationship over their shared passion for the sport.

One day, Chuck presented a business opportunity to Carmine. At this point, Carmine was eager to explore new ventures. Chuck proposed that they partner on a discount saver book promotion.

This seemed like a great opportunity. These types of coupon books were much more popular before the internet made direct marketing to consumers less expensive. However, some still circulate in small-town markets.

Basically, local businesses and franchise operators are approached to participate in coupon book promotions. The business offers specials in these coupon books that are sold by promoters directly to consumers. The promoters are not permitted to change the terms of the coupons, oversell the books, or distribute them outside the company's normal business area. In return, the promoters receive 50 percent of the sales price of the books.

Carmine is an exceptional salesman. He's a blue-collar guy with a sense of humor, personable, relatable. After agreeing to partner with Chuck, in a relatively short time, Carmine lined up dozens of additional businesses to participate and sold a sizable quantity of books.

Then one day, Carmine and Chuck squabbled over some of the finer points of their venture. "We had that argument, and later, he called the house when I was out, and had words with my wife," Carmine says. "I got right in my car, drove to his house, and cracked him. He fell back and I jumped on him and I said, 'How dare you curse at my wife? You got a problem, you take it up with me.'"

After that dust-up, things blew over and the partnership continued, for a time. That was, until Carmine and Chuck vacationed together with their families in Virginia Beach. "While we're down there, we met these kids from Indiana University, and we started a little pick-up football game with them, Chuck on one side, me on the other. I remember it clearly. He came across the middle, and I hit him so hard, laid him out. What a hit. It was great. Felt good."

Not so much for Chuck. When Chuck regained consciousness, he did not share Carmine's appreciation for the artistry of the hit. "Chuck said, 'You're crazy,' and I was, but I told him, 'I play to win,'" he remembers. It not only ruined the game, as everyone fled the field, but dissolved the short-lived partnership between Carmine and Chuck.

"He was another phony, fake telephone tough guy, and I called his bluff. Honestly, I don't know where he played his college football. But trust me, if that clown was on the field, there's no way they won any games."

The Madonna's Revenge

Faith works in mysterious ways for those from South Brooklyn.

There's an old story about a Mafia don and a thief that tells you everything you need to know about religion in this unforgiving place. At the time, circa early 1950s, some said it was a miracle. However, the boys of 13th Avenue knew better. It goes something like this.

Brooklyn Italians take faith *very* seriously. You might even say Italians put Christianity on the map. Emperor Constantine legitimized the faith with the Edict of Milan in AD 313, making it the official religion of the Roman Empire.[154]

Yet Italian immigrants were denied their faith. Back then, America's Protestant majority, and the stern Irish clergy dominating New York's Catholic Archdiocese, discriminated against Italians.[155]

The sons of Erin arrived in America first, fleeing the potato famine of the 1840s that claimed millions.[156] By the 1880s, when the Italians came in large numbers, mostly darker-skinned, unskilled laborers from Southern Italy, the

154. "Roman History: The Edict of Man," Encyclopedia Britannica

155. *All the Nations Under Heaven: Immigrants, Migrants, and the Making of New York*, Revised Edition, by Frederick M. Binder, David M. Reimers, and Robert W. Snyder, Columbia University Press, 1995

156. *City of Dreams: The 400-Year Epic History of Immigrant New York*, by Tyler Anbinder, Houghton Mifflin Harcourt, October 18, 2016

Irish resented their willingness to work for lower wages and longer hours.[157]

Generations of young lovers from these rival groups intermarried, including Carmine's parents (Italian father, Irish mother), even as the animosity between both groups festered. The Irish ridiculed the Italians' devotion to the saints, their garish street festivals, their masses held in the Italian tongue. Services for Italians were relegated to church basements.

So, as proud Italians settled the vast plains of Brooklyn, they built their own churches, and it became known as "the City of Churches" (called such in an 1844 article by *The Brooklyn Daily Eagle*) and later the "Borough of Churches."[158]

The most impressive of these houses of worship sits a mile from where Carmine grew up, the Basilica of Regina Pacis (Latin for "Queen of Peace") on 65th Street and 12 Avenue.[159] The original parish church St. Rosalia-Regina Pacis, erected on the site in 1905, was already known as the "Mother Church of Italian Immigrants" throughout the New York Archdiocese.[160]

During a sermon in 1942, in the midst of World War II, Pastor Angelo R. Cioffi challenged the congregation to replace the church with a votive shrine to the Madonna, the Queen of Peace, to ensure the safe return of parish men fighting overseas. Italians were as patriotic for their adopted homeland as they were passionate about their faith. They scraped together the massive sum for construction, through

157. *An Unlikely Union: The Love-Hate Story of New York's Irish and Italians*, by Paul Moses, New York University Press, July 3, 2015

158. "City of Churches," The Brooklyn Daily Eagle, March 6, 1844, Newspapers.com

159. Official Site of the Basilica of Regina Pacis

160. "Pope Benedict XVI Elevates Brooklyn Church To Minor Basilica," The Roman Catholic Dioceses of Brooklyn, November 24, 2021

street fairs and collections, gathering coins and small donations. Many even ripped stones from their wedding rings and ancient heirlooms.[161] [162]

The jewels not sold to pay for construction were embedded in two crowns: one for the statue of the Virgin Mary and one for the baby Jesus. Crafted by renowned Italian jewelers the DeNatale Brothers, the intricate crowns took three years to create. When completed, Pastor Cioffi took them to the Vatican to be blessed by Pope Pius XII. They were set on display in the basilica when it opened in 1950 to great fanfare.

Then, one morning in 1952, a mortified Father James Russo noticed the crowns (valued at $100,000, a massive sum in 1950s Brooklyn, approximately $1 million when adjusted for inflation) were gone. Stolen.

The story hit the *New York Times* the next morning. More than ten thousand distraught Catholics descended upon the basilica to pray for the return of the crowns. For more than a week, there were no leads. Local investigators were stumped. It seemed as if the crowns were lost forever.

Eight days later, a tightly wrapped, nondescript package arrived at the church rectory through the postal service. It included both crowns, with some of the jewels missing, damaged and requiring repair, but mostly intact. With no letter, no explanation, the delivery was a mystery.

The nation rejoiced.

Beyond the borders of Bensonhurst, the story of the Madonna's stolen crown jewels remained unsolved for years. Technically, this is still a cold case in the annals of the New York City Police Department.

---

161. "Gold Crowns Stolen from Church Shrine are Returned: Church Gets Stolen Gems in Mail; Pastor Hails Recovery as Miracle," *New York Times*, June 9, 1952

162. "Shrine dedicated; 7,000 at services," *New York Times*, August 16, 1951.

Yet South Brooklyn locals know better. Lost in the headlines heralding the return of the jewels, buried way back in papers' police blotters, was a brief report of Ralph "Bucky" Emmino, a low-level Mafia associate and jewel thief, found shot to death in Bath Beach. Emmino was tortured, then murdered, on the orders of gang boss Joseph Profaci.

Or so the old rumors go.

No one provided testimony. There is no evidence.

During the 1950s, Joseph Profaci ruled a broad cut of the South Brooklyn rackets. Following the Castellammarese War of the early 1930s, when a band of young Turks led by upstart Charles "Lucky" Luciano outgunned the old guard "Mustache Petes," Luciano shaped the Mafia Commission. That ruling body consisted of the leaders of the Five Families in New York, as well as the bosses from Chicago and Buffalo, bringing order to the underworld. Profaci assumed a seat on the Commission as founder of one of those five families, the one that bore his name, the predecessor to the Colombos.[163]

Profaci was a murderer, a thief, a racketeer, but also a religious man. He paid to have priests perform masses in his home and also attended the groundbreaking of the basilica. Upon hearing of the pilfering at Regina Pacis, he ordered a manhunt for the thief. And concealing $100,000 in stolen jewels in the Brooklyn underworld ain't easy.[164] [165] [166]

Before Profaci henchmen shot Emmino, they strangled him with rosary beads.

Again, or so the old story goes.

---

163. Law, Crime, and Punishment: Joseph Profaci Biography, Britannica

164. "Mafia Banned Murder – Halted Hits Under Heat," by Steve Dunleavy, *New York Post*, July 12, 2004

165. "A Tip Directs the F.B.I. To Stolen Church Jewels," by Glenn Fowler, *New York Times*, January 22, 1973

166. *Iceman of Brooklyn: The Mafia Life of Frankie Yale* by Michael Newton, McFarland, April 16, 2021

According to FBI informant files from 1962, Greg Scarpa Sr. confirmed that Profaci ordered the execution of Emmino. While Scarpa Sr. did not identify the killer, he suspected Profaci consigliere Charles "the Sidge" LoCicero, as Emmino was "running numbers of LoCicero at the time."[167]

Today, in the church proper, there's a massive ceiling mural that depicts the Coronation of Our Lady Regina Pacis. The few old timers left along 13th Avenue will tell you that for years—joining the blessed mother, the choir of angels, and scores of heavenly saints—buried in that mural was an image of Profaci himself. Yet it was painted over when a reporter started snooping.

Yes, faith works in mysterious ways for those from South Brooklyn.

In the summers of Carmine Imbriale's youth, they still shouldered the massive effigies of their saints through the streets in processions preceding the Italian street festivals the Irish once scorned. These *feasts* were sponsored by ancient societies, like the Festa di Santa Rosalia and the Festa di Santa Fortunata.

Like flocks of slow-shuffling *pinguinos*, the old Italian black shawls still made their early morning pilgrimages to the Italian masses. Sunday services were packed, and still followed by mid-afternoon family feasts. And front yards were still guarded by the blank-staring statues of Saint Anthony and Padre Pio.

The Imbriale family's parish was the Roman Catholic Shrine Church of Saint Bernadette—not as large nor as ornate as Regina Pacis, but still a beautiful church—on 13th Avenue between 82nd and 83rd Streets.[168]

---

167. Top Echelon Criminal Informant Program, New York Division, Federal Bureau of Investigation, FBI Subject File for Gregory Scarpa Sr., Memoranda from SAC to FBI Director, Part 01, Page 10, 8/31/62

168. Official website of The Shrine Church of St. Bernadette, Brooklyn, NY

Young Carmine enrolled at Saint Bernadette's for catechism weekly religious instruction, forced to attend confession regularly. Confession, or the sacrament of penance, is a rite where parish members confess sins committed after baptism to receive absolution administered by a priest. The children attend confession together, separate from the adults.

As all good Catholic boys and girls remember, you wait in a line at the back of the church for your turn to enter a small, dark booth. You kneel and a small screened window slaps open for you to admit your sins to a priest you do not actually see. The priest assigns penance, usually doing some good deed or act of reconciliation, as well as a stack of prayers. Carmine often received a larger number of prayer assignments than most boys of the parish.

One day, in the sixth grade, Carmine attended confession with Mike Sella, a tough Irish kid from the neighborhood who was a couple years older. "Mikey Sella and me, we're in line, waiting to give confession with the monsignor," Carmine remembers. "Bobby DiCarlo comes running in, late. We knew him, so he comes right up to us, tries to cut in line."

Robert J. "Bob" DiCarlo grew up to serve in the New York State Senate in Albany (1993 - 1996) representing Bay Ridge, Brooklyn, and Staten Island's East Shore.[169]

"Mikey wouldn't let him cut, because we'd been waiting and wanted to get outta there and go play ball. But Bobby forced his way in front of us, thinking who he was because of his father. He was being a real jerkoff. That set Mikey off." Bobby's father was Dominick DiCarlo, a local politician who served in the New York State Assembly (1965 - 1981), was Ronald Reagan's first assistant secretary

---

169. Candidate Details for Robert J. DiCarlo, Our Campaigns

of state for international narcotics matters (1981 – 1984), and federal judge.[170]

"So Mikey hauls off and knocks him out cold, then goes into confession and tells the priest. I couldn't believe Mikey owned up to it, but I respected it. Things were different back then. Monsignor must have given Mikey twenty Hail Marys and another twenty Our Fathers to say."

Growing up, both of Carmine's parents were religious. Though his father only attended the occasional Christmas Mass, and funerals and weddings, he was a devout Catholic. He was a hard man, but a man of faith and integrity, values he instilled in his children. However, Carmine's father was not a fan of certain clergy at Saint Bernadette's.

"They didn't disagree on religion, both were very religious," Carmine says. "They just didn't see eye to eye, especially when it came to monsignor. My mother always attended mass, but my father had a problem going and sitting there because he thought the guy was a crook."

One afternoon, the monsignor led a group of priests and nuns door to door in the neighborhood, soliciting donations to add a wing onto Saint Bernadette's. "My father slammed the door, and I mean *slammed it*, loud, right in his face," Carmine says. "I saw the whole thing, thought it was hilarious. My mother did not. And boy, they went at it."

This particular priest may not fit the mold of a traditional monsignor. But after all, this was 1970s South Brooklyn. "The monsignor kind of acted like he was in the mob," Carmine recalls. "He was a big guy, for a priest. Carried himself that way, not like a priest; with, like, a swagger. And he was quicker with his hands than any priest I ever seen. Me and the boys were always fighting with other kids at the church bazaar. He'd drag us into the rectory, and had

---

170. Federal Court Jude Profile of Dominick L. DiCarlo, Federal Judicial Center

no problem slapping us. And that man didn't have no hands like any monsignor you've ever been slapped by."

The monsignor was more casual than what you'd expect from a Roman Catholic priest, which didn't sit right with a traditionalist like Carmine's father. "Monsignor would sit outside the rectory, wearing a muscle shirt, with his big, purple priest hat on backwards." Carmine laughs. "My father would say to my mother, 'That's your priest?' and then complain how she was wasting his money. But she still went to mass, still gave money, and I still had to go to catechism and confession."

The monsignor didn't help matters. He organized casino nights and night-at-the-races events in the church basement to raise money, as well as raffles and sweepstakes. If there was anything Carmine's father disliked more than crooked clergy, it was *bunco* gambling.

When Carmine was 12 years old, St. Bernadette's held a raffle, offering the winner a brand-new Cadillac, donated by a local car dealership. At a time when the median annual household income in America was barely $7,000, the chance of winning a shiny new Cadillac was surreal.

So, as they say in South Brooklyn, *everybody and their mutha* was buzzing about the raffle all summer.

Well, almost everyone. "At the Saint Bernadette Bazaar, they had a booth to get a ticket for a chance to win that Cadillac, and believe me, everybody got a ticket; except my father," Carmine says. "No matter how exciting it got, he refused to play. Said it was a gimmick, said it was rigged, said, 'They're not getting none of my money.'"

But they did. Carmine's mother ignored her husband, buying up dozens of tickets.

Then, as the Saint Bernadette Bazaar drew to a close, the entire neighborhood made its way to the street outside the parish church for the big finale.

Who was going to win that Cadillac?

The crowd hushed, straining to see the elevated stage, packed along 13th Avenue outside St. Bernadette's. Quiet descended, so much so that you could hear the turning balls plinking in that big bingo drum.

Necks craned as a tiny sister of the parish reached into that drum and drew a small slip, stepped to the mic, and did a double take frown before announcing the winner.

Oh my, what a surprise.

The monsignor had won the Cadillac.

Groans flew up and down 13th Avenue that day.

"My father went home and drank a bottle of scotch, pissed my mother had bought so many raffle tickets." Carmine laughs. "But not for nothing, what was she gonna say back?"

In those days, every summer there were dozens of feasts like the St. Bernadette's Bazaar. Long white trailers lined both sides of the street for blocks and blocks, with games of chance, *zeppole* carts, street performers, rides for the kids, Italian bands and, if you were lucky, Lucy's Sausage Stand.

For the hot-blooded boys of South Brooklyn, these were battlegrounds. Carmine and the 13th Avenue Boys most frequent feast brawls were with the Bath Avenue Boys, Carmine usually out in front, swinging wildly.

One summer evening, during a St. Bernadette's Bazaar, Carmine and his boys patrolling 13th Avenue spotted a handful of Bath Avenue Boys, who did not see them.

Nearby were some crab apple trees, the kind that once grew in yards all over Brooklyn. Dozens of overripe apples had fallen into the street.

Ammunition.

Carmine and his boys scooped up armloads of those rock-hard orbs, snuck up on their rivals, and bombarded them. In the melee, Carmine, usually a sure shot, threw wide, striking the statue of the Blessed Virgin Mary right in her precious ceramic head. Carmine paused at the shot, struck by a sense of foreboding, then went back to driving his rivals off the Avenue.

Not more than an hour later, Carmine felt a throbbing pain begin pulsing from the right side of his head. He became nauseous, vomited into the street. The bright lights and loud sounds of the feast grew overwhelming, and he stumbled home in agony.

For a full day Carmine lay in darkness, recovering.

Since that evening, after striking the Madonna in the right side of her head in anger with a stray South Brooklyn crab apple, Carmine has suffered migraine headaches. Carmine went to confession afterward, yet no number of Hail Marys or Our Fathers could save him. The Madonna would have her way with Carmine Imbriale.

In the early 1990s, with the Colombo Family locked in a bitter civil war, the Neddy's Bar crew in turmoil, Carmine Sessa in hiding, Michael Sessa set his sights on Carmine. Sessa assembled a hit team that included Joey Brains Ambrosino and another associate, and headed to Staten Island.

The hit crew arrived at Carmine's home early evening, but not late, with passersby floating by. They circled the block a couple times before rolling into the driveway. Sessa sat in the car as Ambrosino approached, gun ready in his pocket, and rang the bell. The plan was to lure Carmine outside on the false pretense Carmine Sessa had emerged from hiding and called a sit-down for the crew. Then, get Carmine Imbriale in the car, shoot him to death, then dump him in a hole already dug out in Great Kills. Afterward, Michael Sessa would plant the seed that Carmine had been whacked by the Orena faction.

By then, Michael Sessa was desperate to wipe out Carmine, at a time when everyone was distracted by the war. However, Carmine would not budge from his home, which he shared with his wife and children. This was a problem. First of all, according to the rules, involving families in violence was forbidden. Moreover, this was an unsanctioned hit. Michael Sessa never got permission from his brother.

Ambrosino was handpicked to lure Carmine out because of their close relationship. They'd collaborated on dozens of scams, and were friends. Michael Sessa knew that out of anyone in the crew, Carmine would more likely trust Ambrosino.

Yet, at that very moment, the Madonna of 13th Avenue was again punishing Carmine Imbriale.

As the assassin Ambrosino shadowed Carmine's doorstep, gun locked, loaded, Carmine was rocked by a vicious migraine. Any other time, Carmine would answer that bell at his front door, welcome Ambrosino, and go willingly... or be murdered on the spot. Ambrosino had orders to take the shot if he could do it without witnesses.

Instead, Carmine's wife, Janet, blocked the way. Ambrosino insisted. Janet resisted.

Sessa and Ambrosino returned the next evening, meeting the same response. In fact, within a ten-day span, they visited Carmine's home three times. On the third visit, Ambrosino would not be denied.

"They came to my house and Joey insisted to Janet that Carmine [Sessa] needed to see me right away, it was a direct order, and I'm on the bathroom floor in the dark with a really bad migraine. Joey even came into the bathroom, saw me, asked me to take a quick ride. I said, 'Get the fuck out of here.' Right after they left, I went to the hospital and got a Demerol shot. I didn't find out until later they were trying to whack me without telling Carmine."

Did that poorly aimed crab apple, thrown so many years ago, save Carmine's life? Carmine thought about that for a long time. It was part of a religious awakening. Along the dark winding road ahead, Carmine and his family needed all the faith they could muster.

Yet the Queen of Peace was not quite done with Carmine Imbriale.

In the cold winter of 2019, Carmine was diagnosed with cancer. Caught early, the cancer was treatable. Yet at this late stage, the risk was high. It required surgery. Carmine went under the knife. There were complications. The family gathered at the hospital in vigil.

The next day brought more uncertainty. Janet and family members retreated to a Catholic church for a day of prayer.

One of the priests gave each Imbriale family member a healing prayer card. These are like small playing cards with the image of a saint or religious scene on one side, a healing prayer on the other. The priest instructed the family members to pray to the saint on their card.

Then the priest handed Janet a card to place by Carmine's bedside. Janet was distracted, upset, worried, and didn't focus on the card until later, when she pressed it into Carmine's lifeless hand.

When she looked down and realized what the card depicted, it took her breath away.

On the front side of that prayer card were two figures.

One was Saint Bernadette of Lourdes.

Alongside her was the Madonna of the Miracle.

Carmine soon recovered.

Yes, faith sure does work in mysterious ways for those from South Brooklyn.

You Can Never Go Home

Entering the Witness Protection Program, you sever ties with your life.

Under no circumstances may you return to your childhood home, former place of business, or anywhere in that region of the country you knew. Whatever you leave behind, stays behind. If you do return home, you violate your agreement and can be expelled from the program.

What would you take with you? What would you leave behind?

It was months before Carmine's family had a permanent address. They lived out of suitcases in hotels on the outskirts of cities with names you've never heard. They ate out of cardboard containers with plastic cutlery, slept on starchy sheets, passed time slowly, sitting, waiting... hoping.

"I still have my wife and kids and my life and you can't say that about many who were part of this thing," Carmine says. "People think it's a break, and maybe it is, but it's not that easy. Changing your name, changing the names of your kids, changing your entire life, disrupting your family."

The US Marshals Service kept Carmine's family safe. Federal agents kept him busy. He shuttled back and forth from safe houses to the basements of federal buildings. Met with an alphabet soup of government agencies. Cases were built, loops closed. His decades of knowledge of the inner workings of the 13th Avenue mob filled in thousands of blanks.

Within days of Carmine's arrest, the job of packing up the Imbriale family's entire life fell to Carmine's wife, Janet. "I give my sister-in-law a lot of credit for dealing with all that and being there for him," Maryellen Imbriale says. "She is pretty amazing."

Janet had her work cut out for her. This was a one-shot deal. No return trips. Too dangerous. The kids were not allowed to leave the safehouse, and there were no friends or family members to help.

Janet had to move fast. Word was out on the street that Carmine flipped. By the time Carmine was in protective custody, his name was on the lips of every wiseguy in South Brooklyn, especially those he'd done dirt with over the years.

Colombo wiseguys knew Carmine's house was empty, but likely kept it under surveillance, hoping he returned for a favorite sweater or family heirloom.

Federal marshals secured the location, then instructed Janet to work with a vetted team of movers to pack whatever she wanted and they'd load it onto a moving truck. They didn't set limits other than if Janet could fit it onto the truck, it could go.

Good thing they brought a big truck.

These days, the Marshals Service mandates sterner guidelines on what personal property witnesses and their family members can bring when entering the program. For one thing, they disallow items that can in any way identify you. Documents, photographs, pieces of jewelry, unique pieces of clothing, souvenirs... all must be abandoned.

Back in the early 1990s, though, they were more flexible. They assumed Janet, like most wives entering the program before her, would heed their advice, leave most of her former life behind and try and make as clean a break as possible.

They didn't know Janet Imbriale.

"I took it all," Janet laughs. "Anything and everything not nailed down, and even some of the furniture that was nailed down, I had them put on that truck. And not only the furniture inside; I had them take everything in the backyard, down to the patio furniture. We were there all day, but I didn't care. I wanted my stuff. It was bad enough we had to leave."

The two marshals sat by, patiently waiting as the hours dragged on from the morning into the late afternoon.

"They sat there all day and rolled their eyes as I took everything," she says. "But I was not leaving any of our stuff, not the pictures, not the albums, not the photos, all of that stuff they now say you can't take, I took. I don't know if they changed the rules because of us, but they did change the rules, so now you can't take all your stuff like we did. But I got everything."

Well, almost everything.

A few priceless items still needed to be negotiated. These proved more problematic than just bubble-wrapping some lawn chairs.

"They said we couldn't take our dog," Carmine says. "Can you image that? We loved this dog, like part of the family. We were shocked when they told us we had to leave him behind."

Today, federal marshals will not allow pets to relocate with witnesses for good reason. Unlike an old sweater or pictures that can be stowed in closets, pets draw attention. They also respond to their former names. In one case, when Jess Brewer, a narcotics trafficker in Hawaii, entered the program with his wife Rae Devera, the family had to give away its dog, Pono, then asked if they could at least take their cat, Susha, and were denied.[171]

But in the early 90s, this was a grey area.

---

171. "What Happens When You Enter the Witness Protection Program?" by Alex Mayyasi, Pricenomics

"So my wife said, 'If we can't take the dog, then we're not going,'" Carmine recalls. The Imbriales held firm. It was a beautiful dog, a Shetland sheepdog, also known as a Sheltie, like a mini-Lassie.

For crying out loud, who leaves Lassie behind?

"So they all walk out of the room," Carmine says. "Then, after a bit, they come back in, and they agree to let us take the dog."

Both sides seemed relieved to settle what could have derailed months of hard work.

But wait. Not so fast. "What about my cat?" Janet interrupted. "I mean, we love this cat. This was a great cat. We've had this cat forever. We can't leave this cat behind. My kids love this cat. She's like a member of our family."

The Imbriales dug in their heels. Again, the marshals left the room to huddle. After a short while, they returned and relented. The Imbriale cat would join the family in hiding.

Then, an exasperated marshal jokingly asked a question he regretted the moment it left his lips. "You guys got any other pets?"

"Oh yeah, that's right. Sure, we also gotta take the parakeet," Carmine quipped.

He was joking. Sort of. "We could've lived without the parakeet." Carmine laughs. "Bird was kind of annoying anyway."

A dog is one thing. Even a cat is reasonable. But a parakeet? Now you're reaching.

Sure, over the years, program participants submitted unusual requests. Some requested the school grades of their children be doctored.[172] Gangster Aladena "Jimmy the Weasel" Fratiano had the feds pay for breast implants and a face lift for his wife. Another nameless mobster requested funding for a penile implant. Distraught at being unable to

---

172. *Witsec: Inside the Federal Witness Protection Program* by Pete Earley, Bantam, April 1, 2003

satisfy his wife (as well as a mistress), he no longer wanted to testify for the government.[173]

Turns out Carmine's parakeet request was a first for the Witness Protection Program. Such a request needed to be escalated to Washington. The decision took longer to come back. Much longer. Hours, in fact. The government approved the bird.

"Then later, [FBI Agent] Jeff Tomlinson comes to the safehouse. It was raining, he's in a trench coat, all serious, and tells me, 'Bad news, Carmine.' Me, I got a lot on my mind, and I'm here thinking the worst, something real bad happened, like my brother got shot or something. 'No,' they said, 'Sorry, Carmine, but the parakeet didn't make it.'

"What did I care about the stupid bird?" Carmine says. "I even told Jeff, if he didn't make it, musta been a stool pigeon and got whacked."

There was a happy ending to the story, albeit a bit delayed. "Crazy thing, there's a mix-up at the airport, and the cat and dog don't make the flight. So now, you can imagine how pissed the marshals are, having to track down the animals and put them on another flight. My kids are upset, they miss the pets. I tell them don't worry, they're coming tomorrow. So they're sitting there waiting the next day, faces pressed against the glass. And they finally came, in a cab, just the dog, the cat, and the driver."

And so, the Imbriales disappeared, never to be seen again...

.... kind of.

For years, Carmine heeded the warnings of the marshals and never set foot in Kings County. Even after exiting the Witness Protection program in 1998, Carmine and his family continued to live under assumed aliases in an undisclosed location.

---

173. "The Invisible Family," by Robert Sabbag, *New York Times*, February 11, 1996

Carmine had been away for so long, many of the wiseguys he put away were dead, some still imprisoned, but some have been released. Some are still active in South Brooklyn. Even Joel "Joe Waverly" Cacace, whose murder of a police officer was likely the single most egregious crime leading to an all-out blitz from law enforcement, was released from a federal penitentiary in 2019, despite admitting to four murders.

Contacting family has been challenging, but not impossible. Over the years, Carmine quietly reached out to some family members. Mostly long-distance phone calls, Caller ID blocked. Face-to-face encounters were rare.

"We both had daughters born around the same time, his daughter on July 12 on his birthday, and my daughter September 22, born on my husband's birthday, and we tried to keep them close," Maryellen Imbriale remembers. "When they were both around three years old, that's when Carmine left."

Carmine was not supposed to contact any family members, but he did from time to time.

"What we would do was I would buy presents for his kids, and he'd buy presents for mine, and we would not send them, but put tags on them like it was from each other," Maryellen says. "It was very sad, not to be together as a family, but we spoke.

"He would call me out of the blue and it would be short phone calls and I finally did get to see him, after about five years in the program; we met up in North Carolina with all the kids," Maryellen says. "It was like he never changed, but in a happier place. And the kids were growing up and interesting. Carmine's personality, his jokes, his charisma, for him to have maintained all of that, through all he's been through, is amazing."

By 2013, Carmine had been away from the neighborhood for more than 20 years. He decided to visit family in Mill Basin, Brooklyn.

Mill Basin is not Dyker Heights. It's a less congested residential neighborhood in the southeastern part of Brooklyn, about 11 miles east of Neddy's Bar. It's on a peninsula just north of Floyd Bennet Field, abutting Jamaica Bay, once known for its abundant shellfish—crabs, oysters, and clams. It's more family-oriented, a suburban oasis with near 360-degree shoreline views.

So no, Mill Basin is not close to Dyker Heights. But it's close enough.

Traffic was light on that beautiful summer afternoon. There were still a couple hours of daylight remaining. Carmine couldn't help himself. After his visit, he got back in his car, paused, checked the rearview, said fuck it, jumped on the Belt Parkway and headed west for the 15-minute ride to breeze by his old haunts.

Yet a funny thing happened to this former wiseguy on the way to visit his past. As he rolled off the Belt Parkway at the 14th Avenue exit, he realized, sometimes, you know, you can't go home.

Sometimes, home is no longer there.

"I drove down 13th Avenue, fast enough so it'd be hard to see my face or my plates, but not so fast that I'd get pulled over," Carmine says. "Sure, Sirico's was still there, and Mona Lisa. Then I went by Neddy's Bar, and I laughed to myself at a couple of idiots hanging around outside. These guys? I used to shake them down all the time, rob them for their pot. Here they were, playing the part of tough wiseguys, probably *made* by now. What a joke, bunch of jerkoffs."

But even that was different. As Carmine drove through a South Brooklyn he sort of recognized, he saw how the neighborhood had changed in the decades he'd been away. The wiseguys no longer patrolled the sidewalks, scheming with hands cupped over their mouths to throw off federal lip readers. Gone were their cafes and social clubs, replaced by tanning salons and Pan Asian fusion joints.

Sure, on that day, Neddy's Bar was still serving, but it was up for sale. Soon, it faded from view, like Greg Scarpa's Wimpy Boys, reborn as Sal's Hair Stylist and Barber Shop. Tali's Bar, Sammy Gravano's wiseguy spot on 18th Avenue, was a Pho Vietnamese restaurant for a time. Carmine Sessa's Occasions, a car service. Billy Fingers' Friendly Bocce Social Club on 11th and 63rd Street is now the Sun Ray Driving School. The Gemini Lounge, the Flatlands Avenue joint where Roy DeMeo's crew murdered dozens in a side room, is now the Church of God. The Wrong Number on Avenue T is a nondescript storefront.

Gone were the butchers, the bakers, the *braciole di manzo* makers. No more pork barons, no more fish mongers. No more salumerias, no more scents of Sunday sauce spiking the air, nor pungent garlic to punch you in the nose. Where once were mom-and-pops were now Middle Eastern markets, empty bank lobbies, 99-cent stores.

No longer did Italian flags snap in the wind in the front yards. No longer did the blank-stare statues of Saint Anthony and Padre Pio guard the cement gardens. And no sounds of broken *Barese* or clipped *Calabrese* drifted by. Bensonhurst's Little Italy gets littler and littler every year, worn down by waves of immigration from Asia, Russia, and the Middle East.

The feasts are nearly all gone, and the ones left are less than half the size they were when Carmine led the 13th Avenue Boys' assaults against Bath Avenue. The elderly Italian black shawls no longer crawl along the avenues to Italian masses in the morning.

Pastels no longer pumps freestyle on Saturday nights, at least not on 88th Street. A nostalgic version of the South Brooklyn club popped up on the South Shore of Staten Island for a while, drew many of the old regulars, but with less hair, larger bellies, and no more cocaine in the bathroom or sex in the stalls.

Just about all the old movie theaters in the neighborhood have closed down, converted into Asian-themed supermarkets (the Fortway), gyms (the Benson Twin), and retail outlets (the Loew's Oriental and the Walker). And they no longer show the *Rocky Horror Picture Show* Saturdays at midnight at the Marlboro on Bay Parkway. It's now a damn CVS.

Mona Lisa is still on 13th Avenue, or you can drop in at Villabate Alba for a sugar-dusted cannoli. But better get there at the crack of dawn Easter morning because half of New Jersey lines up out front to snag a box of cannoli or grain pies for their holiday tables. The rest, the *Rispolis* and the *Fortunatas* and the *Terminis,* that once stood on every other corner, their ovens were long cold and sold.

There are no longer payphones and fire department call boxes on the corners. The sun still softens the asphalt, but there are no stickball games in the streets. Kids don't hang onto the backs of buses for free rides out to Coney, and the johnny pumps no longer scream out the sun. They no longer throw block parties with the DJ set stacked on milk crates, or chuck their old sneakers up to sag the power lines. Damn, they don't even cruise chromed out caddies under the 86th Street El on Saturday nights anymore—the city put up signs years ago so you're not even allowed to park there at night.

All the old joints—Richelieu's, Chookies, the Cotillion, the Del Rio, Millers, even the Vegas that held out the longest—all gone. Jahn's, Italia Records, Carvel, Gloria's, Seedy Edie's, Sbarros', Ceasar's Bay Bazaar, the Avenue I Flea... *see ya.* Even Nellie Bly is no longer Nellie Bly, and Korvettes is a *frickin'* Kohls.

And the Backwards Wheelchair Lady no longer rolls down 86th Street, and Crazy Vinny no longer talks to his fingers as he sings on Bay Parkway, playing that charming little ukulele.

Sure, as Carmine drove, block after block, he realized the Brooklyn he left behind all those years ago no longer existed, except in fading memories, photographs, and old Super 8 videos.

Sad? Bittersweet?

Sure.

Yet Carmine survived.

Even if the South Brooklyn he no longer knew did not.

Photos

Retired NYPD Detective Thomas "Tommy" Dades

Carmine Sessa

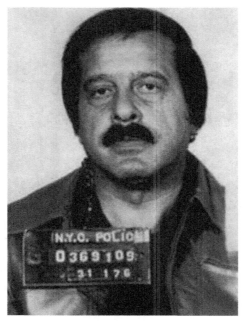

Greg "The Grim Reaper" Scarpa Sr.

Frank "Frankie Notch" Iannaci

Matthew "Matty the Horse" Ianniello

James "Jimmy" Ida

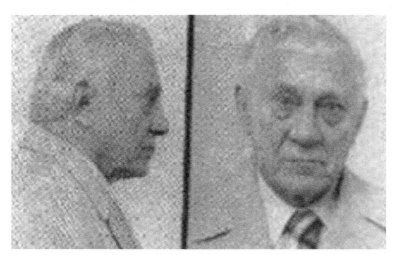

Aniello "Mr. Neil" Dellacroce

Christopher "Christie Tick" Furnari

Salvatore "Sammy the Bull" Gravano

Vittorio "Little Vic" Orena

Joel "Joe Waverly" Cacace

Michael "Mikey Scars" DiLeonardo

William "Wild Bill" Cutolo

Joseph Colombo

Dominick "Baldy Dom" Canterino

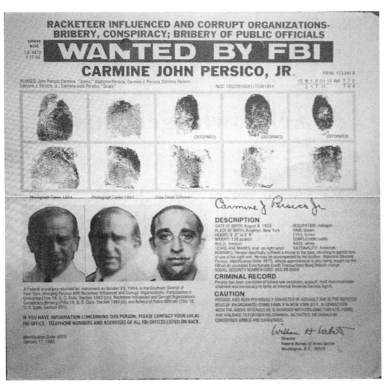

Carmine "The Snake" Persico Wanted Poster

Acknowledgements

This work would not have been possible without the tremendous support of the following people.

CARMINE IMBRIALE WOULD LIKE TO
RECOGNIZE THE FOLLOWING:

To my wife, who is my soulmate, best friend, and partner for life. We wouldn't be where we are if it were not for you. Thank you for sticking with me and never leaving my side. I love you deeply, with all my heart.

To my children, thank you for always loving me through all of our tough times. I am so proud that you are all mine, and I am proud to have you call me Dad. I love each and every one of you all more than life. I thank God for blessing me with all of you.

To my grandchildren, you are all very precious and special to me. Words cannot describe the love I have for you. May God bless you and keep you happy always.

To my sister Maryellen and my brothers, thank you for your loving support through the years.

In devoted memory of my mother, who loved me unconditionally, no matter what I did, you were always by my side. I am happy you saw me with my loving family, still all together, and my close relationship with God. I know you're smiling down on us all.

To my father, who made me who I am today. You taught me to be a man, strong, tough, honest, a man of his word, loyal, respectful, and to stand firm on my own two feet. You also taught me that family is all that matters and to love and cherish them. I now smile every time I remember you say, "Carmine, you're heading to the bullpen."

To all of my aunts (my mother's sisters) who followed my mother's lead and loved me without condition.

To my mother-in-law and my wife's extended family, nieces and nephews, I love you all, and my wife's Nana, who we still talk about when we get together. She was very special and is greatly missed.

Danny Grimaldi and Eddie Beak, for agreeing to comment for this book, and for your friendship for all these years.

A personal thank you to Tommy Dades, who is more like a brother than my friend. From the beginning to the end, you stuck by me, advised me, and even fed me in lock up. Thanks for everything, Tommy.

To Craig McGuire, who made this book possible. After being introduced by my good friend Tommy Dades, from the first conversation, I knew this was a good fit. We laughed a lot and knew we had something here. I consider you not just my writer, but my good friend. Thank you for all your hard work. I couldn't have done this book without you.

In loving memory to those deceased, including my dear sister Joanne and my good friend Joe De Simone.

CRAIG MCGUIRE WOULD LIKE TO
RECOGNIZE THE FOLLOWING:

First and foremost, Carmine Imbriale, for the privilege of allowing me to share these remarkable stories. It's been a long, winding road, one that I hope continues. I consider you a close friend and I look forward to helping share more of your stories.

To Janet Imbriale, for keeping us both honest, adding so much value, remembering so many details, and holding Carmine to task. This work would not have been possible but for your contributions. Thank you.

To Marie McGuire, my mom, who saw something in a scrawny Brooklyn scrub so long ago, believed in me, sacrificing so much for me, and never letting me quit.

To Francis X. McGuire, my dad, for saving me from the abyss and opening that Brooklyn street kid up to the wonderful world of the written word. I regret sadly that you were not part of yet another chapter in this journey you helped start.

Those individuals who allowed me to call for advice, consolation, or to read copy, including Mike Deliso, Bill Donnelly, Robert Katz, Greg Janvier, Ron Valdes, Ivan Avelancio, Steven Matt, Dori Bright, Elizabeth Cahail, Christopher Bayer, Michael McLeer, Joe Pupo, Sean Lawler, Rob Bolstad, Jeff St. Leger, Mick Dorgan, Anthony Ibelli, and so many more. I beg forgiveness for those I have failed to mention.

Special thanks to the most wonderful in-laws a man can have, Tony and Maria, for their patience, their support, and their daughter. Also, Susan McGuire, Bailey, Eddie, and Sophie, as well as Bryan; Barbara and John Ambre; Mary Ellen and Robert McGuire; Carol and Dennis O'Connor; and the rest of the Long Island and Georgia McGuires;

Santino, Enza, Sara, Catia, Marisa, Kelvin, Enza-Marina, Luca, Marco, Zander, the Antonios, and the rest of the South Florida Delisos.

Finally, and especially, to my wife, my rock, my love, my Anna, for seeing something in a South Brooklyn bartender all those years ago, enough so to come back and live in my Gravesend cave, and all the ever after; and to my three sons, Frank, Jace, and Tonio, for their lack of patience, their intolerance of dad jokes, and their barely conceived contempt that convinced me that when you said you were proud I was your dad, I knew you meant it and it meant the world.

JOINT ACKNOWLEDGEMENTS

To our publisher, WildBlue Press, for taking a chance on this work and nurturing it in its long march to market, especially Steve Jackson and Michael Cordova, as well as Publishing Director Ashley Kaesemeyer, Editor Jenn Waterman, and the rest of the crew. There is something amazing going on at WildBlue Press. If you support independent publishing and the arts, support WildBlue Press.

Last, but certainly not least, to retired NYPD Detective Tommy Dades, for bringing us both together at the start of this long road, making the time to guide us along the path when needed, and inspiring us to complete the journey.

Further Reading – Bibliography

1. The Most Popular Zip Codes for Baby Boomers: New York Challenges Sunny Locations for the Title," RENTCafé, July 16, 2019

2. "The Year 1957," ThePeopleHistory.com

3. *Brooklyn's Dodgers: The Bums, the Borough, and the Best of Baseball, 1947-1957,* by Carl E. Prince, Oxford University Press, 1997

4. *Mafia Summit: J. Edgar Hoover, the Kennedy Brothers, and the Meeting That Unmasked the Mob,* by Gil Reavill, Thomas Dunne Books, 2013

5. "Where the Mob Once Found Its Members," by Ed Scarpo, CosaNostraNews.com, 2014

6. *Carmine the Snake: Carmine Persico and His Murderous Mafia Family,* by Frank Dimatteo and Michael Benson, Citadel Press, 2018

7. *Five Families: The Rise, Decline, and Resurgence of America's Most Powerful Mafia Empires*, by Selwyn Raab, Thomas Dunne Books, 2014

8. "Coney Island, home to hot dogs and the Cyclone roller coaster, sees a budding real estate boom," Daniel Bukszpan, CNBC, December 30, 2018

9. *Coney Island: The Decline & Death of an American Icon*, by Michael Malott, November 13, 2010

10. *Underboss: Sammy the Bull Gravano's Story of Life in the Mafia*, by Peter Maas, HarperCollins, 1997

11. "Puparo Presents: The Roaring 1970s," Gangsters Inc.

12. *Anabolic Steroid Abuse*, by Geraline C. Lin, Diane Publishing, 1996

13. *Wiseguy: Life in a Mafia Family*, by Nicholas Pileggi, Simon & Shuster, 1985

14. *My Blue Heaven*, Written by Nora Ephron, Directed by Herbert Ross

15. "Tribal Rites of the New Saturday Night," by Nik Cohn, *New York Magazine*, 1976

16. "Disco's Saturday Night Fiction," by Nadia Khoumami, *The Guardian*, 1996

17. "Two Convicted as Leaders of New York Trash Cartel," by Selwyn Raab, *New York Times,* October 22, 1997

18. *Mob Killer: The Bloody Rampage of Charles Carneglia, Mafia Hit Man*, by Anthony DeStefano, Pinnacle Books, June 1, 2011

19. "Prosecutor to jurors: Mob man Joel Cacace ordered cop Ralph Dols' slay out of envy," by John Marzulli, *New York Daily News*, November 25, 2013

20. "Mob Figure Admits Roles In Murders, Including Judge's," by William Glaberson, *New York Times,* August 14, 2004

21. "Suspected Mob Capo, 51, Shot in Brooklyn," *New York Times*, February 27, 1992

22. "Genovese Family Counselor Is Convicted of Racketeering," by Jan Hoffman, *New York Times*, April 24, 1997

23. The GM Collection: 1964 Buick Electra 225, The General Motors Heritage Center

24. "9 New York Mafia Social Clubs: Then & Now," National.CrimeSyndicate.com

25. "Patient Care & Health Information - Diseases & Conditions: Compulsive Gambling," The Mayo Clinic

26. "Vehicle Identification Numbers (VINs) and the Federal Parts-Marking Program," The National Highway Traffic Safety Administration

27. "Car Reported Stolen Every Five Minutes on New York Streets," by Barbara Basler, *New York Times*, April 18, 1982

28. "Amateurs Fading in World of Car Theft," by M. A. Farber, *New York Times,* December 13, 1983

29. Obituary: James (Jimmy the Gent) Burke, Gangster, 64, of 'Wiseguy' Fame, Reported by The Associated Press, Appeared in the *New York Times*, April 17, 1996

30. "Brooklyn's House of Detention Closes Under De Blasio's New Jails Plan," by Sydney Pereira, *The Gothamist*, January 3, 2020

31. "A Pioneer in Residential Drug Treatment Reaches Out," by Michel Marriott, *New York Times*, November 13, 1989

32. "Catskills: New Uses For Old Hotels," by John Conway, New York Almanac, October 9, 2014

33. Daytop "About" Webpage from 2021, WaybackMachine.com

34. "The Daytop crisis and its impact on the global Therapeutic Community movement," by Phoebus Zafiridis, Published in "Therapeutic Communities: The International Journal of Therapeutic Communities," April 29, 2020

35. "New York Consolidated Laws, Penal Law - PEN § 155.30 Grand Larceny in the fourth degree," FindLaw.com, Current as of January 1, 2021

36. "Paul Vario, 73; Called a Leader Of Crime Group," by Mark A. Uhlig, *New York Times*, May 5, 1988

37. *Mafia Dynasty: The Rise and Fall of the Gambino Crime Family*, by John H. Davis, HarperCollins

38. "Truck Hijacking in City Is a $4.2-Million Business," *New York Times*, May 20, 1974

39. "Reputed Organized Crime Leader Dead at 71," by Rick Hampson, The Associated Press, December 3, 1985

40. "Disgraced FBI agent's attorneys attack credibility of witness," by Scott Shifrel, *New York Daily News*, October 23, 2007

41. "Slain mob boss Frank Cali laid to rest — as authorities look on," by Joe Marino, Kevin Sheehan, Larry Celona and Kate Sheehy, *New York Post*, March 19, 2019

42. "U.S. Jury Convicts Eight as Members of Mob Commission," by Arnold H. Lubasch, *New York Times*, November 20, 1986

43. "Christy Tick, 90, Beats the System, Departs Prison," by Ed Scarpo Saturday, Cosa Nostra News, October 4, 2014

44. "Most Ruthless Mafia Leader Left; Leader on the Lam Runs the Lucchese Family, Agents Say," by Selwyn Raab, *New York Times*, November 28, 1992

45. "Once Shunned, Chinese Population Booms In Bensonhurst And Dyker Heights," by Eric Jankiewicz, *The Bklyner*, January 8, 2014

46. "Career NY Mobster Arrested for First Time in His 80s; Stayed Out of Limelight," by Allan Lengel, TickletheWire. com, July 24, 2011

47. "Thomas Verdillo, 77, Dies; Restaurateur Went from Red Sauce to Blue Ribbon," LightlyNews.com, January 11, 2021

48. "Chef talk: Tommaso Verdillo," by Michael Steinberger, *The Financial Times*, November 26, 2010

49. "Mob sauce summit! Colombos and Bonannos had sitdown over suspected family recipe theft from L&B Spumoni Gardens," by John Marzulli, *New York Daily News*, June 13, 2012

50. "Colombo mobster gets 6-month medical leave from prison," by Selim Algar, *New York Post*, September 26, 2013

51. "Mobster Nicholas Rizzo was ordered back to jail after a judge said he violated conditions of a humanitarian parole," by John Marzulli, *New York Daily News*, October 9, 2013

52. "Start Snitching: Inside the Witness Protection Program," by Marcus Baram, ABC News, October 26, 2007

53. "United States of America v. John A. Gotti, Jr., Defendant DiLeonardo Testimony (04 CR 00690 SAS-1) District Judge Shira A. Scheindlin, United States District Court, Southern District of New York New York, NY, February 22, 2006

54. "The Star 'Scar' Witness; Turncoat vs. 'Junior' Gotti Ready to be Mafia's Next 'Sammy Bull'," by Brad Hamilton, *New York Post*, August 7, 2005

55. "Virginia is for Lovers: On Madison Avenue Advertising Walk of Fame," Tourism Website for the State of Virginia

56. *The Mafia with Trevor McDonald*, ITV, March 23, 2015

57. "*The Mafia with Trevor McDonald*, Review: Nice guy Trevor just isn't cut out for the mean streets," by Ellen E. Jones, *The Independent*, March 24, 2015

58. "The Origins of the Credit Card Trace Back to a Flatbush Bank," by Hannah Frishberg, Brownstoner, March 24, 2016

59. "The Beginning of the Credit Card," by Sydney Vaccaro, Chargeback, November 13, 2017

60. *Credit Card Nation The Consequences Of America's Addiction To Credit*, by Robert D. Manning, Basic Books, December 25, 2000

61. "The History of Credit Cards," by Jay MacDonald and Jason Steele, CreditCards.com, May 24, 2021

62. "What is a Knuckle Buster," Investopedia

63. About EMVCo, EMVCO.com

64. "The rise and fall of the credit card magnetic stripe," by Marcia Frellick, CreditCards.com, June 14, 2011

65. "Matthew Ianniello, the Mafia Boss Known as 'Matty the Horse,' Dies at 92," by Paul Vitello, *New York Times*, August 22, 2012

66. "Shocking Vintage Photos Show Time Square At The Peak Of Its Depravity In The 1970s and 1980s," ByGonely.com

67. "Life on W. 42nd St. a study in decay," *New York Times*, March 14, 1960

68. *The Deuce*, HBO, 2017-2019

69. "HBO'S *The Deuce* Returns for a Second Season With the Mob in Control," by Larry Henry, The Mob Museum, 2019

70. "A Look Back At The Real *Deuce*: Times Square In The 1970s," by Jen Carlson, *The Gothamist*, September 8, 2017

71. "Ianniello Is Sentenced In Racketeering Trial," *New York Times*, February 16, 1986

72. "U.S. Attorney Reports Indictment of Ianniello," *New York Times*, May 16, 1986

73. "The History of Handball," by Tom O'Connor, The United States Handball Association

74. *Deal with the Devil: The FBI's Secret Thirty-Year Relationship with a Mafia Killer*, by Peter Lance, Harper Collins, July 1, 2014

75. *Gaspipe: Confessions of a Mafia Boss*, by Philip Carlo, William Morrow, June 23, 2009

76. "14 Are Charged In 7 Burglaries By Skilled Ring," by Arnold H. Lubasch, *New York Times*, November 15, 1990

77. "The Daily Lottery Was Originally a Harlem Game. Then Albany Wanted In," by Bridgett M. Davis, *New York Times*, February 27, 2019

78. "Tall Tales of a Mafia Mistress," by Tom Robbins, *The Village Voice*, October 23, 2007

79. "Mole's New Slay Shocker – 5th 'Rap' on FBI Man in 'Miss Israel' Triangle," by Alex Ginsberg, *New York Post*, April 28, 2006

80. "Ex-FBI Agent Probed for Aiding Mob Hits," by Jerry Capeci, *The New York Sun*, January 12, 2006

81. *We're Going to Win This Thing: The Shocking Frame-up of a Mafia Crime Buster*, by Lin DeVecchio and Charles Brandt, Berkley, February 7, 2012

82. "Examiner testifies in trial of accused mob informant," by Anthony M. Destafano, *New York Newsday*, October 22, 2007

83. "The Mafia of the 1980's: Divided and Under Siege," by Robert D. McFadden, *New York Times*, March 11, 1987

84. *The Valachi Papers*, by Peter Maas, Harper Perennial, 1968

85. "Gambino Believed Seeking Single Mafia Family Here," by Nicholas Gage, *New York Times*, December 8, 1972

86. "Five Mafia Families Open Rosters to New Members," by Nicholas Gage, *New York Times,* March 21, 1976

87. "Fateful 1976 NYC mob Commission vote to admit new members marked a Mafia turning point in retrospect," by Larry McShane, *New York Daily News*, May 31, 2020

88. *Donnie Brasco: My Undercover Life in the Mafia - A True Story by FBI Agent Joseph D. Pistone*, by Joseph D. Pistone, Dutton Books, 1988

89. "Carlo Gambino, a Mafia Leader, Dies in His Long Island Home at 74," by Nicholas Gage, *New York Times*, October 16, 1976

90. "Criminal RICO (Racketeer Influenced and Corrupt Organizations Act)," Excerpt from Trial, Volume: 22, Issue: 9, Pages: 40-47, By J F Lawless and LR Jacobs, The US Department of Justice, Office of Justice Programs; September 1986

91. "Vincent 'The Chin' Gigante, 'Oddfather' Mob Boss, 77," *The Washington Post,* December 20, 2005

92. "N.Y. crime boss admits he faked mental illness," by Anthony M. DeStefano, *The Baltimore Sun,* April 8, 2003

93. *Chin: The Life and Crimes of Mafia Boss Vincent Gigante*, by Larry McShane, Citadel Press, November 29, 2016

94. "United Stated vs. Michael Sessa 92-CR-351 (ARR), 97-CV-2079 (ARR)," January 25, 2011

95. "Fat Larry Released from Prison: Promises to Go Legit," The Colombo Crime Family

96. United States v. Persico, 853 F.2d 134 (1988) No. 988, Docket 87-1545. United States Court of Appeals, Second Circuit. Argued April 19, 1988. Decided August 4, 1988

97. "Judge Sentences Reputed Mob Figure To 25 Years," by Vera Haller, The Associated Press, December 19, 1987

98. "United States vs. Alphonse Persico, No. 988, Docket 87-1545," Argued April 19, 1988

99. *Body Mike: An Unsparing Expose by the Mafia Insider Who Turned on the Mob,* by Joseph Cantalupo and Thomas C. Renner, St. Martin Press, January 1, 1991

100. "A mobster's trail of bodies," by Dave Goldiner, *New York Daily News,* September 29, 2000

101. "Judge Sentences 8 Mafia Leaders to Prison Terms," by Arnold H. Lubasch, *New York Times,* January 14, 1987

102. "Carmine Persico's 'Commission' case sentencing a miscarriage of justice, insured Colombo family boss' death behind bars: lawyer," by Larry McShane, *New York Daily News,* March 31, 2019

103. Orena v. United States, US District Court for the Eastern District of New York - 956 F. Supp. 1071 (E.D.N.Y. 1997) March 10, 1997

104. "Colombo Family – The Youngest of the 'Five Families'," American Mafia History, October 19, 2015

105. "Double Portrait of a Man on Trial Astounds Friends," by Selwyn Raab, *New York Times,* April 11, 1995

106. United States vs. Monteleone, United States Court of Appeals, Second Circuit, July 20, 2001

107. "The 1990s Colombo Mob War Murder Timeline: NYC Mafia Clan In Chaos As Jailed Don Fought Off Insurgence," by Scott Burnstein, The Gangster Report, June 6, 2017

108. "Organized Crime: A Gang That Still Can't Shoot Straight," by Richard Behar, *Time Magazine,* June 24, 2001

109. "My life as a Colombo hit man," by Brad Hamilton, *New York Post,* March 4, 2012

110. "The G-man and the Hit Man," by Fredric Dannen, *The New Yorker,* December 8, 1996

111. "Settlement in Lawsuit on H.I.V.-Tainted Blood," by Mary B. W. Tabor, *New York Times,* August 30, 1992

112. *The Life: A True Story About A Brooklyn Boy Seduced Into The Dark World Of The Mafia,* by Larry Mazza

113. "Killing Is Tied To Mafia War In Brooklyn," by George James, *New York Times*, December 9, 1991

114. "Brooklyn's Mob War Interrupted With a Quiet Day in Court," by Robert D. McFadden, *New York Times*, December 17, 1991

115. "Street Stories With Ed Bradley," *CBS News*, November 12, 1992

116. Orena v. United States, Judgement, Memorandum, and Order, "Nos. 96 CV 1474, 92 CR" Orena v. U.S., 956 F. Supp. 1071, (E.D.N.Y. 1997), United States District Court, E.D. New York, March 10, 1997

117. "Acting Crime Boss Is Convicted of Murder and Racketeering," by Arnold H. Lubasch, *New York Times*, December 22, 1992

118. "Ailing ex-Colombo family boss Victor Orena, 86, could be released from prison: lawyer," by Noah Goldberg, *New York Daily News*, April 29, 2021

119. "Alzheimer's has the former acting boss of Colombo crime family thinking he's president of the United States," by Noah Goldberg and Larry McShane, *New York Daily News*, October 13, 2021

120. "Greg Scarpa Sr. talked too much, mobster says," by Scott Shifrel, *New York Daily News*, October 26, 2007

121. "From 'Drop-Dead Gorgeous' to DOA," by Jerry Capeci, *The New York Sun*, February 16, 2006

122. "Murderous Mob Canary Sprung," by Christopher Francescani, *New York Post*, September 29, 2000

123. "Judge Throws Out Convictions Of Two Men in Burglary Case," by Joseph P. Fried, *New York Times*, September, 20, 1993

124. State of New Jersey v. Aurelio Ray Cagno, Superior Court of New Jersey, Appellate Division, Argued March 18, 2009

125. "Man Tied to Crime Family Is Shot to Death in Queens," by George James, *New York Times,* October 22, 1993

126. "Mob turncoat says shackled Colombo crime big ordered hit while at grandmother's wake," by Mitchel Maddux, *New York Post,* June 14, 2012

127. United States of America v. Michael Persico, United States District Court, Eastern District of New York, Filed July 19, 2017

128. "John Pappa Failed at Shooting His Way into the Mafia," by Ed Scarpo Friday, Cosa Nostra News, February 4, 2011

129. "Colombo hit man John Pappa makes the most of his time cooking and cheering on the Yankees as he's holed up in high-security prison," by John Marzulli, *New York Daily News*, June 27, 2012

130. "Carmine Persico, Colombo Crime Family Boss, Is Dead at 85." by Selwyn Raab, *New York Times*, March 8, 2019

131. The United States of America v. Appellee Richard Alan Brady, Frank Pontillo, also known as Franky Steel, Robert Montano, Michael DeMatteo and John Pate, Defendants-Appellants, Nos. 590, 613, 760, 762, 842, Dockets 93-1215, 93-1220, 93-1251, 93-1252, 93-1618, United States Court of Appeals, Second Circuit, Decided May 13, 1994

132. "Mob turncoat details the 1997 slaying of NYPD cop Ralph Dols," by Mitchel Maddux, *New York Post*, March 27, 2012

133. "It's not just Whitey Bulger: Meet another Mafia killer aided for decades by the FBI," by Peter Lance, *Salon Magazine*, June 30, 2013

134. "Top Member of Colombo Crime Family Is Ambushed in Brooklyn," by Selwyn Raab, *New York Times*, December 30, 1992

135. "The Mobster Was a Mole for the F.B.I.; Tangled Life of a Mafia Figure Who Died of AIDS Is Exposed," by Selwyn Raab, *New York Times*, November 20, 1994

136. "Ailing Brooklyn mobster blamed in 1980s killings wins compassionate release from prison," by Noah Goldberg, *New York Daily News*, November 11, 2020

137. United States v. Larry Sessa, Gregory Scarpa Jr., United States Court of Appeals, Second Circuit, No. 1363, Docket 96-1631, Decided September 9, 1997

138. The United States Code, Title 18, Part II, Chapter 224, Section 3521, United States Codes and Statutes

139. "Inside the witness protection program," by Gabriel Falcon, CNN, February 16, 2013

140. "How the Witness Protection Program Decides Where To Send People," *Popular Mechanics*, February 8, 2019

141. "Mobster Anthony 'Gaspipe' Casso, who murdered dozens and caught COVID-19 behind bars, dead at 78," by Noah Goldberg, *New York Daily News*, December 16, 2020

142. *Friends of the Family: The Inside Story of the Mafia Cops Case*, by Tommy Dades and Mike Vecchione, with David Fisher, William Morrow, May 12, 2009

143. "Plea Deal Rescinded, Informer May Face Life," by Selwyn Raab, *New York Times*, July 1, 1998

144. "Ex-Lucchese underboss Anthony 'Gaspipe' Casso dies after getting COVID-19 in prison," by Priscilla DeGregory,

Larry Celona and Tamar Lapin, *New York Post*, December 16, 2020

145. "Boston mobster known as 'Cadillac Frank' gets life in prison for an old murder," by Taylor Telford, *The Washington Post*, September 14, 2018

146. "Henry Hill, Mobster and Movie Inspiration, Dies at 69," by Margalit Fox, *New York Times*, June 13, 2012

147. US Marshals Service Witness Protection Program Sheet, US Marshals Service

148. "Tenants' Rights: Knowing Your Rights as a Tenant," By Brette Sember, J.D., Legal Zoom, September 4, 2020

149. Tenants Rights State-By-State, US Department of Housing and Urban Development

150. "The Dyker Heights Christmas Lights Guide," by Collier Sutter and Jennifer Picht, *Time Out New York*, December 1, 2020

151. "This Brooklyn Neighborhood Is a Con Edison Christmas Wet Dream," by Harmon Leon, *The Observer*, December 23, 2019

152. "Witness protection program faces challenges," The Associated Press, NBC News

153. "How Does Rent-to-Owning Work?" Zillow.com

154. "Roman History: The Edict of Man," Encyclopedia Britannica

155. *All the Nations Under Heaven: Immigrants, Migrants, and the Making of New York, Revised Edition*, by Frederick M. Binder, David M. Reimers, and Robert W. Snyder, Columbia University Press, 1995

156. *City of Dreams: The 400-Year Epic History of Immigrant New York*, by Tyler Anbinder, Houghton Mifflin Harcourt, October 18, 2016

157. *An Unlikely Union: The Love-Hate Story of New York's Irish and Italians*, by Paul Moses, New York University Press, July 3, 2015

158. "City of Churches," *The Brooklyn Daily Eagle*, March 6, 1844, Newspapers.com

159. Official Site of the Basilica of Regina Pacis

160. "Pope Benedict XVI Elevates Brooklyn Church To Minor Basilica," The Roman Catholic Dioceses of Brooklyn, November 24, 2021

161. "Gold Crowns Stolen from Church Shrine are Returned: Church Gets Stolen Gems in Mail; Pastor Hails Recovery as Miracle," *New York Times*, June 9, 1952

162. "Shrine dedicated; 7,000 at services," *New York Times*, August 16, 1951

163. Law, Crime, and Punishment: Joseph Profaci Biography, Britannica

164. "Mafia Banned Murder – Halted Hits Under Heat," by Steve Dunleavy, *New York Post,* July 12, 2004

165. "A Tip Directs the F.B.I. To Stolen Church Jewels," by Glenn Fowler, *New York Times*, January 22, 1973

166. *Iceman of Brooklyn: The Mafia Life of Frankie Yale*, by Michael Newton, McFarland, April 16, 2021

167. Top Echelon Criminal Informant Program, New York Division, Federal Bureau of Investigation, FBI Subject File for Gregory Scarpa Sr., Memoranda from SAC to FBI Director, Part 01, Page 10, 8/31/62

168. Official website of The Shrine Church of St. Bernadette, Brooklyn, NY

169. Candidate Details for Robert J. DiCarlo, Our Campaigns

170. Federal Court Jude Profile of Dominick L. DiCarlo, Federal Judicial Center

171. "Fact Sheet: Witness Security, 2021," US Marshals Service, US Department of Justice, 2021

172. "What Happens When You Enter the Witness Protection Program?" by Alex Mayyasi, *Pricenomics*

173. *Witsec: Inside the Federal Witness Protection Program*, by Pete Earley, Bantam, April 1, 2003

174. "The Invisible Family," by Robert Sabbag, *New York Times*, February 11, 1996

175. "Well, the Ices Are Still Italian; Immigration Patterns Shift, Altering the Old Neighborhood," by Joseph Burger, *New York Times*, September 17, 2002

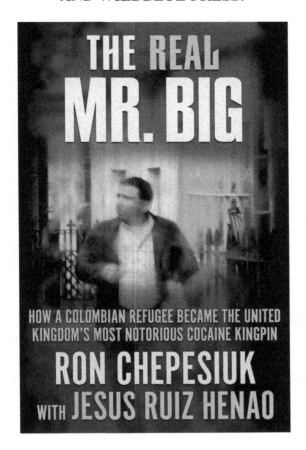

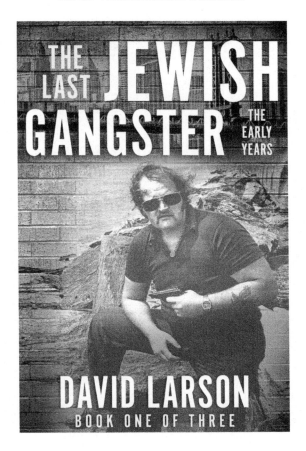